Microsoft

Programming Microsoft® Office Business Applications

D1451198

Steve Fox, Rob Barker, Joanna Bichsel,
Erika Ehrli Cabral, and Paul Stubbs

PUBLISHED BY
Microsoft Press
A Division of Microsoft Corporation
One Microsoft Way
Redmond, Washington 98052-6399

Library of Congress Control Number: 2008920567

Printed and bound in the United States of America.

1 2 3 4 5 6 7 8 9   QWT   3 2 1 0 9 8

Distributed in Canada by H.B. Fenn and Company Ltd.

A CIP catalogue record for this book is available from the British Library.

Microsoft Press books are available through booksellers and distributors worldwide. For further information about international editions, contact your local Microsoft Corporation office or contact Microsoft Press International directly at fax (425) 936-7329. Visit our Web site at www.microsoft.com/mspress. Send comments to *mspinput@microsoft.com*.

Microsoft, Microsoft Press, Active Directory, ActiveX, Excel, Fluent, FrontPage, InfoPath, IntelliSense, Microsoft Dynamics, MSDN, Outlook, PerformancePoint, PowerPoint, SharePoint, Silverlight, SQL Server, Virtual Earth, Visio, Visual Basic, Visual C#, Visual Studio, Windows, Windows Live, and Windows Server are either registered trademarks or trademarks of Microsoft Corporation in the United States and/or other countries.

The example companies, organizations, products, domain names, e-mail addresses, logos, people, places, and events depicted herein are fictitious. No association with any real company, organization, product, domain name, e-mail address, logo, person, place, or event is intended or should be inferred.

This book expresses the author's views and opinions. The information contained in this book is provided without any express, statutory, or implied warranties. Neither the authors, Microsoft Corporation, nor its resellers or distributors will be held liable for any damages caused or alleged to be caused either directly or indirectly by this book.

Acquisitions Editor: Ben Ryan
Developmental Editor: Devon Musgrave
Project Editor: Carol Vu
Editorial Production: S4Carlisle Publishing Services
Technical Editor: Philippe Freddi; Technical Review services provided by Content Master,
                 a member of CM Group, Ltd.
Indexer: Kirsten E. Balayti

Body Part No. X14-55507

Contents at a Glance

List of Figures

Table of Contents

What do you think of this book? We want to hear from you!

Microsoft is interested in hearing your feedback so we can continually improve our books and learning resources for you. To participate in a brief online survey, please visit:

www.microsoft.com/learning/booksurvey/

What do you think of this book? We want to hear from you!

Microsoft is interested in hearing your feedback so we can continually improve our books and learning resources for you. To participate in a brief online survey, please visit:

www.microsoft.com/learning/booksurvey/

Foreword

The Office system has evolved incredibly over the last twenty years. When we look back at our first version of Microsoft Word (Word for Windows 1.0), it's amazing to see the difference in the design of the *then* and the design of the *now*. We notice a core difference when we look at our applications of yesterday: their purpose was specific and discrete. There was little interoperability with other applications beyond copy and paste. Today, the experience of word processing is not just about creating documents; it's about content management, team collaboration, smart and structured documents, extended search, workflow management, and much more.

The Office system as a whole was designed to enable organizations to communicate and collaborate, manage content, search and index information, create and manage workflow, build business intelligence views, and do this in a secure and efficient way. And when we say the Office system, we not only include products from the productivity suite (Word, Excel, PowerPoint, Outlook, etc.), but we also include our newer technologies such as Microsoft Office PerformancePoint Server, Microsoft Exchange Server, Microsoft Office Communications Server, and Microsoft Office SharePoint Server. For the organization, this means more choices and more extensive functionality for the information worker.

At the same time that Office has evolved the experience for our information workers, it's also providing a rich development platform for our professional developer community. As you'll see in this book, the Office system provides many tools, services, and servers that together enable developers to build Office Business Applications (OBAs)—a new breed of applications that bridges the discrepancy between information workers and the necessary business data that allows them to make informed business decisions. In this sense, the Office system operates within a new development paradigm—one that includes Microsoft Office SharePoint Server 2007 and Visual Studio 2008 as part of the key development backbone. And it is with this marriage, perhaps even extended family, that you'll see a new dynamic in Office development surface—one that will take Office solutions to the next level in many different ways.

I'm glad to have the opportunity to introduce you to one of the few technical books on the market that specifically addresses the development of OBAs. Given the breadth and power of the Microsoft Office system, developing OBAs might require knowledge in a number of areas, so having the right guidance is critical. I believe this book provides that for you. The authors show you how to use SharePoint and Visual Studio Tools for Office (VSTO) as key tools for OBA development, provide guidance in the area of service-oriented architecture (SOA) solutions development, provide insight on how to deploy and integrate client and server OBA components, and explain and demonstrate how you can build and deploy workflow to manage your solutions, among a myriad of other abilities.

My hope is that by the end of this book, you will begin to see the true power of the Office platform and will be excited to get started developing your first OBA.

Chris Capossela

Corporate Vice President

Microsoft Office

Introduction

By Steve Fox

Office Business Applications

I don't want to steal any thunder from the authors who helped put this book together, but before you get underway I just want to help set the stage for this book by giving you a glimpse of what's to come.

Office Business Applications (OBAs) are a new type of composite application that integrate line-of-business (LOB) systems (such as SAP, PeopleSoft, and Microsoft Dynamics) to Office, whether it be the client (for example, extending the Excel 2007 Ribbon) or the server [for example, integrating an SAP Web service with the Microsoft Office SharePoint Server (MOSS) 2007 Business Data Catalog (BDC)]. OBAs are an important new development in the realm of enterprise solutions development. They enable companies to leverage the rich Office platform to build composite solutions that bring information workers closer to the business data that helps them in their everyday work. This is, as you'll see as you read this book, quite a high-level representation of the problem that OBAs solve, but it drives at the heart of why organizations would want to build and implement OBAs: a) to better leverage the large-scale LOB systems they pay quite a lot of money to implement and sustain, and b) to ensure the data in these systems is available (in real time) to the people who need it (what is often called the "results gap").

As you might imagine, "Office platform" encompasses not only a lot of the development technology that Microsoft has to offer, but also a lot of options for the developer and the OBA solutions the developer can build using that technology—many of which are covered in this book. This is both exciting and arguably overwhelming, thus necessitating the need for not only books like this but other related support mechanisms for the developer (see Additional Resources later in this section for one such list of related resources). It also necessitates the IT organization as a whole asking a different question, and that is, "How can we best leverage the tools and applications we have in our environment today?" I think one of the underlying themes of this book—leveraging the Office system and the Office platform to build and deploy OBAs that bridge the results gap—will help answer this question, as each of the chapters illustrates how the developer can use the myriad components of the Office platform to help build OBAs for his or her organization.

Who Is This Book For?

Given the nature of the chapters (we tried to follow a concept and code sample and/or walkthrough model), this book is primarily targeted at the professional developer who is new to the idea of developing OBAs. More specifically, this book is aimed at the developer who has some familiarity with either the .NET Framework or with programming against MOSS or the Office object model. This is an interesting marriage in skills because oftentimes it's difficult to find one developer with all of these skills. Historically, Office development skills are often centric to either SharePoint (think SharePoint Portal Server 2003), COM, or VBA development without a lot of cross-over. However, with OBA development you, the developer, may find yourself building smart-client components while at the same time building Web parts on a SharePoint portal—all within one OBA solution.

For the reader who is a professional developer, I think that it helps to have some grounding in object-oriented programming, although it's not a prerequisite for this book. Further, I would also add that the reader of this book should have some knowledge in either Visual Basic or C# and while not covered in this book directly, working within the innards of SharePoint implies knowledge of ASP.NET and COM when it comes to the more general Office object model.

That said, I think developers of all skills can get something out of this book. For example, the more advanced developer may acquire an understanding of how various pieces tie together and pay less attention to the code samples, while the novice or intermediate developer may pay some attention to the code samples to see how we've implemented certain items within the solutions we discuss within the book. One of my key goals for this book is that it is accessible on a grander scale, so in some chapters you'll see code samples that apply to specific solutions, whereas in others you'll see walkthroughs that may appeal to a different type of developer. I'll leave you to explore these on your own to see what you can use in your day-to-day development lives.

While the developer is our primary audience, I do believe that there is some value for other disciplines, including the architect, program or project manager, technical product manager, and even technical field sales or support roles. I say this because Office cuts across many veins of use and practicality, so having a good understanding of *what* can be built using the Office platform and system can hopefully provide some ideas (in multiple areas, like planning, design, architecture, and so on) for people from different disciplines. I think the key takeaway here is that OBAs can be built for many different disciplines and purposes within the enterprise, so even perusing this book to help inspire those ideas may be beneficial to those whose job is not core to development.

About Programming Office Business Applications

Multiple authors contributed to this book, ultimately resulting in eight chapters that cover each of what we thought to be important areas within OBA development. We unfortunately could not cover every area, but where appropriate, each of the authors has added additional resources at the end of his or her chapter for additional consultation. Further, each of the authors either works for the Office product group or the Visual Studio product group, thus bringing some great experience into the fold.

Here is a quick summary of the contents of *Programming Microsoft Office Business Applications*.

Chapter 1, "Introducing Office Business Applications" (Rob Barker, Senior Technical Evangelist, Microsoft)

- This chapter provides a good introduction to OBAs and the different technologies that comprise OBA development. Specifically, it provides an overview of the OBA (and Office) platform capabilities, services, and main technologies developers can use to begin building OBAs.

Chapter 2, "Creating a Smart Client for Your OBA by Using VSTO" (Paul Stubbs, Senior Program Manager, Microsoft)

- VSTO 3.0 is an important component technology within Visual Studio 2008 that helps you create client-side customizations and SharePoint workflow. This chapter provides an introduction to Visual Studio Tools for Office (VSTO) 3.0, and illustrates the different types of things that developers can do to build rich smart-client components to their OBAs. It provides both Visual Basic and C# examples to illustrate how you can extend Office applications such as Excel, Word, and Outlook and take advantage of the Office object model.

Chapter 3, "Building Business Intelligence for Your Office Business Applications" (Steve Fox, Program Manager, Microsoft)

- Business intelligence can mean different things to different people but it represents an important element in enterprise solutions—especially ones where business decisions are made. This chapter introduces you to the different ways in which you can develop business intelligence into your OBAs. Whether it be through smart-client solutions (for example, extending Excel 2007) or through SharePoint development (like using Excel Services to integrate with Excel 2007 spreadsheets), this chapter provides the developer with a number of examples and walkthroughs that illustrate how to build and integrate business intelligence into your OBAs.

Chapter 4, "Integrating Web Services into Your Office Business Applications" (Joanna Bichsel, Program Manager, Microsoft)

- A core part of OBAs is the ability to integrate with Web services—because in many cases you will use Web services to connect to your LOB system. This chapter provides an overview of a recruiting solution that consumes Web services in the client and server to illustrate how developers can integrate Web services using VSTO and MOSS.

Chapter 5, "Building Social Networking into Your Office Business Application" (Fox)

- Social networking is becoming an ever-important part of the enterprise solution. This chapter provides you with an overview of a number of different social networking features that you can take advantage of—some of which are MOSS-specific, but also one that integrates third-party social networking environments (for example, Facebook) with MOSS.

Chapter 6, "SharePoint and Developing Office Business Applications" (Barker)

- MOSS is an increasingly important solution in the enterprise today. It is also a critical part of developing and deploying OBAs. This chapter provides an overview of how SharePoint is critical to OBAs and the types of tools support that developers should look out for.

Chapter 7, "Managing Complex Business Processes with Custom SharePoint Workflow" (Erika Ehrli Cabral, Site Manager, Microsoft)

- Integrating workflow into solutions enables developers to take some of the burden off of information workers and have the system manage key processes within OBAs. This chapter provides an overview of how developers can build and deploy SharePoint workflow to manage business processes within your OBA.

Chapter 8, "Deploying Your Office Business Application in the Enterprise" (Stubbs)

- After you've built your OBA, you obviously need to deploy it somewhere. This chapter provides an overview of how you deploy client-side customizations (built using VSTO), server-side components (SharePoint components), and integrations between client-side customizations to SharePoint.

Support and Downloads

Some of the chapters may have code samples that accompany them. If they do, you can download these samples at the following link: *http://www.microsoft.com/mspress/companion/9780735625365*.

Every effort has been made to ensure the accuracy of this book. Microsoft Press provides support for books and companion content at the following Web site: *http://www.microsoft.com/learning/support/books*.

If you have comments, questions, or ideas regarding the materials in this book, or questions that are not answered by visiting the site just mentioned, please send them to *msinput@microsoft.com*. You can also write to us at:

Microsoft Press
Attn: Programming Microsoft Office Business Applications Editor
One Microsoft Way
Redmond, WA 98052-6399

Please note that Microsoft software product support is not offered through these addresses.

System Requirements

While this book will not provide an exhaustive guide on how to set up the environment for building and deploying OBAs, I can provide you with the baseline system requirements so you can go ahead and set up a sandbox environment where you can build and test your own OBA. These are as follows:

1. Windows Server 2003.

2. MOSS 2007.

3. Visual Studio 2008 (Professional SKU or higher).

4. Visual Studio Tools for Office (VSTO) 3.0. (Note: VSTO ships in Visual Studio now, so if you have Visual Studio 2008 Professional or higher, you will have VSTO.)

5. Microsoft Office 2007 Professional.

6. Office 2007 Programmability Interoperability Assemblies (PIAs), which should install as part of the Visual Studio 2008 installation process.

For your hardware, I would recommend minimum server standards, so at least 2 gigabytes or more of RAM, I gigahertz or more for the processor (preferably dual processor), and at least 60–80 gigabytes of hard-disk space.

Additional Resources

Here are a number of additional resources that you might find useful. Also note that some of the chapters offer more resources in sections called Further Reading, which are specific to the material covered in those chapters.

Resources at Microsoft.com

- OBA Central: *www.obacentral.com*

- MSDN OBA Developer Portal: *http://msdn.microsoft.com/oba*

- MSDN Office Developer How-To Center: *http://msdn2.microsoft.com/en-us/office/bb266408.aspx*

- Office Developer Center: *http://msdn2.microsoft.com/en-us/office/default.aspx*

- Visual Studio Tools for Office Developer Center: *http://msdn2.microsoft.com/en-us/office/aa905533.aspx*

- Excel Services Information Center Portal on MSDN: *http://msdn2.microsoft.com/en-us/office/bb203828.aspxv*

- Ribbon User Interface: *http://msdn.microsoft.com/office/tool/ribbon/default.aspx*

- XML File Formats: *http://msdn.microsoft.com/office/tool/xml/2007/default.aspx*

- Business Data Catalog Information Center:
  http://msdn2.microsoft.com/en-us/office/bb251754.aspx

- Business Data Catalog Software Development Kit:
  http://msdn2.microsoft.com/en-us/library/ms563661.aspx

- Introduction to Content Types: *http://office.microsoft.com/en-us/
  sharepointserver/HA101495511033.aspx?pid=CH101779691033*

- Content Types Software Development Kit:
  http://msdn2.microsoft.com/en-us/library/ms479905.aspx

- Microsoft Office SharePoint Server 2007 Software Development Kit:
  http://msdn2.microsoft.com/en-us/library/ms550992.aspx

- Office Developer Webcasts:
  http://www.microsoft.com/events/series/officedeveloperlive.mspx

- How Do I? Screencasts: *http://msdn.microsoft.com/office/learn/screencasts*

Blogs

- Building Office Business Applications:

  - *http://blogs.msdn.com/oba*

  - *http://blogs.msdn.com/Joanna_Bichsel/*

  - *http://blogs.msdn.com/rbarker/*

  - *http://blogs.msdn.com/javeds/*

  - *http://blogs.msdn.com/steve_fox/default.aspx*

- Brian Randell's blog, for information about SQL Server, Microsoft Office, and Visual
  Studio Tools for Office (VSTO): *http://sqljunkies.com/WebLog/brianr/*

- Eric Carter's blog, for information about Microsoft Office and VSTO:
  http://blogs.msdn.com/eric_carter/

- Microsoft Office fluent interface: *http://blogs.msdn.com/jensenh/*

- Office Developers: *http://blogs.msdn.com/erikaehrli/*

- Open XML File Formats:

  - *http://blogs.msdn.com/brian_jones/*

  - *http://blogs.msdn.com/dmahugh/*

  - *http://blogs.infosupport.com/wouterv/*

- Paul Stubbs' blog, for information about Microsoft Office, VSTO, and OBAs:
  http://blogs.msdn.com/pstubbs/

- Scott Guthrie's blog, for information on a variety of topics:
  http://weblogs.asp.net/scottgu/

- SharePoint Products and Technologies:

    - *http://blogs.msdn.com/sharepoint/*

    - *http://blogs.msdn.com/mikefitz/*

    - *http://www.u2u.info/Blogs/Patrick/default.aspx*

- Visual Studio extensions for SharePoint and SharePoint Designer:
  http://blogs.msdn.com/alexma/

- VSTO: *http://blogs.msdn.com/vsto2/*

Books

- *6 Microsoft Office Business Applications for Microsoft SharePoint Server 2007* by Rob Barker, Joanna Bichsel, Adam Buenz, Steve Fox, John Holliday, Bhushan Nene, and Karthik Ravindran (Microsoft Press)

- *Microsoft Office SharePoint Server Best Practices* by Ben Curry, Bill English, and Mark Schneider (Microsoft Press)

- *Inside Microsoft Windows SharePoint Services 3.0* by Ted Pattison and Daniel Larson (Microsoft Press)

- *VSTO for Mere Mortals: A VBA Developer's Guide to Microsoft Office Development Using Visual Studio 2005 Tools for Office* by Kathleen McGrath and Paul Stubbs (Addison-Wesley Professional)

- *Visual Studio Tools for Office* by Eric Carter and Eric Lippert (Addison-Wesley Professional)

Acknowledgments

After starting out and designing this book, I asked a number of my colleagues, all of whom I have great respect for, to contribute to the writing of this book. I was very pleased when all of them accepted the difficult challenge of contributing to the book—for it is a sometimes cumbersome journey to get one's experience and knowledge on paper. They all bring different, unique, and erudite perspectives to this book, and I hope this is reflected in each of the chapters. So, to Rob Barker, Paul Stubbs, Erika Ehrli Cabral, and Joanna Bichsel I thank you very much for your efforts. I'd also like to thank Carol Vu and the editing team for their tireless review of the content and Ben Ryan and Devon Musgrave for their overall management of the project.

For you, the reader, I hope you enjoy this book as much as I enjoyed the creation process. OBAs are a growing development area, and many organizations are taking note. And to speak for the team, our goal is that you not only have an understanding of what OBAs are by the end of this book, but you also understand the different technologies you can use to build them.

Chapter 1
Introducing Office Business Applications

Getting Started

Office Business Applications (OBAs) is a new development paradigm that leverages the features of the Office platform. This book provides a broad look at the different technologies you can use to build and deploy OBAs, and it represents a good introduction to this emerging area. It is also a good accompaniment to other books currently on the market, like *6 Microsoft Office Business Applications for Office SharePoint Server 2007* (Microsoft Press), in which each chapter provides an overview of an individual OBA; *VSTO for Mere Mortals* (Addison-Wesley Professional), which provides a comprehensive look at VSTO; and *Inside Microsoft Office SharePoint Server 2007* (Microsoft Press), which provides a comprehensive look at SharePoint. This introductory chapter lays out the accepted foundation for OBAs—similar to our "sister" book *6 Microsoft Office Business Applications for Office SharePoint Server 2007*—but it very quickly jumps into discussing individual technologies at a deeper level. So, without further adieu, let's begin our journey on learning about OBAs.

What Is an Office Business Application?

OBAs are a new breed of application that combines the use of the Office system with information and processes defined in line-of-business systems (LOBs). OBAs are a type of *composite application*. Composite applications are focused on enabling an effective way to build business applications that are contextual, collaborative, easy to use, role-based, and

1

configurable. Today's businesses need to be more agile to be competitive, and this need depends on access to information and its integration with various business processes, thus bringing to light this new type of software application called an Office Business Application.

The activities that most affect a company's success today are usually not transactional and transformational jobs that involve mechanization and automation, such as assembly-line work and data entry. An established and growing class of employees can now accomplish work tasks by exchanging information and making judgments about a variety of data gleaned from a variety of interactions. These *information workers* (IWs) typically make business decisions based on people-to-people interactions and information deriving from e-mail, phone conversations, or one-off discussions with colleagues in the hallway. IWs include salespeople, marketing managers, product designers, lawyers, and engineers, and usually make significant contributions to the sustenance and growth of a business. However, this significance often depends on how easily and consistently they can access the information they need to do their jobs and make decisions.

Let's look at a common business process that is illustrated in Figure 1-1. The scenario is related to a basic sales process, beginning with a sales lead and ending with the creation of a customer invoice. The first and most important item to point out is that most people think about the lower box only when discussing a business's *structured process*. In fact, the real business process takes place in a very ad-hoc manner, as illustrated in the top box. No business process is simple, and processes always involve a human element, which gathers information, negotiates, collects data, and, based on all that information, makes immediate business decisions that affect the business in a positive or negative way. This ad-hoc

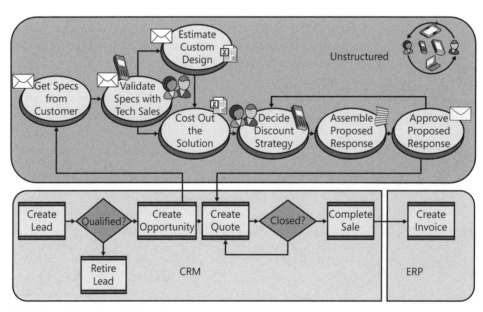

FIGURE 1-1 The real world of work

process is part of the *unstructured business process,* which is where all the most valuable information is assembled. In this unstructured business process, the people taking actions need immediate access to information, but in most cases the people do not have the types of data they need. *OBAs provide the ability to bridge people and information.* Bridging this information provides the ability to surface information in a multitude of ways to applications that are commonly used by IWs, such as Microsoft Office Outlook.

OBAs represent the integration of both structured and unstructured processes, and they are being included in innovative solutions developed by some of the world's largest software companies—including Microsoft with Dynamics Snap and Duet, a partnership of Microsoft and SAP—and solutions from independent software vendors (ISVs) such as Bentley Systems, Autodesk, and KnowledgeLake.

To help you understand what technologies and capabilities make up the foundation of OBAs, the next several sections will describe the platform's capabilities and supporting services.

The Office Business Application Platform

Figure 1-2 shows the different pillars of the Office Business Application platform, along with the services and core infrastructure that enable the platform. Each of the individual pillars, services, and core infrastructure will be discussed in detail in the section that follows.

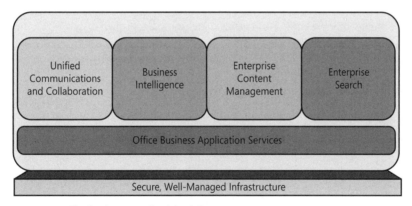

FIGURE 1-2 The business productivity infrastructure

Office Business Application Pillars

With the 2007 Microsoft Office system, some significant investments were made to enable several different core pillars. Each of the pillars contains different technologies, but in the end they all leverage Microsoft Office SharePoint Server (MOSS) 2007 as part of the core infrastructure. The next several sections will detail the various pillars and the different capabilities they provide to the Office Business Application platform.

Enterprise Content Management (ECM)

Even diverse content across an organization can have a consistent design and process for Web, document, and records management, enabling a categorization of content types with metadata, policies, and workflows. ECM allows searches across multiple repositories and LOB systems. Because functionality from Microsoft Content Management Server (MCMS) 2002 has been incorporated into MOSS, users can take advantage of Web content management features directly from the Office system platform. This integrated Web content management system controls consistency by enabling content types that define certain documents or collections of information, master pages that can define the look and feel of an entire site, and page layouts and logos that provide for consistent branding and images for Web pages.

This single content management and collaborative system eliminates the need for the separate solutions offered by Microsoft SharePoint Portal Server 2003 and MCMS. Thus, it's possible to create dynamic Web sites, customized for team or individual need, that are centered on the content the site manages.

Business Intelligence (BI)

MOSS 2007 takes traditional portal and dashboard solutions and builds on them, thus providing users with BI portals that can be used for data manipulation and analysis. Users—both information workers and developers—can create dashboards from single or multiple data sources without using code through, for example, the BDC. Key performance indicators (KPIs) can be defined using a variety of sources, including Excel spreadsheets, SharePoint lists, and SQL Server Analysis Services cubes. When information such as this is hosted in MOSS 2007, it is available for other SharePoint services, such as search and workflows.

The BI functionality allows you to:

- Combine ETL, OLAP, data mining, and reporting capabilities
- Fuse high volumes of LOB business data into your data warehouse with XML, Web services, and RSS sources
- Integrate newer data sources with traditional or legacy LOB data
- Use Excel with SQL Server Analysis Services to bring clarity to large amounts of data
- Tap into LOB data within spreadsheets and reports using the Business Data Catalog (BDC)

We would be remiss if we did not mention Microsoft Office PerformancePoint Server 2007 in addition to the capabilities provided by SharePoint. PerformancePoint Server is built on top of Microsoft SQL Server 2005 and provides an organization the ability to monitor, analyze, and plan its business activities. In addition to a great set of features provided by PerformancePoint, it also integrates well with SharePoint and Microsoft Office 2007 client applications such as Microsoft Office Excel. When considering building business intelligence into your OBA solution, PerformancePoint should be reviewed in conjunction with Microsoft Office SharePoint Server 2007.

Unified Communication and Collaboration

In today's modern workplace, the focus is on the work itself, not the location where work occurs. Individuals collaborate to solve problems, develop plans, and embrace opportunities, but even "coming together" no longer means or implies that a group of people is sitting in the same room or even in the same building or country. The physical and logical barriers that once defined a team or workgroup are disappearing. The 2007 Microsoft Office system supports communication and collaboration through a number of contextual capabilities. Teams can collaborate by using virtual workspaces, for example, which can be large and relatively centralized, supporting entire divisions of business units, or fit the needs of real-time workgroups that need a way to work together quickly.

Office Business Application Services and Technologies

As illustrated in Figure 1-2 there are Office Business Application services provided within the Office Business Application platform that support and enable the capabilities in the overall Microsoft Office platform. The following services define the core technical foundation that enables *developers and architects* to design and build applications that provide access to business data so that IWs can make critical business decisions in the application and contexts that they are used to in their everyday environment.

Workflow

Windows Workflow Foundation (WF) provides a programming model, engine, and tools for developers to rapidly build workflow-enabled applications. WF supports both system workflow and human workflow across a variety of scenarios that include integrating with line-of-business systems, document workflows (for example, routing and approval processing), and more. WF has been integrated into Microsoft Office SharePoint Server 2007 to provide developers the ability to create simple workflows and attach them to SharePoint Server 2007 document libraries. Microsoft Office SharePoint Designer can be used to create custom workflows without coding. For power users and developers, the Workflow object model is available in Microsoft Visual Studio 2008. Included with Visual Studio 2008 are the SharePoint Sequential and State Machine workflows for developers to extend. Each of these workflows will be discussed in more detail in later chapters. Figure 1-3 provides an architecture view of workflow.

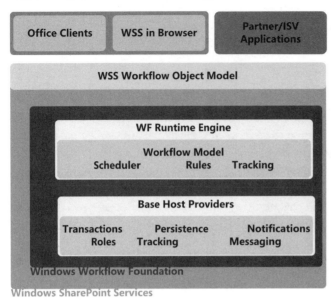

FIGURE 1-3 Architecture of Windows Workflow

Microsoft provides two development tools for authoring workflows for Windows SharePoint Services: Visual Studio Tools for Office in Visual Studio (VSTO) 2008 and Office SharePoint Designer 2007. The major differences between the two tools are as follows:

- Authoring workflows (state machine or sequential) in VSTO is performed by a professional developer. The developer creates a workflow template that can be deployed across multiple sites and contains custom code and activities. From here, the developer passes the workflow template to a server administrator for actual deployment and association.

- Workflow authoring in SharePoint Designer is likely to be done by someone other than a professional developer, such as a Web designer or IW who wants to create a workflow for a specific list or document library. In this instance, the designer is limited to the workflow activities on the Safe Controls List, and the workflow cannot include custom code. The author of the workflow deploys the workflow template directly to the list or document library as part of the workflow authoring process.

Business Data Catalog

One of the main methods for connecting to data in MOSS 2007 is through the BDC. A shared service that can be used with MOSS 2007, the BDC presents business data (read-only) from back-end server applications. The BDC can also display data from SAP, Siebel, or another LOB application through Web services or databases. The BDC exposes enterprise data to Web parts, Office Forms Server, and search. Thus, developers can use this capability to build applications that allow users to interact with LOB data in easy-to-use interfaces designed on the basis of substantial usability studies.

The BDC is essentially a metadata repository that allows you to define business entities such as customers, invoices, purchase orders, and custom entities that are relevant to your organization. Once you define these entities, they can be used throughout your Web sites and portals in the following ways:

- In search results
- In Web parts and lists
- As a filtering mechanism in SharePoint dashboards
- With document properties through integration with the Document Information Panel

These models for business entities will help maintain consistency in data and reduce errors and the re-entering of data. Figure 1-4 provides an architecture view of the BDC and the different data access methods that are supported.

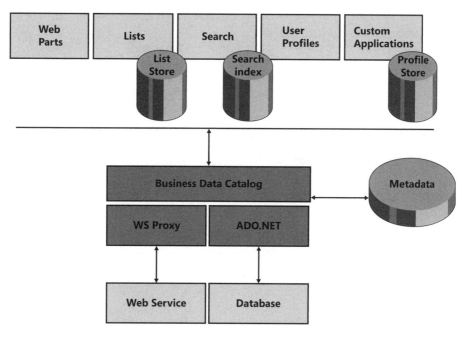

BizTalk, SAP, Siebel, Other LOBs   **SQL Server, Oracle, Other Data Providers**

FIGURE 1-4 Architecture of the BDC

Search

MOSS 2007 Enterprise Search is a shared service that provides broad and extensible content gathering, indexing, and querying, and supports full-text and keyword searches. By coupling the BDC with Microsoft Office Forms Server 2007 and search, organizations can build searchable server-side applications that allow users to interact with data that was previously segregated within the context of the organization's portal. Search is central to the 2007 Office system platform's efforts and provides multiple ways to integrate with and extend search, including:

- Controlling the presentation of search results using XSLT transforms and custom Web parts

- Presenting LOB data in the search index by using the BDC

- Incorporating custom content in the search index using protocol handlers and IFilters

- Consuming the search index from remote clients via Web services

The following list details the different components that are part of search that enable the previous integration scenarios.

- Index engine—Processes the chunks of text and properties filtered from content sources, storing them in the content index and property store.

- Query engine—Executes keyword and SQL syntax queries against the content index and search configuration data.

- Protocol handlers—Opens content sources in their native protocols and exposes documents and other items to be filtered.

- IFilters—Opens documents and other content source items in their native formats and filters into chunks of text and properties.

- Content index—Stores information about words and their location in a content item.

- Property store—Stores a table of properties and associated values.

- Search configuration data—Stores information used by the search service, including crawl configuration, property schema, and scopes.

- Wordbreakers—Used by the query and index engines to break compound words and phrases into individual words or tokens.

Figure 1-5 provides an architecture view of Enterprise Search and the functionality it enables.

The Microsoft Office Fluent UI ("The Ribbon")

The 2007 Office system offered developers a major improvement in the work performed on the extensibility model within the Office Fluent UI. Developers can now customize the Ribbon (through drag-and-drop ease) to expose both core features of the 2007 Office system through these custom extensions they build into the Office applications. The 2007 Office system also offers more managed code support, as well as improved security and management through a common application trust model.

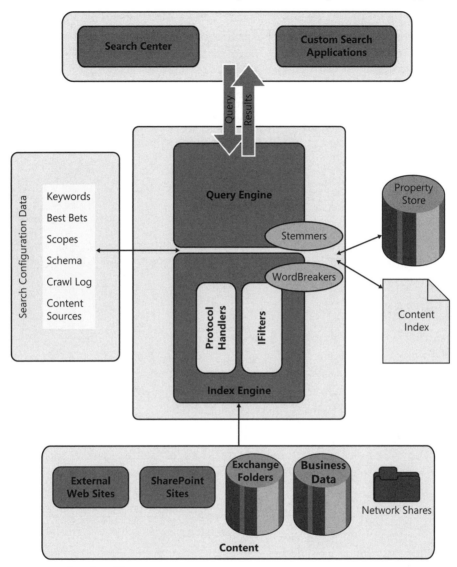

FIGURE 1-5 Search architecture

Most of the features accessed by using menus and toolbars in previous versions of Microsoft Office can now be accessed by using the Ribbon, the new user interface metaphor that brings a unified customization model to many Office applications. This control provides a way to organize related commands (in the form of controls) so that they are easier to find. Controls are organized into groups along a horizontal strip at the top edge of an application window. Related groups are organized on tabs that help users perform tasks. Developers can add or remove controls to provide users with a specific experience or specific functionality. This UI model also provides more consistency for developers by supplying the same Ribbon and task pane model across the applications.

Figure 1-6 is an example of a Ribbon that has been custom developed and shows up as its own *tab* in Microsoft Office Excel 2007. This example Ribbon leverages the investment from Microsoft using the various images that come stock with any of the Office applications that support Ribbon extensibility. There are custom groups and functionality behind each of the buttons that drive a completely custom user experience for an integrated LOB application.

FIGURE 1-6 Example of a custom Ribbon

The new Microsoft Office Fluent UI has been implemented in several applications in the 2007 Microsoft Office suite, including Access, Excel, Outlook, PowerPoint, and Word.

Open XML File Format

Open XML file formats enable developers to access and program Office documents outside of the application that generated them. This standards-based format is a primary data transport between applications and users in an OBA. The substantially smaller file sizes are one benefit of this new format. The Office XML formats are based on XML and ZIP technologies, which make them universally accessible.

With Open XML at the heart of the Office XML formats, solutions can programmatically alter information inside an Office document or create a document by using standard tools and technologies capable of manipulating XML and ZIP. Further, data can be exchanged between Microsoft Office applications and enterprise business systems in a greatly simplified manner. A simple example of this is the ability to create an Excel spreadsheet on the server without the need for Excel.

The Office XML formats were designed to be:

- More robust than the binary formats, thereby helping to reduce the risk of lost information resulting from damaged or corrupted files.

- Open, resulting in more secure and transparent files. You can share documents confidently because you can easily identify and remove personally identifiable information and sensitive business information such as user names, comments, and file paths.

- Backward-compatible with Microsoft Office 2000, Microsoft Office XP, and Microsoft Office 2003. Users of these versions can adopt the new format with little effort and continue to gain benefits from using their existing files.

The benefits of the Office XML formats include:

- Easy integration of business information with documents

- Rapid creation of documents from disparate data sources, thereby accelerating document assembly, data mining, and content reuse

- Improved interoperability through an open, transparent format

- XML- and ZIP file-based compression technologies

- Access to information stored within 2007 documents

- The ability to create and edit 2007 documents without automating the Microsoft Office application object models

Figure 1-7 provides a visual representation of the Open XML file format.

FIGURE 1-7 Open XML architecture

Excel Services

Excel Services, outlined in Figure 1-8, is part of MOSS 2007. It extends the capabilities of Microsoft Office Excel 2007 through the broad sharing of spreadsheets and improved manageability and security. Excel Services also provides a means for reusing spreadsheet models through a scalable, server-based calculation service and an interactive, Web-based user interface.

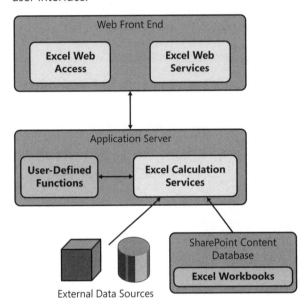

FIGURE 1-8 Architecture of Excel Services

Excel Services has three core components: Excel Web Access, Excel Web Services, and Excel Calculation Services. Excel Services handles communication among the three components and load-balances the requests made to Excel Calculation Services. The Excel Web Access, Excel Web Services, and Excel Calculation Services components can be divided into components that reside on the front-end Web server and those that live on a back-end application server. The Web front end includes Excel Web Services. The Excel Calculation Services component resides on the back-end application server, alongside any user-defined function assemblies that an administrator may have added.

Web Site and Security Framework

The Web Site and Security Framework is a common site framework for intranet, extranet, and public-facing sites. This framework integrates with ASP.NET 2.0 and provides support for ASP .NET master pages and native ASP.NET Web parts.

ASP.NET is Microsoft's Web Application Framework for building dynamic Web applications, sites, and XML Web services. ASP.NET is a core component of the overall Microsoft.NET platform and is central to WSS and MOSS. ASP.NET supports master pages, which provide the user experience, design, and behaviors of the pages within your SharePoint sites. It is through a combination of layout and content provided by master pages and content pages, respectively, that produce the final page for presentation in the browser. A common role-based security model that integrates with Active Directory services, the Web Site and Security Framework also exposes a greatly improved site template model. This model allows solution creators to take required features and combine them into site templates. Users can then provision themselves, and then configure and customize.

A Breakthrough Opportunity for Businesses and Developers

Developers are experiencing a breakthrough now that the common services described in previous sections are being offered in a single platform. With fewer platforms and tools to learn and with a common deployment model, developing OBAs in conjunction with .NET applications and Web services provides for faster development at a lower cost.

Previously, in Figure 1-2, the four major areas show how information is presented and consumed by end users, how information is processed, how collaboration occurs, and how information is stored. Information is made available through a MOSS 2007 portal that has sites composed of pages, and pages composed of Web parts. A Web part is the most basic building block of the portal. Solution providers can develop Web parts and incorporate Web parts that are provided out of the box, one of which provides Excel spreadsheets and charts and another the capability to view lists and tables.

Web parts are aggregated within pages. Users can assemble this aggregation from the collection of Web parts made available to them, or dashboard templates can be created from these pages. For example, developers can create standard dashboards for business functions involved in sales, inventory, or any other business area or provide business intelligence views for specific managers or disciplines within the organization.

Architecture of an Office Business Application

The architecture of an OBA involves leveraging multiple parts of the Office platform. For example, developers can create and package template sites along functional lines. An entire site can be deployed as part of an OBA solution. Users can also work with My Sites, personal sites in which they can create pages from scratch using the Web parts made available to them, or simply pull in links to standard dashboards that are appropriate for their role. Further, these sites can be integrated with a custom Office client.

Within this architecture, information is processed and can be worked on by the users of a site through a number of services within the 2007 Office system. For example, documents live in document libraries, and forms live in form libraries. Document libraries for spreadsheets can be registered with Excel Services, and the worksheets they contain can then be distributed through MOSS-based views of charts and tables. You can also present business data in lists and tables in Office MOSS 2007 through the BDC.

Figure 1-9 provides a high-level architectural overview of the Microsoft Office platform. This figure illustrates the various technologies, tools, and layers that make up an OBA.

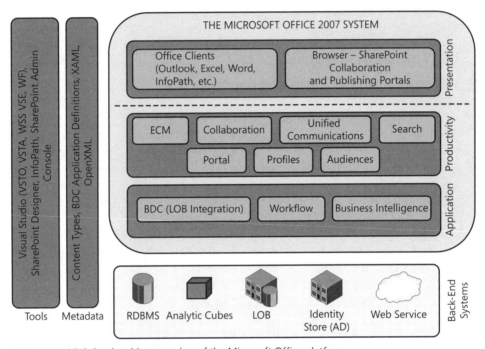

FIGURE 1-9 High-level architecture view of the Microsoft Office platform

Workflows can be created using Visual Studio Tools for Office 3.0 or Microsoft Office SharePoint Designer. Then you can associate these workflows with document and form libraries. You can indicate to SharePoint Server 2007 which workflows to invoke against a document when it is modified or created. These workflows might be related to a business process (document approval, for example) or to document life-cycle management (for example, record expiration dates).

Finally, you can access the information that lives in back-end systems through the BDC or by workflows. This information can be presented through a Web service interface or through direct ADO.NET data connection. The BDC makes information available in lists and tables within MOSS and allows an association of actions to be taken on that data. A drop-down menu on the table, invoking specified URLs and passing in context, then makes these actions available. These URLs can correspond to a Web service or link to an Office document that is prepopulated by the context that is passed in from the BDC.

Attributes of an Office Business Application

OBAs have certain attributes that are enabled by the platform capabilities and the supporting technologies. When building an OBA, the following attributes make your solution more robust and allow you to focus on solving the particular business problem being addressed by your application.

Ease of Use

IWs today often need to request LOB system experts to export useful business data from an LOB system into tools such as Excel. The data, in this case, is presented in a disconnected fashion. OBAs bridge this gap by presenting business data in the user interface that information workers are familiar with. IWs can now analyze the data using tools they already know how to use, thereby facilitating more informed decision making and actions.

Role-Based

OBAs take people-centric processes and map them to system-centric processes to enable workers to perform a particular task from beginning to end without having to shift context, pull data from various data sources manually, or perform analyses in disparate applications. A common identity and security system are also built with OBAs.

Collaborative

Team collaboration is often required to accomplish a business task and typically occurs outside the context of enterprise systems. The OBA platform allows developers to capture many aspects of a business process within a Microsoft Office application so processes and data are centrally located and key information is not lost. The ability to share and connect with others is built into the platform and supports both formal and informal processes (such as workflows), allowing for more complex applications.

Configurable

OBAs are serviceable by their end users, adaptive, and highly customizable by both IT developers and end users. The collaboration and business rules are not hard-coded into the presentation tier, so end users have substantial control over customizing applications to meet their own needs. Power users can arrange their portals in the manner they choose and set business rules for certain tasks using familiar tools. As business needs undergo change, IT developers can rebuild and redeploy the business-tier components, thus maintaining their business applications relatively easily and with less code.

Contextual

OBAs focus on business interactions, analytics, and actions. Users are thus allowed to make informed decisions and act within the context of the business problems at hand by having real-time business data at all times. OBAs do not reinvent the wheel for functions such as data access, data interactions, workflows, analysis, and reporting. However, they leverage these capabilities from the underlying platform. Thus business applications can build on the foundational capabilities of the Office system to provide business capabilities of their own while at the same time doing so in an environment that is comfortable and familiar to the IW.

How Do You Develop an OBA?

There are several development tools and Microsoft Office applications that can be used to create Office Business Applications. The focus of this book is how to leverage the latest capabilities built into Microsoft Visual Studio 2008, but it is important to mention the other array of tools that can be used for development of OBAs.

Microsoft Visual Studio 2008 Tools for the 2007 Microsoft Office System

Microsoft Visual Studio 2008 provides developers with the ability to build applications targeting the 2007 and 2003 Office system. This release of Visual Studio contains the most advanced feature set for developing Office solutions.

Visual Studio 2008 includes the following functionality:

- Visual designers for UI extensibility.
- SharePoint workflow support.
- Data binding in Word content controls.
- VBA —> VSTO interoperability.
- Application-level add-ins for most client programs (both 2003 and 2007).
- Document-level add-ins for Excel and Word 2007.
- Improved deployment and security using ClickOnce. (Yes, ClickOnce is finally here for Office solutions!)

The following illustrations, Figures 1-10 and 1-11, provide views to the different project templates that can be developed using Visual Studio 2008.

One of the greatest features added to Visual Studio 2008 for Office solutions is the support for developing Microsoft Office Outlook 2007 Forms regions. Form regions add custom functionality to standard Outlook 2007 forms. Form regions provide a range of options for presenting a UI, including:

- A customized default page of any standard form
- Up to 30 additional pages to any standard form
- Replacement or enhancement of any standard form
- Custom UI displayed in the reading pane in addition to the Document Inspector

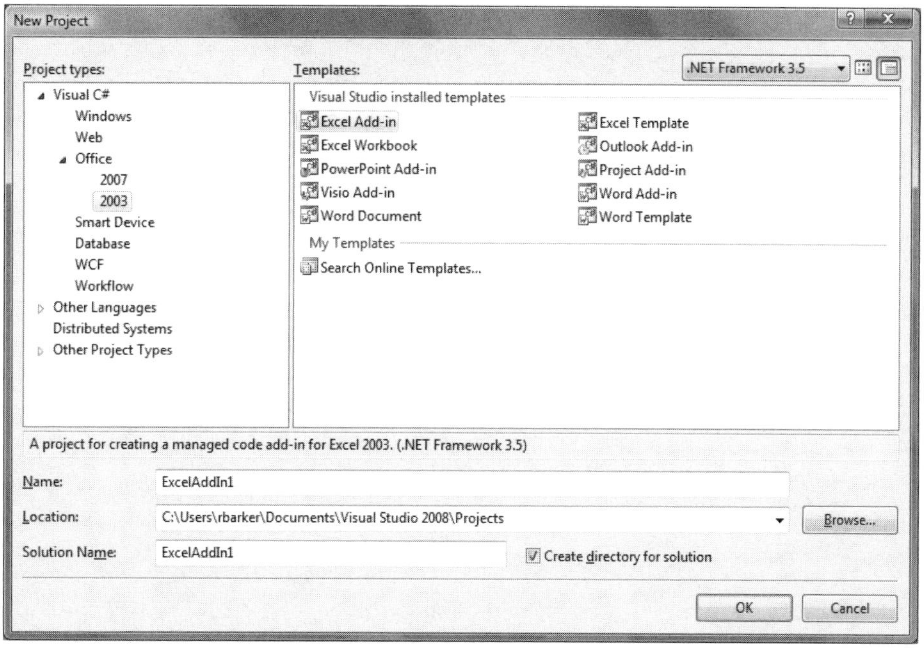

FIGURE 1-10 Office 2003 project templates in Visual Studio 2008

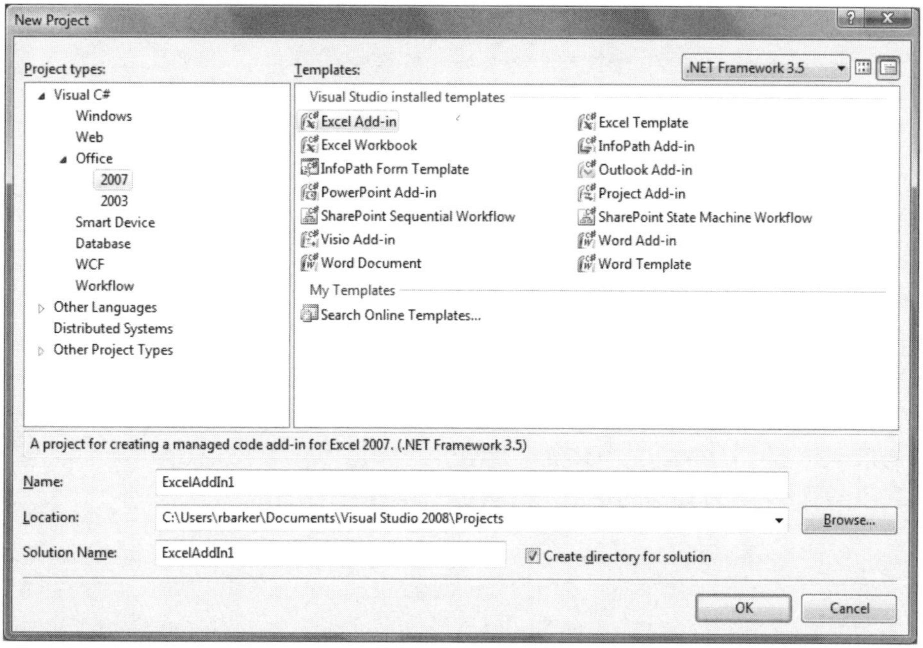

FIGURE 1-11 Office 2007 project templates in Visual Studio 2008

You can design the layout of a form region by using the Outlook 2007 Form Region Designer, as shown in Figure 1-12. You can then import the form region into an application-level add-in project and use managed code to handle events in the form region. Before you test the form region, you define the region's properties and associate the form region with an Outlook message class.

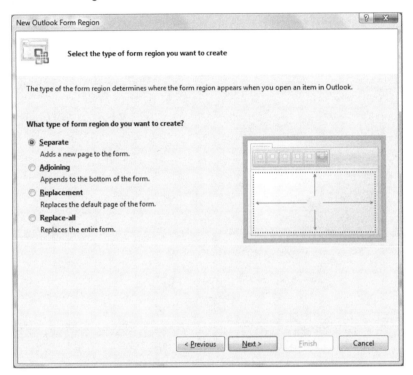

FIGURE 1-12 Visual Studio 2008 Outlook Forms Region wizard

To learn more about an integrated SharePoint development experience, read the next section, which discusses Microsoft Visual Studio 2005 extensions for Windows SharePoint Services version 3.0. Unfortunately Visual Studio 2008 at the time of release does not support integrated SharePoint development, so you will need to run Visual Studio 2005 and 2008 side by side to accomplish a seamless development experience across Office clients and servers.

Microsoft Visual Studio 2005 Tools for the 2007 Microsoft Office System Second Edition

Although this book's focus is Visual Studio 2008, it is important to mention Visual Studio 2005 Tools for the 2007 Microsoft Office System Second Edition (VSTO 2005 SE). A fully supported free add-on to Visual Studio 2005, VSTO 2005 SE gives developers the ability to build applications targeting the 2007 Office system. VSTO 2005 SE includes the following functionality:

- Application-level customizations and add-ins for the most popular Office applications, including the 2003 and 2007 versions of Word, Excel, Outlook, Visio, and Microsoft Office PowerPoint, and the 2007 version of InfoPath. The safe loading, unloading, and management of managed add-ins are some of the most important features of VSTO 2005 SE.

- A programming model and run-time support for the Ribbon, custom task panes, and Outlook forms regions.

- Design-time support for InfoPath 2007 forms so you can build your forms from the Visual Studio IDE.

- Support for Visual Studio 2005 Professional.

- In addition, there is also an additional free add-on, Microsoft Visual Studio extensions for Windows SharePoint Services, that provides the following tools to aid developers in building SharePoint applications:

Visual Studio 2005 project templates

- Web part
- Team site definition
- Blank site definition
- List definition

Visual Studio 2005 item templates

These items can be added into an existing project:

- Web part
- Custom field
- List definition (with optional event receiver)
- Content type (with optional event receiver)
- Module

SharePoint Solution Generator

- This stand-alone program generates a site definition project from an existing SharePoint site. The program enables developers to use the browser and Microsoft Office SharePoint Designer to customize the content of their sites before creating code by using Visual Studio.

Microsoft Office SharePoint Designer

Office SharePoint Designer 2007 is specifically designed to help you create and customize Web sites and workflows built with Windows SharePoint Services and Office SharePoint

Server 2007. It provides tools that IT professionals and solution developers need to develop SharePoint-based applications and workflow solutions that address organizational agility and business process automation.

With Office SharePoint Designer 2007, you can design SharePoint workflows and applications without having to use traditional procedural coding languages or techniques. Instead, SharePoint Designer provides tools that you can use to:

- Build conditional views and forms with validation
- Read, write, and present data from a variety of data sources, including XML files, SQL databases such as Microsoft SQL Server 2005, and Web services
- Compile data from multiple sources to create flexible, customized views and reports
- Build Web part pages and connect Web parts to create business applications

What Does an OBA Look Like?

We have been talking throughout this chapter about all the different aspects of an Office Business Application: the attributes that make up an OBA, the technologies and capabilities it provides, the various types of integration that can be achieved, and lastly the development tools that can be used. As you very well may imagine, OBAs can be implemented in a multitude of ways using the various client applications provided by the 2007 Microsoft Office system. Figure 1-13 illustrates a sales forecasting scenario.

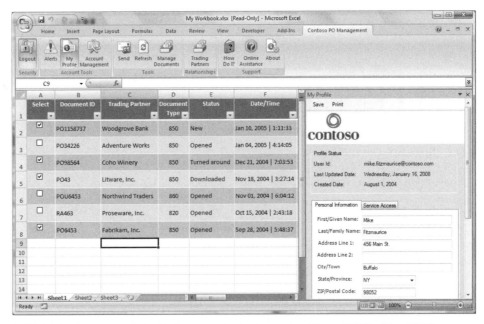

FIGURE 1-13 An example Office Business Application leveraging Microsoft Office Excel 2007

As mentioned earlier in this chapter, the focus of this book is on providing examples of and guidance on what can be accomplished with Microsoft Visual Studio 2008; the following OBA was built using Microsoft Visual Studio 2008.

The example OBA illustrated in Figure 1-13, shows some of the individual capabilities discussed earlier in this chapter, such as a custom Ribbon, task pane, and LOB integration.

All of the capabilities talked about in this chapter will be elaborated on further in subsequent chapters. You will also find code samples to help you jump start your development efforts.

Summary

This opening chapter introduced what OBAs are all about and the various Microsoft tools and technologies that can be used to develop Office Business Application solutions. The remainder of the book will take an in-depth look at the different tools and technologies mentioned in this chapter. Specifically, other chapters will explore:

- Chapter 2 – "Creating a Smart Client for Your Office Business Application by Using VSTO"
- Chapter 3 – "Building Business Intelligence for Your Office Business Applications"
- Chapter 4 – "Integrating Web Services into Your Office Business Applications"
- Chapter 5 – "Building Social Networking into Your Office Business Application"
- Chapter 6 – "SharePoint and Developing Office Business Applications"
- Chapter 7 – "Managing Complex Business Processes with Custom SharePoint Workflow"
- Chapter 8 – "Deploying Your Office Business Application in the Enterprise"

Enjoy the remainder of the book and developing your first Office Business Application solution!

Further Reading and Related Technologies

A number of new technologies, acronyms, approaches, designs, experiences, and architectures will be introduced in the remainder of this book. No single individual can know *everything*, and that is why we count on the many resources that are created by Microsoft and, most importantly, the community of developers focused on productivity solutions based on the Microsoft Office system. This is by no means a comprehensive list of resources, but it definitely provides pointers to sites, blogs, and other related reading materials that will get you started in your quest to develop an OBA solution.

- *6 Microsoft Office Business Applications for Office SharePoint Server 2007* by Rob Barker, Joanna Bichsel, Adam Buenz, Steve Fox, John Holliday, Bhushan Nene, and Karthik Ravindran (Microsoft Press)

- Microsoft Office Developer Center: *http://msdn.microsoft.com/office*

- Windows SharePoint Services 3.0: Software Development Kit (SDK):
  http://www.microsoft.com/downloads/details.aspx?FamilyId=05E0DD12-8394-402B-8936-A07FE8AFAFFD&displaylang=en

- *Inside Microsoft Windows SharePoint Services 3.0* by Ted Pattison and Daniel Larson (Microsoft Press)

- *Inside Microsoft Office SharePoint Server 2007* by Patrick Tisseghem (Microsoft Press)

- *Windows SharePoint Services 3.0 Inside Out* by Errin O'Connor (Microsoft Press)

- Microsoft Office SharePoint Server 2007 Developer Center:
  http://msdn2.microsoft.com/en-us/office/aa905503.aspx

- Microsoft Windows SharePoint Services Developer Center:
  http://msdn2.microsoft.com/en-us/sharepoint/default.aspx

- Microsoft Office Visual How-to Center:
  http://msdn2.microsoft.com/en-us/office/bb266408.aspx

- Microsoft Visual Studio Developer Center:
  http://msdn.microsoft.com/vstudio

Chapter 2

Creating a Smart Client for Your Office Business Application by Using VSTO

One of the main strengths of creating an OBA is leveraging Office as your client platform. This smart client application brings together your business application with the Office clients. You are able to tightly integrate your business data and processes into an experience with which the user is comfortable and familiar. As the application developer, you are able to create a richer experience in a shorter period of time using the tools and services provided by Office and Visual Studio. In this chapter, you will see how Visual Studio Tools for Office makes it easy to bring together SharePoint and LOB data into Office applications such as Outlook, Word, and Excel using visual designers and the .NET Framework.

Getting Started with Visual Studio Tools for Office

Visual Studio Tools for Office (VSTO) is a set of technologies that allows Visual Studio developers to create Office applications. VSTO version 3.0 installs as part of Visual Studio Professional 2008. VSTO supports creating Office 2003 and 2007 applications for Word, Excel, Outlook, PowerPoint, Visio, Project, and SharePoint Workflow. VSTO supports creating document-level solutions for Word, Excel, and InfoPath. A document-level solution is loaded when the document, workbook, or form is open; it is unloaded when any of them is closed. VSTO also supports creating add-in solutions. An add-in solution is loaded when the Office application starts, and it is unloaded when the Office application closes. VSTO add-ins are the replacement for the old shared add-ins model.

A Brief History of VSTO

So that you understand where VSTO is today and where it is going tomorrow, you should know how we got here. One of the biggest challenges for VSTO is the fact that the developer division at Microsoft, which includes the VSTO team, is separate from the Office division at

Microsoft. This means that they both have their own sets of priorities and ship schedules. Office 2003 was the current version when the VSTO team was formed. The first version of VSTO shipped shortly after for Visual Studio 2003 and targeted Office 2003 Professional Edition. This was a targeted release to get some Office tools to market and generate feedback for the next version. Version 2.0 of VSTO shipped as a standalone SKU based on the Visual Studio 2005 IDE. Version 2.0 was a giant leap forward for VSTO. It included add-in support for Outlook and visual designers for Word and Excel solutions. The number of new features was enormous (for a complete list of features, read the book *VSTO for Mere Mortals™: A VBA Developer's Guide to Microsoft Office Development*). Version 2.0 still targeted Office 2003 Professional, but Office 2007 was about to be released the following year. This put VSTO in a tough position because the next version of Visual Studio wasn't due for a couple of years. What was needed was an add-on to Visual Studio 2005 that targeted the new Office 2007. That release of VSTO was called VSTO Second Edition (SE). It added support for Office 2007 add-ins and increased the number of Office 2003 add-ins as well. And the best part was that it was a free download for Visual Studio. Although VSTO SE enabled Office 2007 developers to create add-ins, they couldn't easily take advantage of all the new features in Office, such as the Ribbon. This brings us to where we are today. The next major release, Visual Studio 2008, now has VSTO version 3.0 built into the SKU. VSTO version 3.0 adds visual designers for creating Ribbons and Outlook form regions. It supports both Office 2003 Professional and Office 2007 Standard or above.

You will see in this chapter how to take advantage of some of these features to create your Office Business Applications.

Integrated Development Environment (IDE)

VSTO is part of Visual Studio 2008 Integrated Development Environment (IDE). This gives the Office developer all of the power and features of Visual Studio and all of the power and features of the .NET Framework. Figure 2-1 shows what an Excel 2007 project looks like in the IDE.

Project Templates

VSTO ships with a number of Visual Studio project templates. These templates are divided into two major categories: Office 2003 and Office 2007 for both VB and C# languages.

Office 2003

The Office 2003 project folder, seen in Figure 2-2, contains document-level projects for Word, Excel, and InfoPath, and add-in projects for Word, Excel, PowerPoint, Visio, InfoPath, and Outlook. If you are targeting Office 2003 users with your OBA solution, you should install Office 2003 Professional on your development machine to use all of these templates. But if you are targeting a mixed set of users—some on Office 2003 and some on Office 2007—you should install Office 2007. Then you will be able to create a 2003 add-in that will run for both

FIGURE 2-1 A VSTO Excel project open in Visual Studio 2008

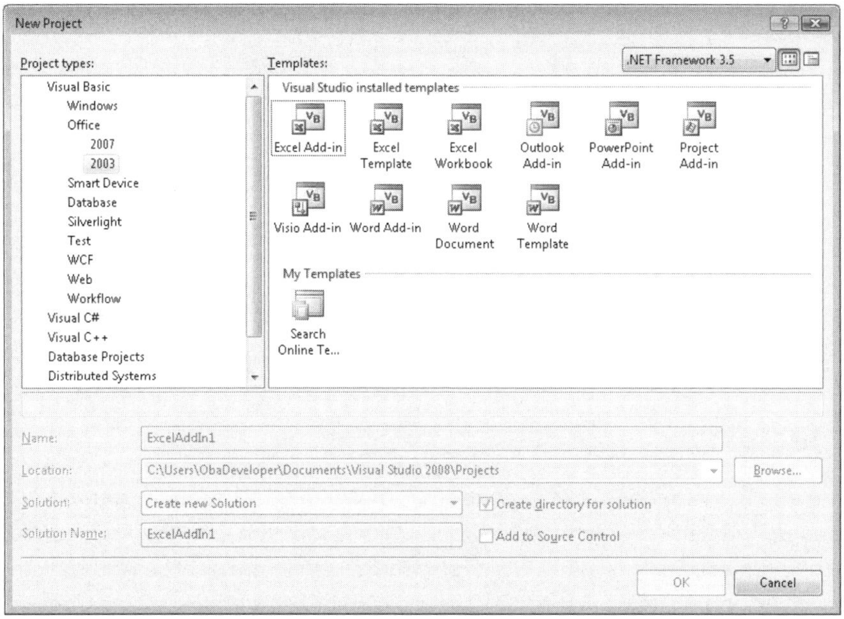

FIGURE 2-2 The project types available for Office 2003 development

Office 2003 and Office 2007 users. The caveat, of course, is that you must use the lowest-common denominator of features, in this case Office 2003. You could also do work to "light up" Office 2007 features if you detect the version of Office in which your add-in is running.

Office 2007

The Office 2007 project folder, seen in Figure 2-3, contains document-level projects for Word, Excel, and InfoPath. There are add-in projects for Word, Excel, PowerPoint, Project, Visio, InfoPath, and Outlook. There are also two SharePoint server projects for creating sequential and state machine workflows. The two SharePoint projects require that Visual Studio runs on a machine with SharePoint installed. You will use some of these templates in this chapter to create OBAs targeting Office 2007 users.

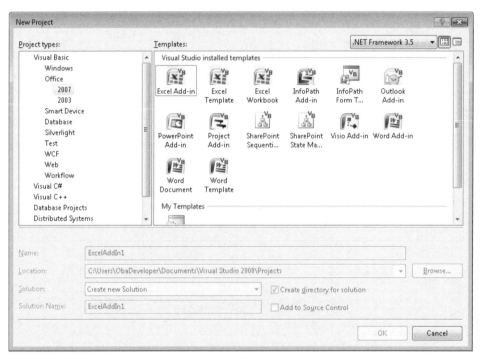

FIGURE 2-3 The project types available for Office 2007 development

Item Templates

There are also a number of item templates that ship with VSTO, seen in Figure 2-4. Item templates are the items that you add to your project. You can open the Add New Item dialog by selecting Project, and then Add New Item from the main menu. The Add New Item dialog contains many project items, but three are for Office projects: Actions Pane Control, Ribbon (XML), and Ribbon (Visual Designer).

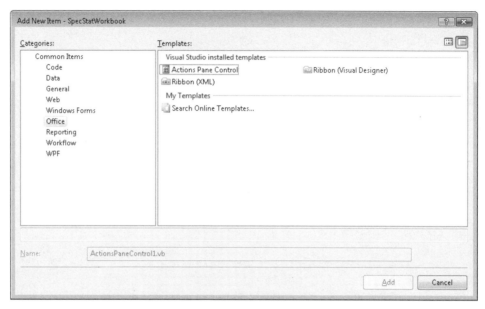

FIGURE 2-4 The project item types available for Office 2007 development

Debugging

Debugging Office projects with VSTO is just like other Visual Studio applications, such as a Windows Forms application. You simply need to press F5 to build and run the solution. The VSTO project system will build, deploy, and launch the Office application, and attach the debugger. All of the standard Visual Studio debugging features work with your Office project as well, such as break points, edit and continue, immediate window, and the autos window.

OBA Smart Client Samples

An OBA at its essence is about surfacing your line-of-business data using Office as the interface. In this chapter, you will see various examples using VB and C# of how to surface a SharePoint list using Office 2007 and VSTO. There are two ways to access a SharePoint list. One uses the SharePoint COM API, which is available only if you are actually running the code on the SharePoint Server. The second way uses the SharePoint Web services API. You can access this API if you are not on the server, such as the case with Office client applications. The difficulty is that Web services API is complicated and more challenging to program against. For this chapter, you will use a hybrid approach by creating a custom Web service component that will use the COM API to return the list as a simple XML document. This solves the problem of using the COM API on the server but calling it from the Office client. Listing 2-1 shows you the Web service method called GetListData, which returns the SharePoint list as an XML document. Creating SharePoint custom Web services is outside the scope of this chapter, but the complete source code is included with the book.

LISTING 2-1 GetListData returns the SharePoint list as an XML document.

```
[WebMethod]
public XmlDocument GetListData(String ServerName, String ListName)
{
   String str;
   SPList oSPList;

   XmlNode oXmlNode;
   XmlElement oXmlElement, oXmlParent;
   XmlDocument oXmlDocument = new XmlDocument();

   oXmlDocument.LoadXml ("<SPListItems/>");

   using (SPSite oSPSite = new SPSite(ServerName))
   {
      using (SPWeb oSPWeb = oSPSite.OpenWeb())
      {
         oSPList = GetList(oSPWeb, ListName);

         if (oSPList != null)
         {
            foreach (SPListItem oSPListItem in oSPList.Items)
            {
               oXmlParent = oXmlDocument.CreateElement("SPListItem");
               oXmlNode = oXmlDocument.DocumentElement.AppendChild(oXmlParent);

               foreach (SPField oSPField in oSPListItem.Fields)
               {
                  if (oSPField.Hidden)
                  continue;

                  str = oSPField.InternalName.Replace(" ", " ");
                  oXmlElement = oXmlDocument.CreateElement(str);
                  oXmlParent.AppendChild(oXmlElement);

                  try
                  {
                     str = oSPField.Title;
                     str = oSPListItem[str].ToString();
                  }

                  catch (Exception e)
                  {
                        str = "Field error:" + e.Message;
                  }
```

```
                oXmlElement.InnerText = str;
                }
            }
        }
      }
    }

    return oXmlDocument;
}
```

The GetListData function runs on the SharePoint server and uses the SPSite class to get an instance of the SharePoint server. The OpenWeb method will open the site. Once you have the site open, Listing 2-2 shows how to iterate over the lists collection to find the list you are looking for.

LISTING 2-2 GetList returns the list from the lists collection.

```
private SPList GetList(SPWeb oSPWeb, String strListName)
{
    SPList oRet = null;

    strListName = strListName.Replace("%20", " ");
    strListName = strListName.ToUpper();

    foreach (SPList oSPList in oSPWeb.Lists)
    {
        if (oSPList.Title.ToUpper() == strListName)
        {
            oRet = oSPList;
            break;
        }
    }

    return oRet;
}
```

Once you have the list, you can iterate over each item and over each field within each item. The requirements for getting this all working correctly with a SharePoint server is a lot, even just to demonstrate the features of VSTO on the client, so we have coded the examples to cache the result set in the projects. The examples use a compiler flag to signal if you are running online or offline. If you are offline, you do not need a SharePoint server, just Office 2007 and VSTO. But we want you to see that the real goal of OBAs is to connect to live business data on the server. Listing 2-3 shows a sample list returned from the custom Web service call to GetListData.

LISTING 2-3 Sample list XML document record returned by the custom SharePoint Web service

```xml
<?xml version="1.0" encoding="utf-8" ?>
<SPListItems xmlns="">
    <SPListItem>
        <Title>Wenauer</Title>
        <FirstName>Peter</FirstName>
        <FullName>Peter Wenauer</FullName>
        <Email>Peter.Wenauer@Contoso.com</Email>
        <Company>Contoso</Company>
        <JobTitle></JobTitle>
        <WorkPhone>229-555-0100</WorkPhone>
        <HomePhone>229-555-0101</HomePhone>
        <CellPhone></CellPhone>
        <WorkFax></WorkFax>
        <WorkAddress>1 Main St</WorkAddress>
        <WorkCity>Albany</WorkCity>
        <WorkState>GA</WorkState>
        <WorkZip>31707</WorkZip>
        <WorkCountry></WorkCountry>
        <WebPage>http://www.Contoso.com</WebPage>
        <Comments></Comments>
        <Gender>male</Gender>
        <ID>13</ID>
        <ContentType>Contact</ContentType>
        <Modified>9/22/2007 4:26:45 PM</Modified>
        <Created>9/22/2007 3:53:27 PM</Created>
        <Author>1;#Paul Stubbs</Author>
        <Editor>1;#Paul Stubbs</Editor>
        <_UIVersionString>1.0</_UIVersionString>
        <Attachments>False</Attachments>
        <Edit></Edit>
        <LinkTitleNoMenu>Wenauer</LinkTitleNoMenu>
        <LinkTitle>Wenauer</LinkTitle>
        <DocIcon></DocIcon>
    </SPListItem>
```

Office Add-Ins

The most common way to surface your LOB data is through Outlook. Many users are in Outlook most of the day and conduct much of their business processes using Outlook. One action that users commonly take is using Outlook rules to sort their incoming e-mail. We will create an Outlook add-in that makes a rule that automatically moves e-mail from our customers in SharePoint to a customer folder. You could also just write code to handle the new mail event and move the mail without creating a rule. But a rule has one big advantage in that it runs on the Exchange server. The rule will even sort your mail when Outlook is not running. For this first version, the sync customers rule will run when the add-in is loaded. Later you will create an Office Ribbon tab to start the sync.

Open Visual Studio and create a new Outlook 2007 add-in project in VB. The add-in project will contain a ThisAddin.vb class, seen in Listing 2-4. This is the main entry point for all VSTO add-ins. You will put the method to sync the customers rule in the Startup method.

LISTING 2-4 ThisAddin class contains the Startup and Shutdown methods.

```
Public Class ThisAddIn

    Private Sub ThisAddIn_Startup(ByVal sender As Object, ByVal e As System.EventArgs) _
    Handles Me.Startup
        Dim RulesHelper As New Rules
        RulesHelper.SyncCustomerRule()
    End Sub

    Private Sub ThisAddIn_Shutdown(ByVal sender As Object, ByVal e As System.EventArgs) _
    Handles Me.Shutdown

    End Sub

End Class
```

This creates a new instance of the rules class. The rules class contains all of the methods for managing our Outlook rules. It then calls the SyncCustomerRule to create an Outlook rule with our customers.

SyncCustomerRule first checks if Outlook is in online or offline mode by calling the IsOnline function shown in Listing 2-5. Outlook rules can be accessed only if you are connected to Exchange, so you need to check this first. One way to do this is to try and access the Public folder. If you can access it, then you are online; if not, then you are offline.

LISTING 2-5 Check to see if Outlook is online with Exchange.

```
'Check if Outlook is Online with Exchange
Private Function IsOnline() As Boolean
    Try
        'This will throw an exception if not online
        Dim cnt As Integer = Globals.ThisAddIn.Application. _
        Session.Folders.Item("Public Folders"). _
        Folders.Item("All Public Folders").Items.Count
        Return True
    Catch ex As Exception
        Return False
    End Try
End Function
```

Next you need to get the list of customers from SharePoint by calling the GetList function seen in Listing 2-6. If the Offline custom compiler flag is set, then just return the customer XML document from the embedded resource.

LISTING 2-6 Return the SharePoint list of customers.

```
    'return the List from SharePoint
    Public Shared Function GetList(ByVal serverName As String, ByVal ListName As String)
    As XElement
        'Check if we have SharePoint Online
#If Not OFFLINE Then
        'Custom webservice
        Dim SharePointLists As New ListServices.ListServices

        'Set the current user for the SharePoint lookup
        SharePointLists.Credentials = System.Net.CredentialCache.DefaultCredentials

        'Call the custom webservice
        Dim SPListXml As Xml.XmlNode = SharePointLists.GetListData(serverName, ListName)

        'Convert the XML Node to an XElement
        Dim SPList As XElement = XElement.Parse(SPListXml.OuterXml)
#Else
        Dim SPList As XElement = XElement.Load(New IO.StringReader(My.Resources.OBACustomers))

#End If

        'return the xml results
        Return SPList

    End Function
```

Listing 2-7 shows the GetCustomerRule function, which creates an Outlook rule named
"Customers." If this rule already exists, then just return the existing rule. The rule will move
incoming mail that matches to a folder called Customers. If the Customers folder does not
exist, it will also be created.

LISTING 2-7 Create an Outlook rule called "Customers."

```
  'Return the existing rule or create a new one
 Private Function GetCustomerRule() As Outlook.Rule

    Dim store As Outlook.Store
    store = Globals.ThisAddIn.Application.Session.DefaultStore

    Dim rules As Outlook.Rules = store.GetRules()
    Dim customerRule As Outlook.Rule = Nothing

    'Get or create the Customer rule
    For Each rule As Outlook.Rule In rules
       If rule.Name = "Customers" Then
          Return rule
       End If
    Next
```

```
'Not found so create a new one
customerRule = rules.Create("Customers", Outlook.OlRuleType.olRuleReceive)

'Add the action to move to the Customers folder
Dim moveAction As Outlook.MoveOrCopyRuleAction
moveAction = customerRule.Actions.MoveToFolder
'We need a folder so get it or create it
moveAction.Folder = GetFolder("Customers")
moveAction.Enabled = True

rules.Save()

Return customerRule
End Function
```

At this point, the Customer rule has been created. Your next step is to add all of the customers' e-mail addresses to the Address rule condition, seen in Listing 2-8. The Address property takes an array of string objects, which are the e-mail addresses. You can use Language Integrated Query (LINQ) for XML to quickly create a string collection of addresses. In this sample, we take the first ten customers. The ToArray method of the collection will turn the collection into an array, which is the type the Address property requires. In the past, this would take many lines of code, but LINQ makes this work trivial.

LISTING 2-8 Use LINQ to create a collection of customer e-mail addresses.

```
'get the customer emails from the SharePoint list
Dim customerEmailAddresses = (From emailColumn In _
                        SPListXElement.Elements("SPListItem").Elements("Email")

                        Where emailColumn.Value IsNot Nothing _
                        Select emailColumn.Value).Skip(0).Take(10)

'Add the customers
Dim from As Outlook.AddressRuleCondition
from = customerRule.Conditions.SenderAddress
from.Address = customerEmailAddresses.ToArray
from.Enabled = True
```

Listing 2-9 completes the sync by saving and running the rule.

LISTING 2-9 Save and run the customer rule.

```
'save the rule
Dim rules As Outlook.Rules = customerRule.Parent
rules.Save()

'Run the rule now
customerRule.Execute(True)
```

Press F5 to build and run the solution. This will launch Outlook and attach the Visual Studio debugger. When the add-in loads, the Startup method will call the SyncCustomerRule. You can verify that the rule was created by opening the Rules and Alerts dialog from the Tools main menu. If you double-click on the Customer rule, you can see the rule's details in Figure 2-5.

FIGURE 2-5 Customer rule detail

Office Document Solutions

VSTO supports the creation of document-level solutions. Document-level solutions are tied to a specific document. When the document is opened, the solution is loaded, and when the document is closed, the solution is unloaded. The lifetime of the solution is tied to the document, whereas with add-ins the lifetime of the code is tied to the application. VSTO supports document-level projects for Word, Excel, and InfoPath. Another interesting feature of document-level projects is that the host application becomes the designer inside of Visual Studio. This enables you to drag and drop items from the toolbox, including WinForm controls and content controls, onto the surface of the document. It also allows drag-and-drop data binding from the data sources window.

Excel ListObject Data Binding

VSTO enables drag-and-drop data binding from a database, an object, and Web services. But in order to data bind to the Web service, it needs to be in a dataset format. It is not always possible to dictate the Web service format, so you will see how to create a list object data bound to a custom SharePoint Web service. You will use the Web service previously discussed in Listing 2-1. First create a new Excel 2007 workbook project. The default project creates four project items—one for the workbook and one for each of the three default sheets that a new Excel workbook contains. Open the code window for sheet1.vb and create a new method called CreateListObject. The code, in Listing 2-10, will call SharePoint to get the customers list. The XML must be converted to a dataset so that it can be data bound to the list object. Next you can programmatically add a list object control to the cell A1 on sheet1 and name it "List1." When data binding to a dataset, you can specify the columns you wish to bind to. In this example, you can use LINQ for XML to return a collection of all of the column names. You have all of the parameters needed to call the SetDataBinding method of the list object. You can call the CreateListObject from the startup method of sheet1 to create this when the worksheet is opened. Figure 2-6 shows the Excel document with the custom data binding.

LISTING 2-10 Create a list object data bound to a custom Web service.

```
Private Sub CreateListObject()
    'populate the gallery from the SharePoint List
    Dim SPListXElement As XElement

    'Get the customers list from SharePoint
    SPListXElement = SharePoint.GetList("http://pstubbs-moss", "OBACustomers")

    'convert the xml to a dataset that can be databound to the Excel ListObject
    Dim tr As New System.IO.StringReader(SPListXElement.ToString())
    Dim SPListDataSet As New DataSet
    SPListDataSet.ReadXml(tr)

    'Create a new ListObject and add it to the sheet
    Dim List1 As Microsoft.Office.Tools.Excel.ListObject = _
        Me.Controls.AddListObject(Me.Range("A1"), "List1")

    List1.AutoSetDataBoundColumnHeaders = True

    'get the customer emails from the SharePoint list using Xlinq
    Dim ColumnNames = From columnName _
                    In SPListXElement.Elements("SPListItem")(0).Elements _
                    Select columnName.Name.LocalName

    'Bind the ListObject to the SPList
    List1.SetDataBinding(SPListDataSet, "SPListItem", ColumnNames.ToArray())
End Sub
```

Office Ribbon Designer

The most visible new feature of Office 2007 is the Ribbon. The Ribbon replaces the menus and toolbars of previous Office versions. Office developers can customize the Ribbon using RibbonX, which is an XML representation of the Ribbon. While VSTO supports customizing

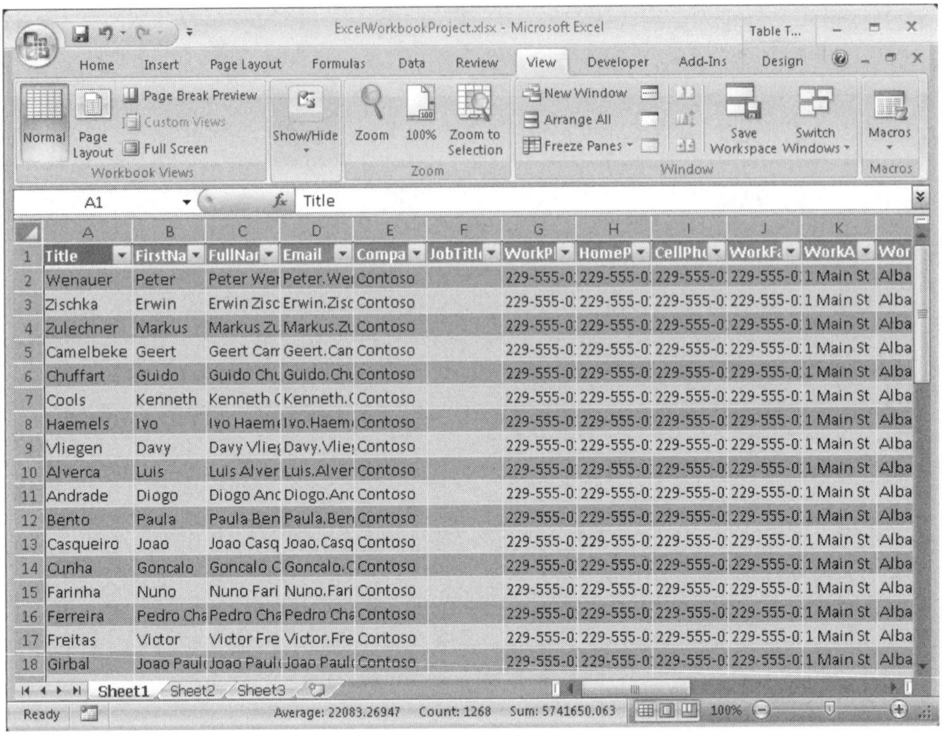

FIGURE 2-6 List object data bound to a custom Web service

the Ribbon using RibbonX, there is now a better way of using a visual designer. Figure 2-7 shows the visual Ribbon designer in VSTO that allows you to simply drag and drop tabs, groups, and controls onto the designer to visually build a Ribbon. This model is very much like creating a WinForm application. In fact, you simply double-click on the control to write the event handler code. The Ribbon designer in VSTO also contains an object model that makes developing interactions with the Ribbon more natural to a .NET developer. The RibbonX model is a callback model where you provide callback methods, and Office calls those methods when it thinks it's necessary. There is no way in the RibbonX model to set the label of a button directly. You must invalidate the controls and Office will re-fire all of the callbacks in which you can set the new label. In the VSTO designer model, you can set properties like you would on any other object, and the Ribbon designer object model will take care of updating the Ribbon.

In the first section, you created an Outlook add-in that synchronized a SharePoint list with a custom rule when the add-in was loaded. But calling a Web service and updating a rule in Exchange can take a few seconds. This delay when opening Outlook may not be desirable. A better solution would be to move the synchronize button to the Ribbon. Open the Outlook add-in project and add a new Ribbon designer item from the Add New item

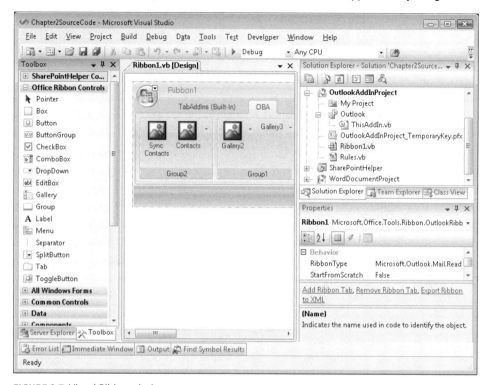

FIGURE 2-7 Visual Ribbon designer

dialog box. This will create a new project item called Ribbon1.vb. The default Ribbon type is associated with reading a mail item. This means that when you open an e-mail message, this Ribbon will be displayed in the inspector window. The Ribbon designer also creates a default tab in the Ribbon called TabAddins. This is the same tab that Office uses to put any legacy menu customizations you may have had. What you want to do is create a new tab called "OBA." On the OBA tab, add a group and a button from the Visual Studio toolbox on the left. Set the label property of this button to "Sync Contacts." Double-click on the button to add the code in Listing 2-11, which will call the SyncContactList method. Also remember to remove the call from the startup method of the add-in.

LISTING 2-11 Call the SyncContactList method from the button click event.

```vb
Private Sub Button1_Click(ByVal sender As System.Object, ByVal e As
Microsoft.Office.Tools.Ribbon.RibbonControlEventArgs) Handles Button1.Click
    Dim RulesHelper As New Rules
    RulesHelper.SyncCustomerRule()
End Sub
```

Press F5 to run the project. Open a mail message to see the OBA Ribbon.

Outlook Commandbars

Outlook has a hybrid implementation of the Ribbon and Commandbars. The Outlook main window uses Commandbars to add menus and toolbars. This is the traditional way that you would customize the Office user interface. You saw previously how to use the Ribbon designer to create a new Ribbon that can be attached to the various inspectors, but if you want to modify the main window, you will need to use code similar to Listing 2-12.

LISTING 2-12 Create Outlook menu using the CommandBars.

```
namespace CustomNewMail
{
  public partial class ThisAddIn
  {
    Office.CommandBarButton myButton;

    private void ThisAddIn_Startup(object sender, System.EventArgs e)
    {
      Office.CommandBar standardCommandBar;
      Office.CommandBarPopup ctrlNewButton;
      Office.CommandBarButton ctrlNewMailMessageButton;

      standardCommandBar = Application.ActiveExplorer().CommandBars["Standard"];
      ctrlNewButton = (Office.CommandBarPopup)standardCommandBar.Controls["New"];
      ctrlNewMailMessageButton = (Office.CommandBarButton)ctrlNewButton.Controls["Mail
                        Message"];

      myButton = (Office.CommandBarButton)ctrlNewButton.Controls.Add(Office.
                 MsoControlType.msoControlButton, missing, missing,ctrlNewMail
                 MessageButton.Index,true);

      myButton.Caption = "Steve's Mail Message";
      myButton.Visible = true;
      myButton.FaceId = ctrlNewMailMessageButton.FaceId;
      myButton.Style = Office.MsoButtonStyle.msoButtonIconAndCaption;

      myButton.Click += new Office._CommandBarButtonEvents_ClickEventHandler
                     (myButton_Click);

      ctrlNewMailMessageButton.Delete(true);
    }

    void myButton_Click(Microsoft.Office.Core.CommandBarButton Ctrl, ref bool
                     CancelDefault)
    {
      Outlook.MailItem newMail;

      newMail = (Outlook.MailItem)Application.CreateItem(Microsoft.Office.Interop.
                Outlook.OlItemType.olMailItem);
      newMail.MessageClass = "IPM.Note.SteveMail";
      newMail.Display(false);
    }
    ...
  }
}
```

Another common scenario is to populate a drop-down list with items from your line-of-business data. In this example, you will add customers from the SharePoint site to a Ribbon drop-down button. Add a gallery control from the toolbox to the OBA tab next to the Sync button. In the properties window for the gallery, double-click on the Items loading event to create an event handler. Listing 2-13 shows the code to load the items from the SharePoint list.

LISTING 2-13 Code to populate a Ribbon gallery from SharePoint with super tooltips

```
Private Sub Gallery1_ItemsLoading(ByVal sender As System.Object, ByVal e As
Microsoft.Office.Tools.Ribbon.RibbonControlEventArgs) Handles Gallery1.ItemsLoading

  'populate the gallery from the SharePoint List
  Dim SPListXElement As XElement

  'Get the customers list from SharePoint
  SPListXElement = SharePoint.GetList("http://pstubbs-moss", "OBACustomers")

  'get the customer emails from the SharePoint list
  Dim DropDownItems = From contact In _
                       SPListXElement.Elements("SPListItem") _
                       Where contact.Element("Email").Value IsNot Nothing _
                       Select New RibbonDropDownItem With { _
                          .Label = contact.Element("FullName").Value, _
                          .ScreenTip = contact.Element("Email").Value, _
                          .SuperTip = contact.Element("Company").Value, _
                          .OfficeImageId = "ClipArtinsert" _
                          }

  'clear the list before adding new ones
  Gallery1.Items.Clear()

  'add the contacts to the drop down list
  For Each galleryItem As RibbonDropDownItem In DropDownItems
     Gallery1.Items.Add(galleryItem)
  Next

End Sub
```

This code, like all of the other samples, gets the customer list from SharePoint. LINQ for XML makes it easy to turn the XML document into a collection of RibbonDropDownItem objects. This single LINQ statement parses the XML, creates a new RibbonDropDownItem object, and sets some of the properties. LINQ has done all of the work, and all that remains is to iterate through the collection and add each item to the Ribbon gallery control. You can see in Figure 2-8 the names of the customers, and when you hover over each, you see the super tooltip with the corresponding e-mail address and company name. You can see from this code that programming the Office Ribbon is very natural and what you would expect as a .NET developer.

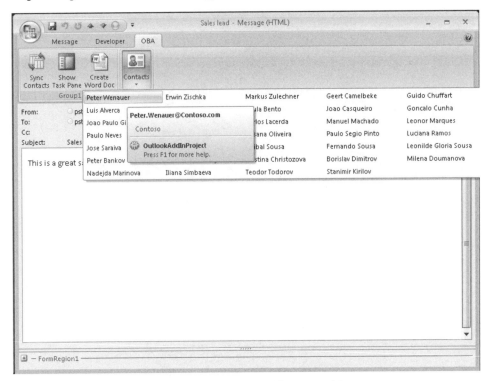

FIGURE 2-8 Ribbon gallery populated from SharePoint with super tooltips

Custom Task Panes

Custom task panes are a new feature in Office 2007 that allow developers to provide an application UI that can be docked to the left, right, top, or bottom of the host application. In this example, you will create a custom task pane that populates with a list of the customers from the SharePoint site. Using VSTO, you can easily add Windows Forms controls to the task pane, including the Windows Presentation Foundation (WPF) host control. This opens up the power of WPF to your Office applications. Open the existing Outlook project that you created in the previous examples. Add a WPF user control to the project from the Add Item dialog. Open the usercontrol1.xaml file that was created. You will use the designer to help you create a WPF style resource that dynamically creates buttons for each customer. The style will define the look and feel for the button and give it a cool rollover effect. In Listing 2-14, you can see that there is a style defined named "BlackGlassButton." This is the name we will use when creating our buttons for each customer.

LISTING 2-14 XAML resource for a glass-looking button with a rollover animation

```
<UserControl x:Class="UserControl1"
    xmlns="http://schemas.microsoft.com/winfx/2006/xaml/presentation"
    xmlns:x="http://schemas.microsoft.com/winfx/2006/xaml" Width="300" Height="100">
```

```
<UserControl.Resources>
  <Style x:Key="BlackGlassButton" BasedOn="{x:Null}" TargetType="{x:Type Button}">
    <Setter Property="Height" Value="50" />
    <Setter Property="Foreground" Value="#FFFFFFFF" />
    <Setter Property="Template">
      <Setter.Value>
...
    </Setter>
  </Style>
</UserControl.Resources>


<ScrollViewer HorizontalScrollBarVisibility="Auto">
<StackPanel x:FieldModifier="Public"  Name="StackPanel1" >

  <Button x:FieldModifier="Public"
      Style="{DynamicResource BlackGlassButton}"
      Name="Button1"
      Content="Button 1"/>
  <Button x:FieldModifier="Public"
      Name="b2"
      Style="{DynamicResource BlackGlassButton}"
      Content="Button 2"/>

</StackPanel>
</ScrollViewer>
</UserControl>
```

In the ThisAddIn.vb class, add a new method called "CreateCustomTaskPane" and add
the code in Listing 2-15. The first thing this code does is retrieve the list of customers
from SharePoint. You need to create an instance of the usercontrol so that we can get
a reference to the BlackGlassButton style that was defined in Listing 2-14. A LINQ for
XML query will extract all of the customer names and e-mail addresses from the XML
document and create a new WPF button with the BlackGlassButton style. The query
returns a collection of the WPF buttons that you will add to the usercontrol after clearing
any existing buttons. At this point you have a WPF usercontrol and need to create an
ElementHost control, which is the bridge between Windows Forms controls and WPF
controls. The WPF control is added to the ElementHost control, which is added to a
WinForm usercontrol, which is added to the custom task pane. There are a number of
layers here to get everything working, but after you understand the basics of the control
model, it is straightforward.

LISTING 2-15 Create a custom task pane for the glass-looking buttons with a rollover animation.

```
Public Sub CreateCustomTaskPane()

  Dim SPListXElement As XElement

  'Get the customers list from SharePoint
  SPListXElement = SharePoint.GetList("http://pstubbs-moss", "OBACustomers")
```

```
'create an instance of the WPF control
Dim u As New UserControl1

'get the customer emails from the SharePoint list
Dim CTPItems = (From contact In _
               SPListXElement.Elements("SPListItem") _
               Where contact.Element("Email").Value IsNot Nothing _
               Select New System.Windows.Controls.Button With { _
               .Style = u.GetStyle("BlackGlassButton"), _
               .Content = contact.Element("Title").Value _
               }).Take(10)


u.StackPanel1.Children.Clear()

'add a button for each customer
For Each b As System.Windows.Controls.Button In CTPItems
    u.StackPanel1.Children.Add(b)
Next

Dim WPFControl As New Windows.Forms.Integration.ElementHost
    With { _.Child = u, _
    .Dock = System.Windows.Forms.DockStyle.Fill}

'wrap the wpf control in a winform user control
Dim uc As New Windows.Forms.UserControl
uc.Controls.Add(WPFControl)

CustomTaskPanes.Add(uc, "OBA Task Pane").Visible = True

End Sub
```

Add a button to the OBA Ribbon to call the CreateCustomTaskPane method. This will look like Figure 2-9 when it is populated with all of the customers.

Actions Pane

Prior to custom task panes, there was only the Actions Pane in Office 2003. The Actions Pane is very similar to the custom task pane except that the scope of the Actions Pane was at the document level only. The Actions Pane gives you a document-specific way to display information that pertains only to a specific document instance. Let's modify the previous custom task pane example to work as an Actions Pane instead. Open a new Word document project and add the usercontrol1.xaml file previously mentioned. Copy the CreateCustomTaskPane method, changing the last couple of lines in Listing 2-16 to use the Actions Pane instead of the custom task pane. Figure 2-10 shows the running Word document with the custom WPF actions pane on the right.

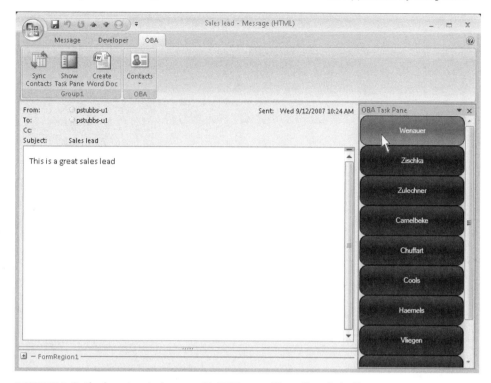

FIGURE 2-9 Outlook custom task pane with WPF control from SharePoint list

LISTING 2-16 Modified to use the Actions Pane

```
...
    'wrap the wpf control in a winform user control
    uc.Controls.Add(WPFControl)
    'resize usercontrol to fit the actionspane
    uc.Height = Me.CommandBars("Task Pane").Height

    'add the user control to the actions pane
    Me.ActionsPane.Controls.Add(uc)
```

Open XML File Format

OpenOffice XML is the new file format standard for Word, Excel, and PowerPoint in Office 2007. The documents are described using XML parts and are packaged together in a ZIP file. You can see what this looks like if you rename a .docx file to .zip. Then using any ZIP tool, you can explore the contents of the package. The .NET Framework 3.0 contains some classes in the System.IO.Packaging namespace to create and manipulate the parts and packages. But even with the help of the System.IO.Packaging classes, this can still be

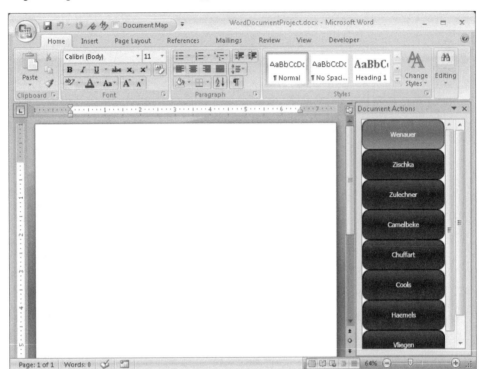

FIGURE 2-10 Word Actions Pane with WPF control from SharePoint list

a little complicated. Microsoft has created a higher level API to create Office Open XML documents. You can download the Microsoft SDK for Open XML Formats from this site: *http://www.microsoft.com/downloads/details.aspx?FamilyId=AD0B72FB-4A1D-4C52-BDB5-7DD7E816D046&displaylang=en*. The SDK contains samples, documentation, and an API to get you started. In this example, you will create a Word document that contains the names of the customers from the SharePoint site. One of the benefits of using the Office Open XML format is that you can also create these documents on the server or from your Web site without requiring Office to be installed on the server. Open the Outlook add-in project and add a reference to the Microsoft.Office.DocumentFormat.OpenXml.dll from the SDK for Office Open XML formats. Add the method in Listing 2-17 to your ThisAddIn class. This will create a new WordProcessingDocument class. Then add the main document part. The main document part is described in the next section, but this is the body of the document. Next you need to define the styles for your document. In this case, I want to use the built-in styles, so I created a blank Word document and extracted the styles.xml part from that document and imported it into my project as a resource file. Reading the styles.xml file into the new style part will save you a lot of time and complexity and allow you to focus on the document body for now.

LISTING 2-17 Create a new Word document using Office Open XML.

```
Public Sub CreateNewWordDocument(ByVal documentPath As String)

    Dim wordDoc As WordprocessingDocument = WordprocessingDocument.Create(documentPath,
    WordprocessingDocumentType.Document)
    ' Set the content of the document so that Word can open it.
    Dim mainPart As MainDocumentPart = wordDoc.AddMainDocumentPart()

    SetMainDocumentContent(mainPart)

    Dim stylePart As StyleDefinitionsPart = mainPart.AddNewPart(Of StyleDefinitionsPart)
    ()
    Dim stream As IO.Stream = New FileStream(ThisAddIn.AppPath & "\Sample\styles.xml",
    FileMode.Open)
    stylePart.FeedData(stream)

    wordDoc.Close()

End Sub
```

The SetMainDocumentContent method in Listing 2-18 does the heavy lifting for creating the document body. The first thing is to get the list of customers from SharePoint. Once again, this uses LINQ for XML to convert the XML document to a collection of contact objects. You need to iterate through each contact to build the WordprocessingML XML that contains the Fullname with a Title style and the e-mail address as normal text. This uses a new feature of VB called XML Literals. XML Literals allow you to put the literal XML in-line with your code and the VB compiler will understand it. Also within the XML Literal string, you can insert variables using an ASP.NET-style syntax with the <%=*variable*%>. In this case, you will insert the full name and the e-mail address from the contact. Finally, after you build the paragraphs with all of the customers, you need to wrap it in the document element to make a valid document part and stream it back into the part object. One last step you need to take for the XML Literals, since you are using namespaces, is to add an import at the top of the file to define the "w" namespace:

Imports <xmlns:w="http://schemas.openxmlformats.org/wordprocessingml/2006/main">

LISTING 2-18 Create the document body with data from SharePoint.

```
'Set content of MainDocumentPart.
Public Sub SetMainDocumentContent(ByVal part As MainDocumentPart)

    'populate the document from the SharePoint List
    Dim SPListXElement As XElement

    'Get the customers list from SharePoint
    SPListXElement = SharePoint.GetList("http://pstubbs-moss", "OBACustomers")

    'get the customer emails from the SharePoint list
    Dim Contacts = From contact In _SPListXElement.Elements("SPListItem") _
                Where contact.Element("Email").Value IsNot Nothing _Select contact
```

```
            Dim docXmlBody As List(Of XElement) = New List(Of XElement)

            For Each contact As XElement In Contacts
                docXmlBody.Add( _
                                <w:p>
                                    <w:pPr>
                                        <w:pStyle w:val="Title"/>
                                    </w:pPr>
                                    <w:r>
                                        <w:t><%= contact.Element("FullName").Value %></w:t>
                                    </w:r>
                                </w:p>)

                docXmlBody.Add( _
                                <w:p>
                                    <w:r>
                                        <w:t><%= contact.Element("Email").Value %></w:t>
                                    </w:r>
                                </w:p>)
            Next


            Dim docX As XDocument = _
                                <?xml version="1.0" encoding="UTF-8" standalone="yes"?>
                                <w:document xmlns:w="http://schemas.openxmlformats.org/
                                wordprocessingml/2006/main">
                <w:body>
                    <%= docXmlBody %>
                </w:body>
            </w:document>

            Dim stream As IO.Stream = part.GetStream()
            Dim buf As Byte() = (New UTF8Encoding()).GetBytes(docX.ToString)
            stream.Write(buf, 0, buf.Length)
        End Sub
```

Add a button to your Ribbon to call the CreateNewWordDocument ("OBACustomers.docx")
method to create the Word document. Running this will generate a document like Figure 2-11
in the user's documents folder.

Content Controls

Content Controls are a new feature in Word 2007 that encapsulate sections of
a document. They are the next generation of bookmarks. Bookmarks had many
shortcomings that have been addressed by content controls; now, for example, they
have an ID and are data bindable. In this example, you will create a fax template that
data binds the To and From fields from the SharePoint customer list. Create a new Word
document project using the fax template. In order to data bind to the content controls,
you need to create a prototype class of the customer object. Listing 2-19 shows what the
customer prototype class looks like.

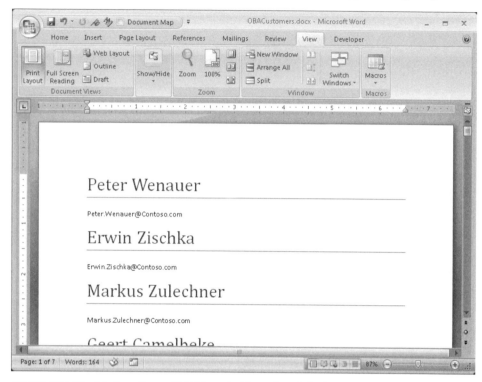

FIGURE 2-11 Word Actions Pane with WPF control from SharePoint list

LISTING 2-19 Customer prototype class

```
Public Class Customer

    Private TitleValue As String
    Public Property Title() As String
        Get
            Return TitleValue
        End Get
        Set(ByVal value As String)
            TitleValue = value
        End Set
    End Property

    Private FirstNameValue As String
    Public Property FirstName() As String
        Get
            Return FirstNameValue
    End Get
        Set(ByVal value As String)
            FirstNameValue = value
        End Set
    End Property
```

```
    Private FullNameValue As String
    Public Property FullName() As String
       Get
           Return FullNameValue
       End Get
       Set(ByVal value As String)
          FullNameValue = value
       End Set
    End Property

    Private EmailValue As String
    Public Property Email() As String
       Get
           Return EmailValue
       End Get
       Set(ByVal value As String)
          EmailValue = value
       End Set
    End Property

    ...

End Class
```

Now that you have a customer class object, add a new data source with the customer object as the data source. Drag a BindingSource control from the toolbox onto the document called FromCustomerBindingSource. Use the drop-down to pick the customer object as the data source property. Add another BindingSource control called ToCustomerBindingSource, setting the data source to the customer object as well. With the fax document open in the designer, you can select text in the document and map it to content controls by dragging the appropriate content control from the toolbox onto the selected text. In this example, you can use the PlainTextContentControl for most of the fields except for the date field, in which case you should use the DatePickerContentControl. Once you have all of your fields wrapped in content controls, you can set the data binding mapping to the correct fields in the customer class. Select the field you wish to map to and set the data binding text property to the correct field. You will have two data sources to choose fields from—the To and the From—so be sure to map to the correct ones. Once you have all of the fields mapped, your document will look like Figure 2-12.

So far, all of the data binding has been done using the VSTO visual designers. Now you must drop to code to fill the data sources with data. Open the ThisDocument.vb code window and add the method in Listing 2-20. The code pattern at this point will be familiar. First retrieve the customer list from SharePoint. Using LINQ for XML, parse the customer XML document and create a collection of customer objects. The last step is to set the data source property of the two data binding source objects to an instance of a customer object. For this example you can randomly pick two, one for the To and one for the From. Add the DataBindContentControls method call to the document start-up method so that the data is populated when the document is opened.

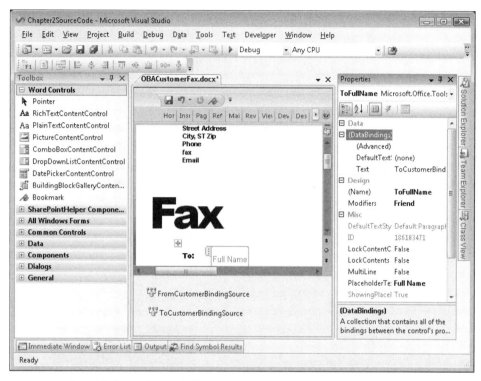

FIGURE 2-12 Data binding a SharePoint list to Word Content Controls

LISTING 2-20 Fill the data sources with data from SharePoint.

```
Private Sub DataBindContentControls()
    'populate the gallery from the SharePoint List
    Dim SPListXElement As XElement

    'Get the customers list from SharePoint
    SPListXElement = SharePoint.GetList("http://pstubbs-moss", "OBACustomers")

    'get the customer objects from the SharePoint list
    Dim Customers = From customer In _
                SPListXElement.Elements("SPListItem") _
                Where customer.Element("Email").Value IsNot Nothing _
                Select New Customer With { _
                .FullName = customer.Element("FullName").Value, _
                .Email = customer.Element("Email").Value, _
                .Company = customer.Element("Company").Value, _
                .WorkAddress = customer.Element("WorkAddress").Value, _
                .WorkCity = customer.Element("WorkCity").Value, _
                .WorkState = customer.Element("WorkState").Value, _
                .WorkZip = customer.Element("WorkZip").Value, _
                .WorkPhone = customer.Element("WorkPhone").Value, _
                .Title = customer.Element("Title").Value, _
```

```
                          .WorkFax = customer.Element("WorkPhone").Value, _
                          .WebPage = customer.Element("WebPage").Value _
                          }

        'for this demo just take 2 random people
        ToCustomerBindingSource.DataSource = Customers(New Random().Next(40))
        FromCustomerBindingSource.DataSource = Customers(New Random().Next(40))


    End Sub
```

Press F5 to build and run the document. When the document loads, the data-bound content controls will be populated with data from the SharePoint list, like in Figure 2-13.

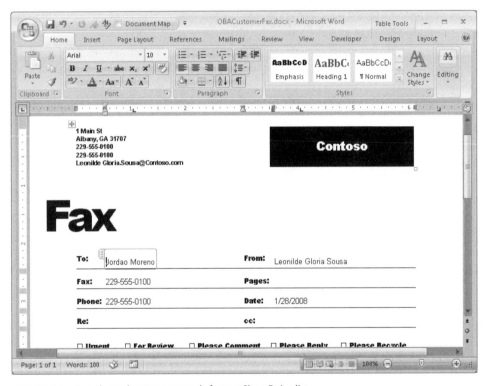

FIGURE 2-13 Data-bound content controls from a SharePoint list

Outlook Form Regions

Users for years have been looking for ways to integrate their business applications seamlessly into Outlook. While Outlook has provided various ways to edit parts of the UI, such as the menu, there was never a good solution until now, using form regions. Form regions are areas of the Outlook form that can be customizable by an add-in. There are a number of different places to display your form region, such as a separate form that the user can switch to, or completely replace the Outlook form with your own. You can also attach your form region to a number of different message types, such as mail, contact, or a calendar appointment. VSTO now provides a wizard and the infrastructure to easily make a WinForm user control be the form region. This opens a whole new area of customization for the Office Business Application developer. In this example, you will add a Web browser control as the form region and browse to different Web sites based on the company name selected in the Ribbon gallery of the message inspector.

Add an Outlook form region item from the Add New Item dialog box. This will start a wizard that will walk you through the choices to create a form region. Choose all of the defaults, except make it an adjoining form region. An adjoining form region will display at the bottom of the mail message, similar to a task pane. In some sense, you can think of it as an inspector-level task pane, in that the lifespan is tied to the inspector, in this case your e-mail message. The form region designer looks and behaves just like the user control designer. You can drag and drop controls from the toolbox onto the design surface. You can add WinForm controls and WPF controls just like any other user control. In this example, we will add the Web browser control onto the form region, which will dock to the parent control by default. Listing 2-21 shows the code call to the navigate method of the Web browser control from the Ribbon gallery.

LISTING 2-21 Click event handler for the Ribbon gallery

```
Private Sub Gallery1_Click(ByVal sender As System.Object, ByVal e As Microsoft.Office.
Tools.Ribbon.RibbonControlEventArgs) Handles Gallery1.Click

  Globals.ThisAddIn.FormRegionWebBrowser.Navigate( _
 "http://search.live.com/results.aspx?q=stock+" & Gallery1.SelectedItem.SuperTip)
  End Sub
```

You need to create a variable on the ThisAddIn class to hold a reference to the Web browser control from the form region, like in Listing 2-22.

LISTING 2-22 Variable to hold Web browser reference

```
 Public FormRegionWebBrowser As System.Windows.Forms.WebBrowser
```

When the form region is displayed, Listing 2-23 sets this reference so that it can be called from the Ribbon gallery.

LISTING 2-23 Set Web browser reference on form region display event.

```
'Occurs before the form region is displayed.
'Use Me.OutlookItem to get a reference to the current Outlook item.
'Use Me.OutlookFormRegion to get a reference to the form region.
Private Sub FormRegion1_FormRegionShowing(ByVal sender As Object, ByVal e As System.
EventArgs) Handles MyBase.FormRegionShowing

'add a reference to the webbrowser
Globals.ThisAddIn.FormRegionWebBrowser = WebBrowser1

End Sub
```

Press F5 to build and run the project. Open an e-mail message and select a contact from the OBA Ribbon tab. You will see the search page for the contact's company in the form region similar to Figure 2-14.

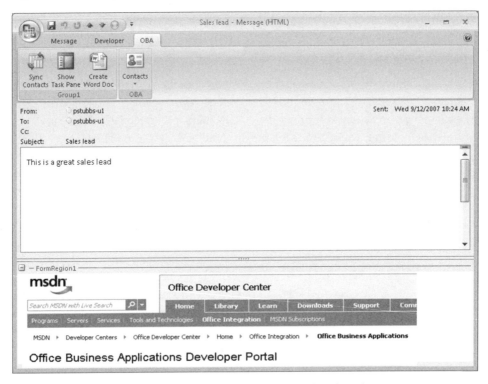

FIGURE 2-14 The form region with the company information for the selected contact

Summary

You have seen many examples of how VSTO makes it easy to visualize your back-end business data on the client machine using Office. This allows users to work in a comfortable environment using the data at the right time, in the right place, and in the right context. Users don't need to task switch between Outlook, Excel, or any other Office application they work in during the day to handle their business processes and make important and informed decisions. VSTO enables you, the application developer, to do things with Office that before would have been too difficult, time consuming, or impossible to achieve.

Chapter 3
Building Business Intelligence for Your Office Business Applications

Business intelligence (BI) is not a new concept. In fact, BI has been around in some fashion since the late 1980s, and in many ways data still lies at the heart of much of the application development that is done today. You might argue that over time the *function* of BI has not changed drastically; that is, it still represents a way of processing and visualizing data so as to make business decisions. That said, the way in which we *process* and *visualize* this data has changed quite a bit.

The modern organization is undergoing some major changes. Some of these are in reaction to the ever-changing behaviors around the workplace—for example, the speed with which people change jobs. Others are through technological changes that are exposed through a collision of legacy systems and newer technologies. While the integration of legacy systems is always a concern, this chapter is mainly interested in discussing more modern technologies vis-à-vis these organizational changes.

Specifically, there are trends that are making it more difficult to harness and centrally manage data and to adequately serve the needs of business intelligence. More specifically, trends such as e-mailing data, saving data on local hard drives, and processing data away from its source are causing an *n degrees of separation*. (See Figure 3-1.) That is, data is withdrawn from a line-of-business (LOB) system, and then that same data is being manipulated, reviewed, and amended outside of that core LOB data source. What this eventually causes is wider discrepancies in business data the further one travels away from the LOB data source.

The goal of OBAs is to reduce this distance between the consumer of business data and the actual data. Thus, the *n* degrees of separation is mitigated by a tightly held bridge between consumer and data. A practical example of this might be the review and approval

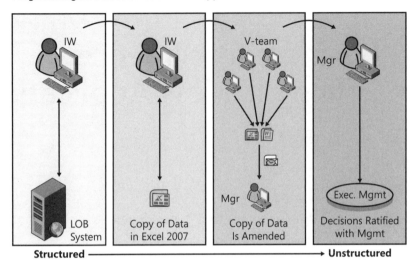

Structured ——————————————————————————————————→ Unstructured

FIGURE 3-1 *n* degrees of separation

of a quarterly budget. The success of the process (or accurate decision pivots on the data that is used in the budget review process) is directly tied to the business data that is used to fuel the process. Thus, if the budget process incorporates many manual steps (for example, e-mailing spreadsheets for review, offline reviews, and amendments, and no synchronization with the core business data store), then the likelihood for success is less than if the review and approval process is tightly coupled with the business data. Architecturally, this type of OBA solution would include Excel customizations that bind directly to the LOB system (for example, a push-and-pull data model), a Microsoft Office SharePoint Server (MOSS) dashboard for quick-view reporting, and potentially reporting and analytics through SQL Server. And although SQL Server is one of Microsoft's flagship products and is extremely important in terms of business intelligence, the focus of this chapter is on the client-side [that is, Visual Studio Tools for Office (VSTO)] and server-side (i.e., MOSS-based) customizations that are available to developers so they can build robust and powerful business intelligence solutions into their OBAs.

Office Business Application Framework

Microsoft's BI offerings include SQL Server, PerformancePoint Server 2007, Business Scorecard Manager, Microsoft Excel 2007, and Microsoft Office SharePoint Server 2007. The focus of this chapter is on the business intelligence offerings within the Microsoft Office development platform (that is, Microsoft Excel 2007 and MOSS 2007). More specifically, we'll discuss how developers can take advantage of new features within Visual Studio Tools for Office 3.0 and MOSS 2007 to build powerful business intelligence applications within their Office Business Applications.

Before we do this, however, let's take a quick look at a high-level view of the architecture of the Office Business Applications Framework, shown in Figure 3-2.

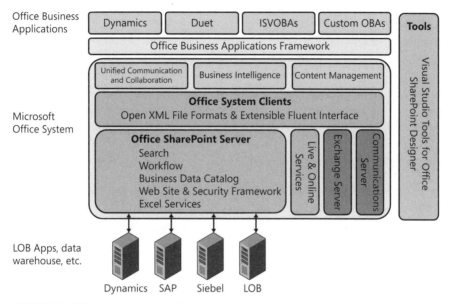

FIGURE 3-2 Office development platform

In this view, you can see types of OBAs running along the top of the diagram. These OBAs range from out-of-the-box solutions like Duet, a solution that integrates SAP and Office using predefined scenarios, to custom OBAs. With the custom solutions, you have a number of tools and services that you can use to build your custom OBAs. Among the tools, you could use OpenXML to manipulate content in documents, you could use Visual Studio Tools for Office 3.0 to build client-side customizations and some server-side customizations like SharePoint workflow, or you could also use the MOSS 2007 platform to customize your SharePoint site. You can further use these different components of the framework to integrate your custom OBAs with LOB systems such as SAP, Microsoft Dynamics, or Siebel. Regardless of what your development goals are, the Office Business Application Framework provides you with a number of tools, servers, and services to build powerful composite applications that bridge the gap between your business data and the consumers of that data.

The goal of this chapter is to introduce you to some of these capabilities. The nice thing about a lot of the business intelligence solutions discussed in this chapter is that they don't always require a great degree of coding. Thus, for the designer you could create OBA business intelligence solutions with some relative ease, and for the hardcore developer, you could create an interface for your business intelligence solution and then use the Office platform to build greater custom logic into your solution.

To start, let's discuss how you can develop client-side BI customizations. We'll then discuss server-side, that is, more SharePoint-centric solutions, in the latter half of the chapter.

Developing Client-Side Business Intelligence Customizations

When developing OBAs, there are a range of opportunities that can be used to integrate business intelligence into your solutions. These options range from automated data connection string binding to more sophisticated Web service consumption. With each of the options, you'll have varying degrees of control and reach on your business intelligence logic. In this section, we'll cover the integration of business intelligence into an OBA either through a) using native Office functionality or b) using VSTO to develop custom client-side business intelligence solutions.

Integrating Data into Excel 2007 Using Native Office Features

Microsoft Excel 2007 has native functionality that enables you to directly connect to different data sources and then manipulate the presentation of that data. More specifically, Excel enables you to build a connection (that is, information such as type of connection, server name, table name, and so on, that is needed to identify a data source) and to connect to that data source so you can import that data. You can find this functionality on the Data tab within Excel 2007. For example, Figure 3-3 illustrates some of the possible data sources you can directly connect to your Excel spreadsheet, including Access, Web, and text.

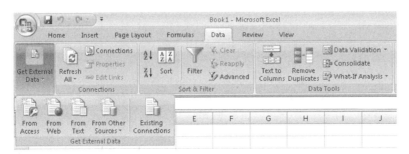

FIGURE 3-3 Excel 2007 Data tab

Essentially, this new functionality creates a connection string for you and then saves that connection string in association with the specific Excel document. Thus, connection information is stored either inside (default mode) of Excel or in a separate Office data connection file (that is, a .odc file). Excel uses these files when a specific Excel document is opened to establish the connection to the connected data source.

From the From Other Sources option, you can also create a connection to a SQL Server database. Since I predominantly use SQL Server in my application development, I chose to create a connection to my Excel 2007 spreadsheet using a budget database—a database I use a lot when developing demo projects. To make this connection, select From Other Sources, click From SQL Server (see Figure 3-4), and then complete the Data Connection Wizard.

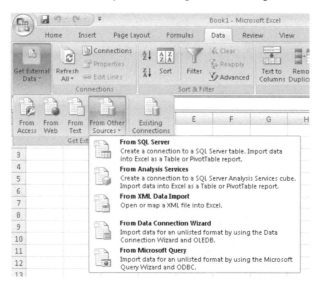

FIGURE 3-4 Connecting data from SQL Server

The Data Connection Wizard prompts the user for the database server name and asks for a choice on credentials. Provide a local server name and then choose to use Windows Authentication.

After you've finished, click Next to take you to the next dialog box in the wizard. The next dialog box in the Data Connection Wizard asks you to select a database within the SQL Server you selected and also enables you to connect to a specific table, as shown in Figure 3-5. In the following example, I have selected the Budget database and then selected a table I have in this sample database called the BudgetSummary.

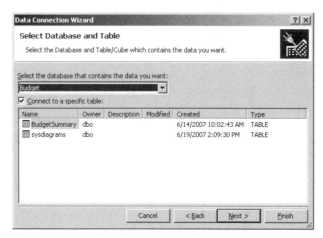

FIGURE 3-5 Data Connection Wizard—Select Database and Table

After you've completed this step, click Next and the wizard will prompt you with the final dialog box, Save the Data Connection File and Finish, shown in Figure 3-6.

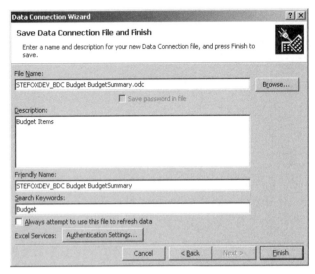

FIGURE 3-6 Data Connection Wizard—Save Data Connection File and Finish

In this dialog box, you can change the name of the connection (.odc) file, add a description, edit the display name, add search keywords, and set the Excel Services authentication services on the file as well. After you've completed these steps, click Finish. Your database connection has been created.

What results is the auto-population of your Excel spreadsheet with the data from the table in the SQL Server that you designated in the wizard. With the data in the spreadsheet, you can now alter the presentation of the data (for example, change table styles, create a pivot table, and so on) or use the auto-added filters to manipulate the views on the data. See Figure 3-7 for the final table with data from the budget table.

Though this may not be a business intelligence solution that employs, for example, Online Analytical Processing (OLAP) and more complex reporting and analysis, it is a fairly simple way to connect, present, and visualize data from a variety of sources in a quick and efficient way through the Microsoft Excel 2007 functionality.

Further, you can leverage many of the native formatting features of Excel for simple reporting and presentation of data. For example, Figure 3-8 illustrates some of the charting and formatting capabilities within Excel—namely, the conditional formatting, which allows you to shade based on cell value, and the 3D pie chart. Not only can you do this through the Excel 2007 menu, but you can also build this functionality into your reporting programmatically.

The native Excel 2007 functionality offers you an extensive list of features, but there are limitations to this, so if you're looking for something with more flexibility, extensibility, complex filtering capabilities, connectivity to Web services, and so on, then there is another powerful option that you can employ to integrate business intelligence into your Office Business Application: Visual Studio Tools for Office.

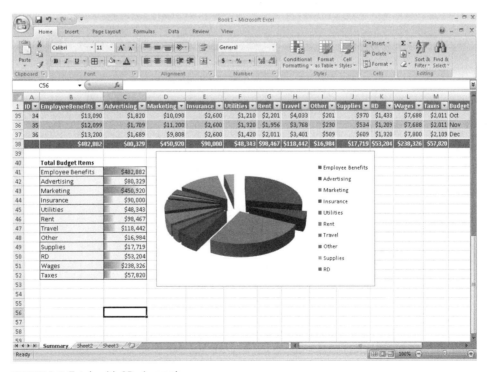

FIGURE 3-7 Connected DB in Excel table

Figure 3-7 (partial visible data):

ID	EmpBenefits	Advertising	Marketing	Insurance	Utilities	Rent	Travel	Other	Supplies	RD	Wages	Taxes	BudgMonth
1	$15,000	$2,300	$13,000	$2,400	$1,400	$3,200	$2,900	$670	$430	$1,400	$5,600	$1,200	Jan
2	$15,000	$2,300	$13,023	$2,400	$1,399	$3,200	$3,001	$500	$430	$1,400	$5,689	$1,210	Feb
3	$14,666	$2,411	$13,044	$2,400	$1,403	$3,200	$2,976	$429	$430	$1,400	$5,689	$1,210	Mar
4	$13,222	$2,511	$12,976	$2,400	$1,405	$3,200	$2,900	$600	$475	$1,450	$5,800	$1,235	Apr
5	$15,000	$2,001	$12,077	$2,400	$1,388	$3,200	$2,890	$680	$430	$1,450	$5,800	$1,235	May
6	$13,287	$2,300	$13,043	$2,400	$1,402	$3,200	$3,022	$651	$450	$1,450	$5,800	$1,235	Jun
7	$15,778	$2,401	$13,039	$2,400	$1,400	$3,200	$3,100	$522	$430	$1,450	$5,890	$1,255	Jul
8	$16,333	$2,508	$12,900	$2,400	$1,322	$3,200	$4,500	$489	$410	$1,450	$5,890	$1,255	Aug
9	$15,233	$1,901	$12,967	$2,400	$1,406	$3,200	$5,066	$502	$400	$1,450	$5,890	$1,255	Sep
10	$13,289	$2,011	$13,056	$2,400	$1,408	$3,200	$2,099	$499	$457	$1,500	$5,945	$1,279	Oct
11	$14,022	$1,967	$13,098	$2,400	$1,388	$3,200	$1,500	$428	$432	$1,500	$5,945	$1,279	Nov
12	$13,998	$2,013	$13,009	$2,400	$1,378	$3,200	$350	$410	$430	$1,500	$5,945	$1,279	Dec
13	$14,500	$1,922	$12,076	$2,400	$1,401	$3,255	$2,900	$645	$445	$1,600	$6,011	$1,300	Jan
14	$15,066	$1,856	$12,096	$2,400	$1,400	$3,255	$3,122	$630	$450	$1,600	$6,011	$1,300	Feb
15	$15,000	$2,013	$13,045	$2,400	$1,395	$3,255	$2,866	$624	$412	$1,600	$6,011	$1,300	Mar
16	$12,300	$2,015	$12,009	$2,400	$1,450	$3,255	$2,800	$660	$440	$1,620	$6,121	$1,322	Apr
17	$16,500	$2,099	$13,595	$2,400	$1,455	$3,255	$3,012	$489	$450	$1,620	$6,121	$1,322	May
18	$13,120	$2,067	$14,000	$2,400	$1,307	$3,255	$3,211	$650	$432	$1,620	$6,121	$1,322	Jun
19	$15,120	$3,012	$12,967	$2,400	$1,398	$3,255	$3,300	$622	$455	$1,650	$6,121	$1,322	Jul
20	$16,241	$2,967	$12,009	$2,400	$1,460	$3,255	$4,600	$599	$465	$1,650	$6,121	$1,322	Aug
21	$12,099	$2,087	$13,566	$2,400	$1,430	$3,255	$5,244	$550	$477	$1,650	$6,121	$1,322	Sep
22	$13,600	$3,012	$13,900	$2,400	$1,412	$3,255	$1,899	$490	$410	$1,650	$6,277	$1,400	Oct
23	$14,109	$3,016	$12,365	$2,400	$1,450	$3,255	$1,350	$603	$398	$1,650	$6,277	$1,400	Nov
24	$14,255	$3,066	$12,099	$2,400	$1,470	$3,255	$298	$621	$401	$1,650	$6,355	$1,435	Dec
25	$12,008	$2,819	$14,033	$2,400	$1,396	$3,350	$3,025	$561	$412	$1,725	$6,355	$1,435	Jan

FIGURE 3-8 Totals with 3D pie graph

Figure 3-8 (visible data):

ID	EmployeeBenefits	Advertising	Marketing	Insurance	Utilities	Rent	Travel	Other	Supplies	RD	Wages	Taxes	Budget
34	$13,090	$1,820	$10,090	$2,600	$1,210	$2,201	$4,033	$201	$970	$1,433	$7,688	$2,011	Oct
35	$12,099	$1,709	$11,200	$2,600	$1,320	$1,956	$3,768	$230	$534	$1,209	$7,688	$2,011	Nov
36	$13,200	$1,689	$9,808	$2,600	$1,420	$2,011	$3,401	$509	$609	$1,320	$7,800	$2,109	Dec
	$482,882	$80,329	$450,920	$90,000	$48,343	$98,467	$118,442	$16,984	$17,719	$53,204	$238,326	$57,820	

Total Budget Items

Total Budget Items	
Employee Benefits	$482,882
Advertising	$80,329
Marketing	$450,920
Insurance	$90,000
Utilities	$48,343
Rent	$98,467
Travel	$118,442
Other	$16,984
Supplies	$17,719
RD	$53,204
Wages	$238,326
Taxes	$57,820

Creating Business Intelligence Solutions Using Visual Studio Tools for Office

Visual Studio Tools for Office (VSTO) is a powerful way to build customizations for a number of Office applications, including Excel, Word, Outlook, and PowerPoint. VSTO 3.0 ships with Visual Studio 2008 Professional Edition and enables developers to, for example, extend the Office Fluent Ribbon (using Visual Ribbon Designer), create custom task panes that can host managed and Windows Presentation Foundation (WPF) controls, customize Outlook form regions, integrate VBA macros with VSTO managed code, and much more. In terms of Office customizations, VSTO 3.0 is one of the key technologies professional developers should have in their toolkits.

With regard to business intelligence, you can use VSTO to build and integrate customized solutions into your OBA. In this chapter, we'll discuss how you can customize the user interface of Excel to provide rich database and reporting capabilities, show you how you can use Language Integrated Query (LINQ) to integrate data into the customized user interface components, and finally show you how you can call Web services to consume line-of-business business data—or other data provided through Web services. All of these will again work toward the goal of more closely integrating information workers with the business data they need to do their job. Some of them require some development, whereas others will require more configuration to native Excel 2007 features.

Customizing the Excel 2007 User Interface

As you saw in Chapter 2, "Creating a Smart Client for Your Office Business Application by Using VSTO," there are different options for customizing the Excel 2007 interface using VSTO. For example, you can create custom task panes for application add-ins (for document-level solutions, the task panes are custom action panes), extend the Fluent Office Ribbon, and data bind to Word content controls, among other customization opportunities. As an example of one such business intelligence solution, specifically, a search keyword solution, Figure 3-9 illustrates a solution that integrates a custom Ribbon (with custom Office images), custom actions pane, and reporting and analysis that combines both native Excel 2007 functionality with custom business logic.

The actions pane enables you to create an instance of an actions pane object (using the ActionsPane object) and then add controls such as WinForm controls or WPF controls onto the actions pane surface. You can then integrate the controls to, for example, local or external data sources or Web services. That's the nice thing about actions panes: You can design them with either simplicity or complexity in mind. For example, a useful control is the tab control, which allows you to build out a tabbed view within an actions pane. This does a couple of things. First, it enables you to build more data-centric logic (for example, complex filtering through the use of drop-down lists bound to data or calculations that are triggered by specific data being loaded into the spreadsheet) into your actions pane, and second, it enables you to maximize the real estate of the actions pane (for example, having multiple

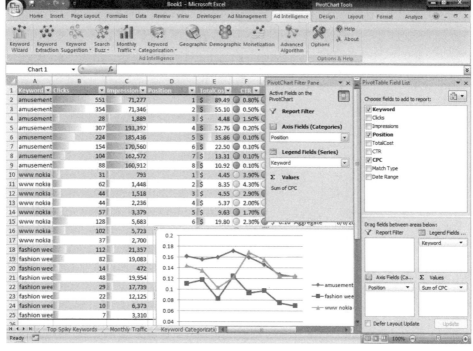

FIGURE 3-9 Search keyword business intelligence solution

tabs within the actions pane to provide multiple tab views). This helps filter data into your Excel 2007 spreadsheet, which can further control views into your data—while at the same time managing single or multiple data connections simultaneously.

Another way to integrate data in a straightforward way into your VSTO project is using the ListObject control. This requires a specific type of VSTO project; specifically, a VSTO document-level solution. To create this type of project, open Visual Studio and click File, New, and Project. Browse to the Office node (in either C# or VB) and then click the 2007 node and select the Excel Workbook project. Name your project and click OK.

Visual Studio prompts you to either create a project from a new workbook or load an existing workbook into the project. After you've got your project created, you now create a new data source. To add a new data source, click Data, Add New Data Source, and then work through the wizard.

The first dialog in the Data Source Configuration Wizard is the Choose a Data Type dialog box, which prompts you to select a specific data type. Click Database and then click Next. The next dialog box prompts you to add a connection with specific database information, as shown in Figure 3-10.

The final dialog box provides a view of the database objects you want to bind to the ListObject. Here you select the objects you want to bind and click Finish.

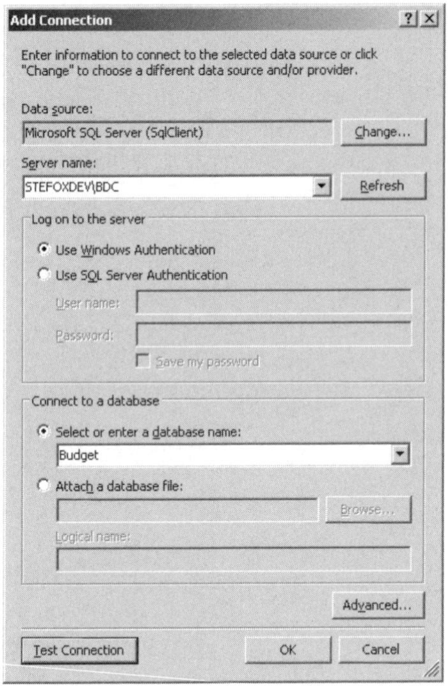

FIGURE 3-10 Add Connection dialog box

After the data source is bound to the ListObject, you can drag and drop the data-bound ListObject directly onto the worksheet as a host control in your VSTO project. When you do this, VSTO automatically loads the column headings as per the header rows within your bound data source. Figure 3-11 illustrates the data-bound ListObject in the worksheet within the VSTO project.

Using the ListObject within your VSTO project is interesting in a couple of ways. First, it's relatively straightforward to bind the ListObject to a dataset. And second, you can build some custom functionality against the data that is bound to the ListObject. One thing to remember is that the ListObject is bound to the dataset, so if you want to develop specific filtering mechanisms or functions that apply to the underlying data, you can do so but you'd be building your logic against the bound dataset as opposed to the ListObject that binds the data to the cells in the worksheet. Remember that here we have created the ListObject binding in the context of a VSTO project, so you open up other business intelligence customization opportunities to integrate into your OBA.

Another way to customize your OBA and integrate more business intelligence functionality is to extend the Office Fluent Ribbon and then associate business-data event handlers with the new Ribbon elements that you've added. For example, you might add additional filters, add code that controls the visibility of other custom components (for example, actions pane), or even have a review cycle around your business data that is started from your Excel

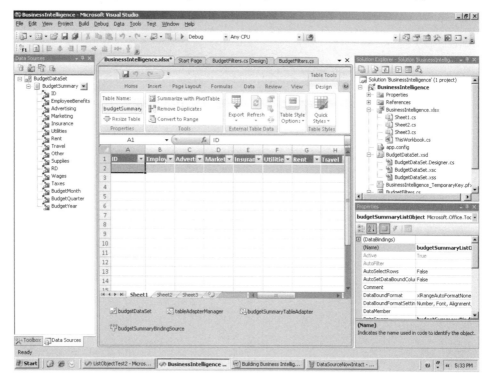

FIGURE 3-11 ListObject bound to SQL Server database

2007 client interface, thus the mapping of the client functionality to the server (for example, SharePoint). The Ribbon extension is important because it enables you to extend Office functionality to fit your design goals, while at the same time keep your end user within the context of the Office experience. Thus, tools development and support costs are mitigated through the deployment of in-context (to Office) applications.

Chapter 2 outlined how you can use the Visual Ribbon Designer to create a new Ribbon. After you've created your Ribbon, you add event handlers by double-clicking the Ribbon element you've dragged and dropped on the designer surface. Customizing the Ribbon enables you to build your business intelligence customizations directly into the context of the Excel 2007 Ribbon. This strikes at the heart of the whole concept of OBAs—that is, extending the user interface to bridge the results gap (or gap between the business data and the information worker). Figure 3-12 illustrates a Ribbon that has a number of different business intelligence features built into it. In some cases, this Ribbon can provide you with shortcut functions to features like charting or calculating the averages; however, there are other cases where you can build functionality that is specific to your data, such as specific analytical or sales report generation or quick-filtering based on specific business data.

A more recent technology that is easy to use and enables you to develop powerful business intelligence customizations into the Ribbon is the use of the .NET LINQ. LINQ essentially evolves your older SQL queries (for example, "SELECT * FROM . . .") into a newer

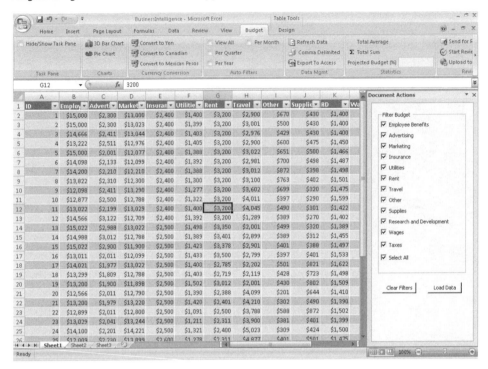

FIGURE 3-12 Custom Office Fluent Ribbon in context

querying programming model so you can develop against databases as if they were objects within your project—that is, model your data sources as if they were classes within your application. This means quick and easy expression creation, support for IntelliSense, straightforward data manipulation and transformation, and full type-safety and expression checking as you compile your applications.

You can combine VSTO customizations like Ribbon extensibility and LINQ in a number of ways to create a powerful and rich business intelligence customization within your Office Business Application. For example, you can add specific filtering capabilities, call stored procedures, and transform the presentation of data. Let's take a look at a relatively straightforward example to show how you can add some specific filtering capabilities to your application.

Before you can use LINQ within your application, though, you must first create what are called entity classes within your project. Essentially, you must create objects that represent your data in the form of classes. Assuming you have a new project created, you right-click your project and select Add New Item. This will invoke the Add New Item dialog box, shown in Figure 3-13, where you select the LINQ to SQL Classes item. Provide a name, and then click Add.

After you've added your relational database to your project, the Object Relational Designer view will open, and here you can create a model of your classes or what are also referred to as entity classes (see Figure 3-14).

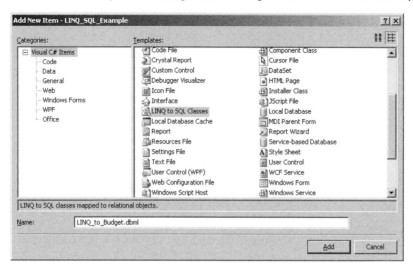

FIGURE 3-13 The Add New Item dialog box

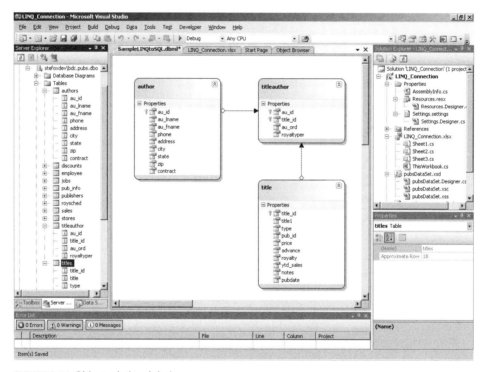

FIGURE 3-14 Object relational designer

Of note is that properties of the entity class map to the table's columns and each entity class you define does not necessarily derive from a root base class. Thus, you have more flexibility when it comes to inheritance and object definition. The following example uses the pubs database, which is composed of multiple tables.

To create the entity class for the one table in your database, select the Server Explorer tab and expand the Tables view. You can then select specific tables to drag and drop into the designer. You can model associations and inheritances between your tables within the designer. After you complete this step, Visual Studio will automatically generate entity classes for you. At this point, you can begin to build LINQ statements against your entity classes.

One example I added to my project was the ability to quick-filter on author's state. The Ribbon element that provides the user interface to the LINQ statement is a combo box comprising all states in the United States. In the following example, I illustrate an event handler extending from the combo box to assign the currently selected text in the combo box to authorState and use this as a parameter to build the LINQ statement. Thus, all authors from the selected state are selected through this LINQ statement.

```
private void cmboBxState_TextChanged(object sender, RibbonControlEventArgs e)
{
    string authorState = cmboBxState.Text;

    LINQ_Connection.SampleLINQtoSQLDataContext db =
    new LINQ_Connection.SampleLINQtoSQLDataContext();

    var stateInfo = from authors in db.authors
                    where authors.state == authorState
                    select authors;


        . . .

}
```

Another example of a BI customization you might add is currency calculation or other predefined and specific algorithmic functions that may not be native to Excel. Again, these types of customizations can be treated as shortcuts that are particular to your environment and Office Business Application. Previously, in Figure 3-12, I added three buttons for currency conversions. You could either update the data in the spreadsheet based off of hard-coded exchange rates or you could call a Web service that provides up-to-the-minute exchange rates. And while I used buttons to be the Ribbon elements that triggered my events, you could also use other Ribbon elements such as the combo box to optimize Ribbon real estate and further tie the available currencies to a back-end data source. In the code sample below, I've created an instance of the Web service and then called that Web service currency exchange method (CurrencyRate), passing the specific currency I want exchanged.

```
private void btnCDN_Click(object sender, RibbonControlEventArgs e)
{
    double exchRate = 0.00;

    XL_Sample.CurrencyRate.CurrencyConvertor currencyConversion = new
    XL_Sample.CurrencyRate.CurrencyConvertor();
```

```
    exchRate = currencyConversion.ConversionRate(XL_Sample.CurrencyRate.Currency.USD,
        XL_Sample.CurrencyRate.Currency.CAD);

    updateBudgetExchangeRate(exchRate);
}
```

I used the returned exchange rate as part of the algorithm that is then used to update my spreadsheet by passing the exchange rate to the updateBudgetExchangeRate method. I've added the code that maps to the updateBudgetExchangeRate method below to illustrate how I used the exchange rate in the presentation of my data.

For this example, I used a free Web service (from *www.xmethods.net*) that ships with predefined rates. However, you could just as easily use other Web services (remembering some will require authentication and/or licensing) to add business intelligence to your application. However, key to OBAs are connectivity to line-of-business systems (such as Microsoft Dynamics, PeopleSoft, and Service Advertising Protocol), and this often requires the consumption of Web services. For example, take the scenario in which an organization wants to integrate SAP within Excel 2007 to expose BI data to the information worker in an environment she is familiar with. Using SAPs Web services, you can programmatically access SAPs Business Application Programming Interface (BAPI) to each SAP Remote Function Call (RFC). Ultimately, BAPIs are Web services accessed via the Web Service Definition Language (WSDL) they publish.

Using the SAP GUI, developers can create and set up Web services manually or opt to use SAP's generic Web service that creates a WSDL for a particular BAPI. For this example, we used the latter approach to build the custom Web service, which consumed a BAPI called the BAPI_FLTRIP_GETLIST. The purpose of this BAPI was to get flight data from SAP (based on the parameters passed into the BAPI).

After you create your custom Web service, you can then add a Web reference to your project so you can then access the methods within that Web service. To do this, right-click your project, select Add Service Reference, click Advanced, and then click Add Web Reference. Figure 3-15 illustrates this dialog box.

The URL associated with your custom Web service (in this case, the BAPI BAPI_FLTRIP_GETLIST URL) can be passed into the URL combo box, which enables a reference to be created between the current project and the SAP Web service.

Once this URL is selected, succeeding screens will ask for valid SAP credentials. After these credentials are provided, Visual Studio will generate a proxy class that can then be used to programmatically access the aforementioned BAPI. The following code sample demonstrates how to access one of the defined Web services (SAP_FLIGHTTRIPLIST).

```
public bool GetList(string customerNumber, string travelAgency)
{
    flightTrip = new SAP_FLIGHTTRIPLIST.BAPI_FLTRIP_GETLISTService();
```

```
flightTrip.Url = Properties.Settings.Default.ContosoTours_SAPServices_SAP_FLIGHTTRIPLIST_BAPI_
                FLTRIP_GETLISTService;
flightTrip.Credentials = SAPIdentity;

bapiBookDateRange = new SAP_FLIGHTTRIPLIST.BAPISCODRA[0];
bapiTripDateRange = new SAP_FLIGHTTRIPLIST.BAPISCODRA[0];
bapiExtIn = new SAP_FLIGHTTRIPLIST.BAPIPAREX[0];
bapiExtOut = new SAP_FLIGHTTRIPLIST.BAPIPAREX[0];
bapiTripData = new SAP_FLIGHTTRIPLIST.BAPISTRDAT[0];
bapiReturn = new SAP_FLIGHTTRIPLIST.BAPIRET2[0];
bapiFlightTripList = new SAP_FLIGHTTRIPLIST.BAPISTRDAT[0];

flightTrip.BAPI_FLTRIP_GETLIST(ref bapiBookDateRange, customerNumber, ref bapiExtIn,
    ref bapiExtOut, ref bapiFlightTripList, 0, false, ref bapiReturn, travelAgency,
    ref bapiTripDateRange);

...
}
```

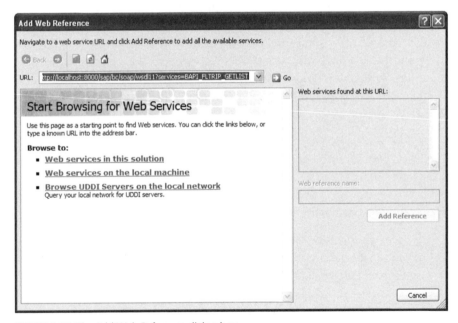

FIGURE 3-15 The Add Web Reference dialog box

This code sample illustrates a number of parameters that are passed into the call to SAP to get the flight list. The output of this call is a list of available flights that map to the input parameters. The method is further tied to a VSTO customization, which again reinforces the fact that you can tie Web service integrations to user interface customizations (that is, VSTO add-ins) to integrate business intelligence solutions into your OBA. Further, this method is part of a larger OBA that includes some interesting BI customizations. For example, the previous example used flight data to generate specialty sales packages, and as a part of tracking those sales, the OBA provides reports on which packages are selling versus other available packages. Figure 3-16 provides an overview of one of these reports.

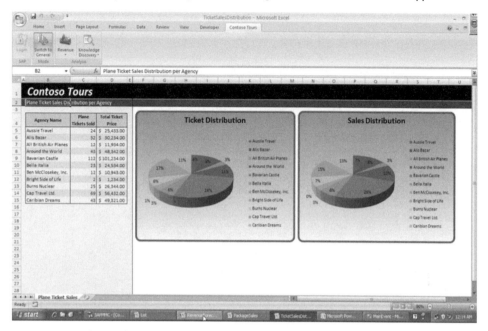

FIGURE 3-16 Package sales

The previous SAP sample is a part of the OBA Starter Kit for SAP, a developer kit that provides code samples, a white paper, and an installation guide to help get you on your way to creating your first OBA integrated with SAP. For more information, go to *http:// msdn2.microsoft.com/en-us/library/bb498189.aspx* on MSDN.

Thus far, we've predominantly discussed client-side customizations and development that have hopefully shed some light on how you might integrate BI into your OBA. Let's now move on to discussing how you can develop and integrate BI by using Microsoft Office SharePoint Server 2007.

Business Intelligence in MOSS 2007

As discussed earlier in the chapter, Microsoft provides a number of BI offerings ranging from SQL Server Analysis Services (SSAS) to PerformancePoint Server 2007. Figure 3-17 provides an overview of the different BI offerings from Microsoft. You can see from this figure that the BI components within MOSS 2007 (SharePoint Server in the figure) comprise a number of different options, including reports, dashboards, Excel workbooks, and so on. MOSS also represents the primary entry point and delivery mechanism for the BI offerings that are located beneath the SharePoint layer.

Because we're discussing Office Business Applications in this chapter, we'll focus on those BI features built into Microsoft Office SharePoint Server 2007 (Enterprise edition). Specifically,

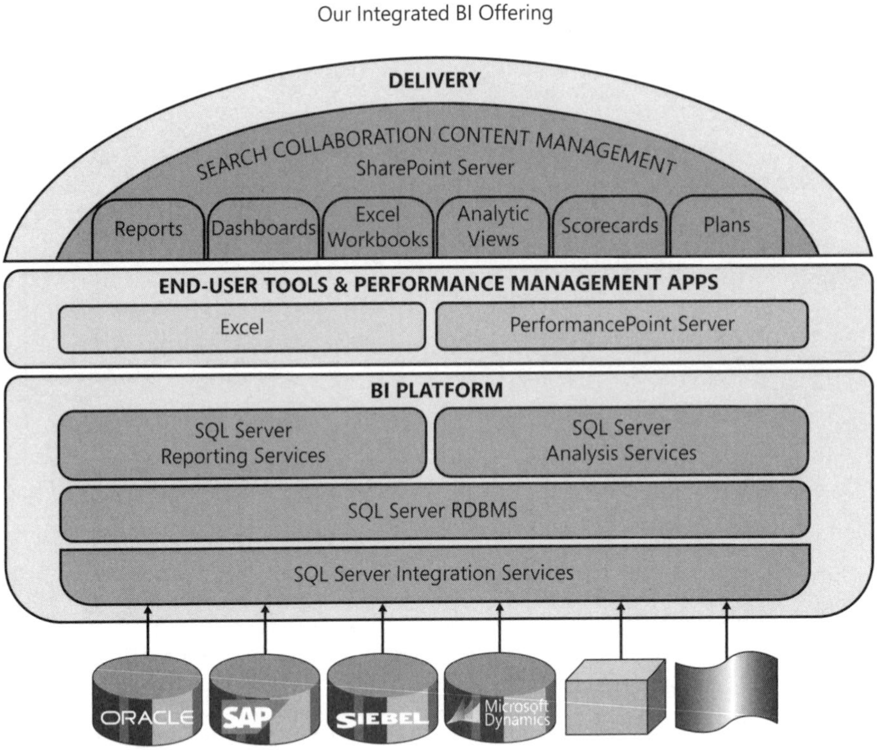

Our Integrated BI Offering

FIGURE 3-17 Microsoft business intelligence offerings

we'll discuss Excel Services, key performance indicators (KPIs), and the Business Data Catalog, all represented through the creation of a top-level BI dashboard.

The Business Intelligence Dashboard

The MOSS Reports Center dashboard is a critical component of any BI solution. It is a new Enterprise Site Template that facilitates the storage and management of BI content artifacts like Office Data Connections, KPI definitions, reports (both Excel and SSRS reports), dashboards created using Excel Services, and report schedules. It provides you with a view into your business data and ideally provides you with a way to filter and manage your data to enable decisions for specific scenarios, for example, filter fiscal year historical data to create next year's forecasts. MOSS 2007 makes it easy to build a dashboard.

To do so, click Reports on your site, and then New Dashboard. This will prompt you to complete some properties for your dashboard, like the name of the dashboard and the layout. Figure 3-18 illustrates the New Dashboard page. After you've filled in the properties, click OK. This creates your dashboard.

FIGURE 3-18 New Dashboard page

At this point, you can edit the existing Web parts and add new ones to the portal. Depending on your properties, you will have a set of default Web parts added to the site already. Figure 3-19 illustrates the dashboard created—a simple Publication Business Intelligence dashboard that will help report on some book sales data. You can see here that there is a KPI Web part and a couple of Excel Web Services Web parts, both of which will be discussed later in this chapter. In both cases, open the tool pane to edit these Web parts. Also notice that you can add either custom HTML code or rich text to the top of the dashboard to provide some explanatory context around the dashboard. You can also add profile information and allow other people (for example, team members or managers) to be able to view your portal as well. When you've finished with all of your customizations, you then click Publish and all of your changes will be saved and published to your SharePoint site.

For my BI dashboard, illustrated in Figure 3-20, I included a number of different Web part types. For example, I wanted to provide some context for my dashboard, so I added a content Web part to the top of my dashboard. I used the rich text editor and simply added some text. Because the content Web part was a default part of my dashboard, I only had to open the tool pane and then click Rich Text Editor to edit the content part.

I next wanted to add some sales KPIs to indicate which books I manage are doing well versus ones that are not doing well. You can see the KPI indicators display a red diamond where sales are lagging and a green orb where sales meet or exceed expectations. I've also added

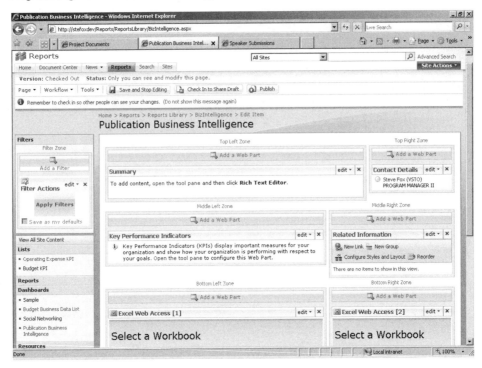

FIGURE 3-19 New Dashboard options

an Excel Services Web part to provide a quick chart view into the book sales data. I've also got a couple of other Web parts, one with my profile information and another with some contextual information about the dashboard. You could choose to keep these types of Web parts included, which again were default Web parts within my dashboard, within your dashboard or make your dashboard entirely data-centric.

Let's now turn to talking more in detail about Excel Services, KPIs, and the Business Data Catalog.

Excel Services

Excel Services represents a smart front end to worksheets that you've uploaded to your SharePoint site. You might think of Excel Services comprising three main parts, Excel Calculation Service, Excel Web Service, and Excel Web Access. The Excel Calculation Service loads the spreadsheets published to MOSS, calculates them, refreshes external data, and maintains session state for interactivity. This is the heart of Excel Services. The Excel Web Services provides programmatic access to the Excel Calculation Services. It is a Web service hosted in SharePoint. You can use methods in this Web service to develop custom applications that incorporate calculations performed by Excel Services and to automate the refreshing of Excel spreadsheets. Excel Web Access is a Web part in SharePoint that performs the "rendering"

FIGURE 3-20 My Publications Business Intelligence dashboard

of Excel Workbooks on a Web page. This is perhaps the most visible component for the end user. You can use it like any other Web part in SharePoint to create a wide range of Web pages.

Excel Services ships with MOSS 2007 Enterprise edition and offers a thin client browser rendering of Excel Workbooks published to MOSS, and exposes Web service interfaces that enable using Excel Formulas and Calculation Services from within custom client applications. Let's take a look at how we can create a view into our business data using Excel Services.

Figure 3-21 illustrates a worksheet created to track book sales. This maps to the dashboard, which manages a specific set of (very much theoretical) books that track as part of a phantom portfolio. The worksheet comprises two objects: a table and a chart. This is what I would call a static worksheet; that is, I've manually entered data into the worksheet to run business calculations. However, you could develop customizations into your worksheet using VSTO or map data to the spreadsheet (as we discussed earlier in the chapter), and this would provide you with a more dynamic experience where you are exposing more centrally located and fresh data.

The goal now, then, would be to create a thin client view into this business data within our Excel Services Web part. To do this, you first have to upload the worksheet to a library on

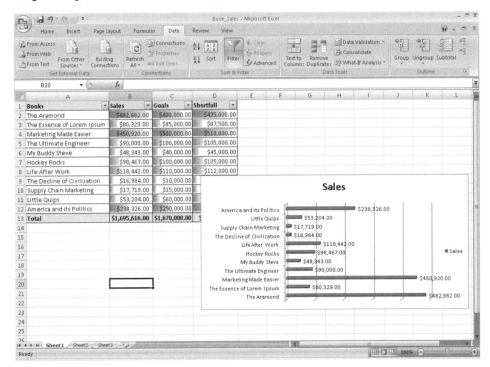

FIGURE 3-21 Book sales data

your SharePoint site. I would recommend having a document library tied to your Reports Center (i.e., your dashboard) that is specifically dedicated to sales sheets like these. For those who are familiar with MOSS, this is a very simple action. You merely navigate to the document library and click Actions, Upload, and then browse to the worksheet, and then click OK.

After you have your worksheet uploaded to the document library, it is important to remember that to expose the objects from your worksheet within the Web part, you must publish them to Excel Services first. To do this, open the document library where your worksheet was uploaded, click the document, and select Edit Document. This will open an instance of the document. You then click the Office button, Publish, and then Excel Services. In the resulting Save dialog box, select Excel Services Options. It is here where you select which parts of the worksheet you want to expose. In my case, I've selected to expose only the sales chart, which was called Chart1.

After you've selected the objects you want to expose in the Excel Services Web part, click Save. You can now go to your dashboard and configure the Excel Services Web part to point to the object you have published to Excel Services.

The last step, then, is to expose the published object in your Excel Services Web part. To do this, open the dashboard and click Edit Page. This will open the dashboard page in Edit mode.

For the Web part that you want to configure, open the tool pane and then provide a link to the Excel spreadsheet and a name for the object (in my case this was Chart1) that you want to expose. There are other properties that you can set, such as the name of the object in the Web part, dimensions for the Web part, and so on. After you've completed configuring the Excel Services Web part, click OK and the Web part will refresh with the object you've chosen to expose.

Key Performance Indicators

Another aspect of business intelligence within your OBA is the ability to surface and track key metrics through KPIs. KPIs are metrics that allow you to gauge the health of a particular item within your project or business. In the dashboard created earlier, I use them to provide indicators of how well the books in my phantom portfolio are selling: a red flag indicates the books are selling below expectation, a yellow flag indicates a warning, and a green flag indicates that the books are meeting or are above sales expectations. They could equally be applied to many other variables.

The nice thing about KPIs is that you can create them quickly, and they can serve as a good view into the performance of business data. Thus, KPIs are good for executive and managerial reporting—or reporting at the top level of a dashboard. For deeper-level business reporting, you would want to use other features of MOSS (for example, Excel Services).

To create a KPI list, navigate to your dashboard. In my dashboard, the KPI list is a default Web part, so I just needed to configure it. You add the KPI list by clicking Site Actions, Site Settings, and then Modify All Site Settings. In the Site Administration of the Site Settings page, click Site Libraries and Lists. Click the Create New Content link, and in the Custom Lists column select KPI List, provide properties for the list, and then click Create.

After you create the KPI list, map the KPI Web part to the business data on which you want to report in three ways. The first is by creating the KPI values manually. The second is to map them to a SharePoint list. And the third is to tie them to values in an Excel 2007 spreadsheet. To select one of these options, in your KPI list select New and then select the appropriate choice that maps to one of the three options mentioned.

To create a KPI using manually entered data is the easiest of the three ways. However, the values are obviously static, so you may need to update them on a regular basis. Oftentimes I'll use the manual KPIs for metrics that don't change often (for example, quarterly report snapshots), or capture longer intervals of tracking, so managing them is less costly to me. Figure 3-22 illustrates how you define the values for the manual KPI.

Essentially you enter the appropriate values for the different KPI indicators and then click OK.

FIGURE 3-22 Manually created KPI list

For more dynamic reporting, or reporting that may be mapped back to an algorithm, project status, or central data source, I like to use KPI lists that either map to a spreadsheet or a SharePoint list. In either case, when you configure your KPI list you need to provide a link to the list or spreadsheet and provide a mapping to the values that will create your KPIs. Figure 3-23 illustrates the mapping of the KPI list to an Excel 2007 spreadsheet. Using this type of KPI list, you can either add the mapping of the indicator values directly into this form or you can invoke an alternate form (Figure 3-24) that enables you to select the specific cell that then maps to a specific indicator.

The final result of this type of mapping, then, is that the indicator values of the KPI rely on the values to which they map in the Excel 2007 spreadsheet. Referring back, Figure 3-20 illustrates an example of what results from this process. I would definitely recommend using KPIs as part of your OBA business intelligence solution. This is because oftentimes you need high-level views for those who may not be familiar with the details of your project or business data. KPIs are not only very good for this, but similar to Excel Services, they require very little coding and are straightforward to configure. Let's finish off this part of the chapter by discussing the Business Data Catalog.

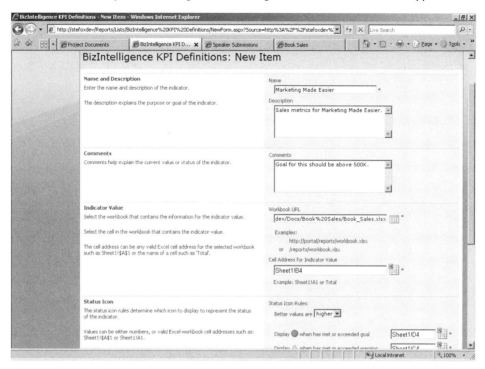

FIGURE 3-23 KPI definitions

Business Data Catalog

A very important part of the OBA is the ability to integrate line-of-business systems with your Office customizations in the client and in SharePoint. This might mean connections to SQL Server databases or larger systems such as SAP, PeopleSoft, or Microsoft Dynamics. Several services within SharePoint are supported through the Business Data Catalog (BDC), which are listed as follows:

- Business Data List Web part
  - ❑ The most commonly used Web part. It displays data (or, more precisely, a list of instances for a specific entity) that is registered in the Business Data Catalog.
- Business Data Related List Web part
  - ❑ Displays related data for which there exists an association with data registered in the Business Data Catalog.
- Business Data Item Web part
  - ❑ Displays details for a particular entity instance.
- Business Data Actions Web part
  - ❑ Displays the actions that can be performed for a specific entity instance.

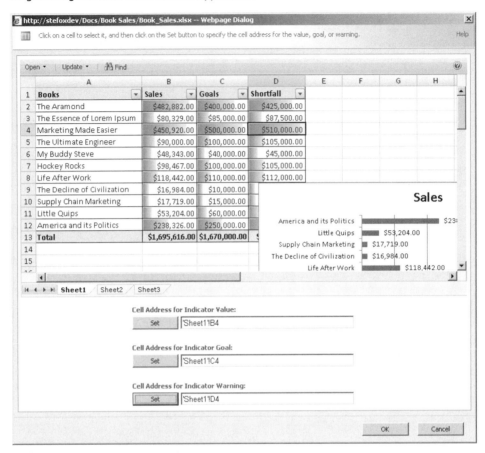

FIGURE 3-24 KPI value definition

- Business Data Item Builder Web part
  - ❏ A normal SharePoint page on which details are displayed through a programmatic call and passing of query string information and identifier information.

The BDC essentially integrates LOB systems with MOSS 2007 through an abstracted XML layer. The XML layer, called the application definition file (ADF) defines and describes how the BDC Web part will integrate with the LOB system. For example, the ADF will define the entities within the data source and the SQL queries that are supported through the connection with the LOB system data. The BDC can further integrate with the LOB system data source through either an ADO.NET-supported connection or a Web service proxy, thus supporting integration with custom Web services in PeopleSoft, SAP, and other large-scale ERP systems—or your own custom Web services.

The creation of ADFs was once cumbersome because the developer had to hand-code the XML; however, today there are tools that allow the developer to more easily create the ADF file. You can find in the MOSS SDK a tool called the Microsoft Business Data Catalog Definition Editor. Using the Microsoft BDC Definition Editor, you can create and edit metadata for OBAs. You can use the Business Data Catalog Definition Editor to connect to LOB systems via Web services or databases. After you create and configure an instance of the LOB in the tool, you export the ADF and save it as an XML file. You can then add the XML file to the Business Data Catalog. You can also import an existing application definition file and edit that file by using the tool.

There are also other tools that developers can use, such as the BDC Meta Man or Simego's MOSS BDC Design Studio. Either way, these tools support much easier creation of the ADF, which is just plain good for the developer. Given these tools abstract the ADF, I will not spend time in this book going over the actual XML structure of the ADF; rather, I will walk through how you can use the Microsoft BDC Definition Editor to create the ADF and then show you how you import the ADF into a BDC Web Part.

To begin with, you must make sure that you've installed the MOSS 2007 SDK. You can download this SDK from the following link:

http://www.microsoft.com/downloads/details.aspx?familyid=6d94e307-67d9-41ac-b2d6 -0074d6286fa9&displaylang=en

After installing the SDK, you must then install the Microsoft BDC Definition Editor. To do this, open Windows Explorer and navigate to the following folder: ...\Program Files\2007 Office System Developer Resources\TOOLS\BDC Definition Editor. To install, click setup.exe.

After you've installed and opened the tool, your default view will display any existing connections you have created. Figure 3-25 illustrates this view and shows the type of information that is displayed within the tool. In this instance, there is an existing connection to a simple Budget database, so let's go ahead and add an LOB system (or ADF) for the pubs database that is being used in this example.

The first thing we need to do is to click Add LOB System and then select Connect to Database. This will prompt you with a dialog box in which you must enter the connection string to the database. The connection string I entered is as follows: **Data Source=<servername>;Initial Catalog=<database>;Integrated Security=True.**

After you've entered the connection string, you can use the designer to add tables to the connection (see Figure 3-26). Because we're discussing business intelligence in this chapter, I added the table Sales to the designer. In practice, you might create relationships among tables and then add specific methods or filters, but I wanted to keep things simple to illustrate the process.

After you add a table, click OK. Note that you can also connect to a Web service in the designer and also define the ADF in much the same way you do the database connection. This is discussed more in Chapter 4, "Integrating Web Services into Your Office Business Applications."

After you click OK, the BDC Definition Editor takes you back to your default view and generates a taxonomy view of the definition. In this view, you can now test the connection by executing methods against the tables.

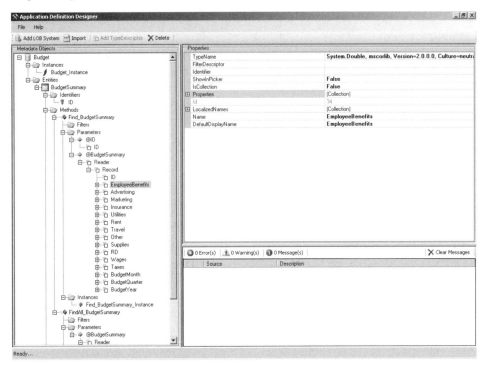

FIGURE 3-25 Default BDC Definition Editor view

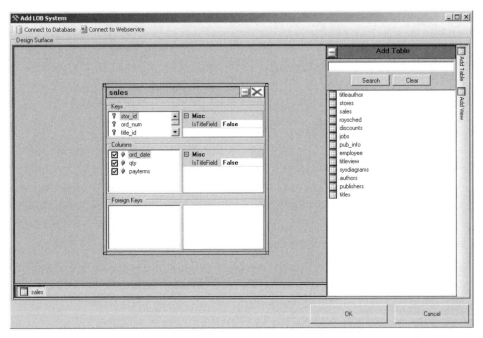

FIGURE 3-26 Add LOB System

To test my connection, I've selected the FindAll_sales_Instance, which selects all of the sales and their associated store IDs, order numbers, and title ID, which is a straightforward "SELECT *" query. And while the results view does not include much information other than returned data, it does provide a good test of whether the connection will succeed and the results that are returned from the execution of this definition. Figure 3-27 illustrates this view.

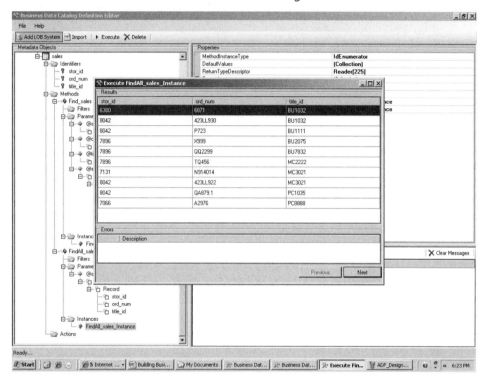

FIGURE 3-27 Executing a test connection

Hopefully, the testing of your connection will have been similarly successful because the next step is to export the definition. To do this, select the root node of the LOB instance and click Export. In my case, the root node is LOB_Book_Sales. This will export the ADF file to a location you select.

After you export the file, you can now import the ADF into SharePoint and associate that ADF with a specific BDC Web part. To do this, navigate to your SharePoint Administration page by clicking Start, All Programs, Microsoft Office Server, and then SharePoint 3.0 Central Administration.

In the left-hand navigation, click your Shared Services. Under the Business Data Catalog, click Import Application Definition. You can then browse to your ADF and then click Import. During the import process, SharePoint will validate the XML definition file against a master BDC XSD, and if there are any errors the import will fail with a specific line number where the failure occurred. Conversely, you'll be notified if the import is a success. Click OK on the Application Definition Import Success page to complete the process.

At this point, you have now successfully imported the ADF, so the last remaining step is to associate the entity definitions with a specific BDC Web part. The view for your database entities automatically invokes after you complete the import process, so navigate to Business Data Catalog Applications to view the definitions available for your use. In my case, I've got three definitions imported in my sandbox environment. Notice that LOB_Book_Sales is among them in Figure 3-28.

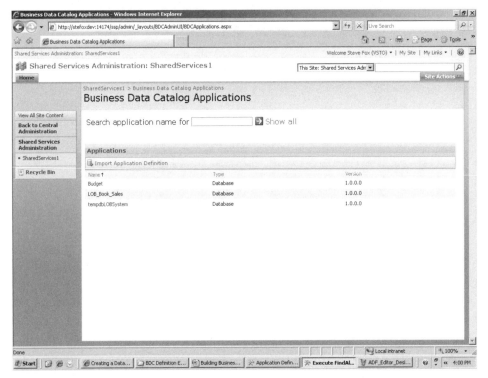

FIGURE 3-28 Business Data Catalog Applications

To add the ADF, navigate to where you want to add your BDC Web part. In my case, I added the BDC Web part to my Book Sales dashboard. Once you've navigated to where you want to add the Web part, click Site Actions and Edit Page.

You can now click Add a Web Part, which invokes the Add Web Parts dialog box. Select the Business Data List Web Part and click Add.

With the BDC Web part added, you need to open the tool pane and then associate the definition with the Web part. You can see in Figure 3-29 the new BDC Web part that displays the sales data from the pubs database.

There are many more types of customizations that you can develop using MOSS 2007, and I encourage you to set up your own sandbox environment for a couple of reasons. First, this will give you some experience in setting up the MOSS environment. And second, you'll have your own environment to explore all of the features of SharePoint.

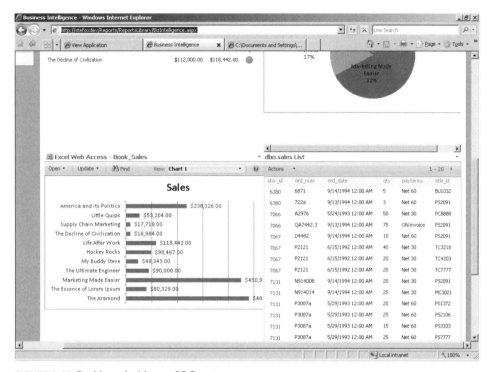

FIGURE 3-29 Dashboard with new BDC part

Further Reading and Related Technologies

As many of you know, knowledge doesn't just magically appear. The great thing about Office Business Applications is that they plug into existing communities for support and technical creativity. I am always humbled and surprised to see the extent to which technologists take Microsoft products and not only write great content around it, but also extend it beyond its original design. Some of the great resources I leverage in my day-to-day work life, including the writing of this chapter, are listed below. I hope you get as much out of them as I do.

Additional details on how to create a database or Web service connection to BDC:

- OBA Web site: *www.obacentral.com*
- Creating a Database Connection by Using the Business Data Catalog Definition Editor: *http://msdn2.microsoft.com/en-us/library/bb736296.aspx*

- Creating a Web Service Connection by Using the Business Data Catalog Definition Editor: *http://msdn2.microsoft.com/en-us/library/bb737887.aspx*

- VSTO Developer Center: *http://msdn2.microsoft.com/en-us/office/aa905533.aspx*

- Office Developer Center: *http://msdn2.microsoft.com/en-us/office/default.aspx*

- Eric Carter's blog: *http://blogs.msdn.com/eric_carter/*

- Andrew Whitechapel's blog: *http://blogs.msdn.com/andreww/*

Have fun building OBAs, and enjoy reading the rest of this book.

Chapter 4
Integrating Web Services into Your Office Business Applications

The Need for S+S in Today's Enterprise Solutions

The demand on enterprises to be leaner, to have greater agility, to be more efficient, and at the same time to surpass customer expectations is growing continuously with the competitive market. Enterprises have been increasing their spending steadily in IT. In fact, Forrester Research says that in 2007, "enterprises expect to increase their IT budgets by 3.8 percent, up from a 3.2 percent planned increase at this time last year." This huge amount of money that goes into IT results in tools that are often disparate and not familiar to the end users who need to learn to use these complicated line-of-business (LOB) applications. More often than not, end users are most comfortable working in Microsoft Office environments and interfaces than in these older, traditional LOB systems that have a very steep learning curve and require a lot of content switching, like copying and pasting, which result in work inefficiencies and general loss of productivity. One example of this happens when a salesperson needs to go into several different systems to update his customer's information after the sale has been made. Mistakes are made, and often the task is forgotten. This is one reason why 42 percent of customer relationship management (CRM) licenses that are purchased are never actually deployed (Gartner Group) and why 57 percent of SAP customers don't believe they've achieved a positive ROI from their implementations (Nucleus Research). This is something that we call the "results gap"—the disconnect between IT solutions and the real workflow of the information worker.

While LOB systems are foundational to enterprise productivity, it's important to step back and ask what the source of the competitive factor and profit driver for the company is. Is it the LOB systems or is it the people—the individuals completing the sales, the employees meeting with customers, and those creating the products? I believe it is the people who drive businesses since it is the employees who create the customer leads, who raise the bottom line, who innovate, who develop strong customer relationships, and who improve operations. Once we've identified the source of the competitive factor and profit driver, it would be wise to start building the processes and applications around the source and make the technology support the people rather than make the people conform to the software and infrastructure. There is no need to throw out any existing investments; it would be best to leverage our current investments and bridge the gap between the back-end and the front-end applications.

Across organizations, and for all information workers, there is the problem of too much data in too many disparate places. Enterprises have data stored in their LOB systems, in their corporate portals, on employees' hard drives, in e-mail, in records repositories...we are in the era of information overload. One of the big challenges that IT faces today is giving end users the ability to work productively by not requiring them to go to all of the systems in which the enterprise has been invested. Creating solutions based on Software + Services results in systems that bring data from all these systems together into one application, so that while the reality is that all this data still exists, managing the data becomes easier.

IT departments have long suffered with the problem of deploying fixes and updates to each employee in the organization. Luckily, this is a challenge that is easily solved by creating solutions based on S+S as a result of the natural code reuse inherent in the architecture. The code is centralized so if a fix needs to be made to the service, this automatically gets picked up by the clients with no interruption to the application.

With the challenges that enterprises face today, like getting a positive ROI from their existing LOB systems, challenging IT to create solutions that mimic the real information worker processes, not just those of the LOB system, and unifying all of our disparate systems to combat information overload, it is easy to see why enterprises are starting to turn to a more agile, service-oriented approach that works around the information worker. So how do we get from disparate, hard-to-use systems to integrated and interoperable applications? That's where S+S and OBAs enter the picture.

S+S and the 2007 Microsoft Office System

Office 2007 is a natural fit for Software + Services for two main reasons:

- Office has exposed a rich set of services that include features such as security, calculation, Enterprise Search, workflow, and single sign-on.

- Office provides the presentation layer for displaying the results of this rich data retrieval into the client applications with which end users are most often comfortable.

The goal of the Office platform here is to achieve integration between software and services and to simplify the consumption of these services for the developer. In addition, Visual Studio 2008, which contains Visual Studio Tools for Office, provides RAD development tools so that teams involving anyone with the skillset of the designer to the professional developer can work collaboratively to create rich, service-oriented Office Business Applications. Let's take a closer look at the services available in Office today.

Services Available in Office 2007

Windows SharePoint Services 3.0 sits at the base of the SharePoint Products and Technologies stacks and offers a lot in terms of administrative and management services, as shown in Figure 4-1.

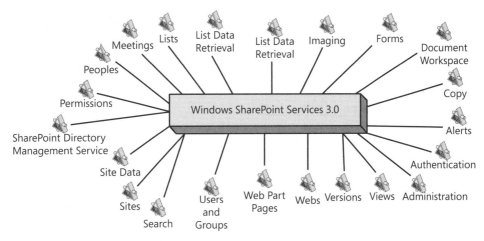

FIGURE 4-1 Web services exposed off of Windows SharePoint Services 3.0

Microsoft Office SharePoint Server (MOSS), which sits on top of WSS architecturally, contains the bulk of the services. MOSS contains many powerful new features, such as Excel Services (the Excel spreadsheet publishing tool, which we will talk more about later on), Forms Services (a thin client of InfoPath), the Business Data Catalog, which enables you to connect to any LOB system and surface that data into your portal without writing any code, Enterprise Search, workflow, and more. Here is a reference of all the Web services available in MOSS:

Microsoft.Office.DocumentManagement.Server	Microsoft.Office.Workflow
Microsoft.Office.DocumentManagement .WebControls	Microsoft.Office.Workflow.Utility
Microsoft.Office.Excel.Server.Udf	Microsoft.SharePoint.Portal
Microsoft.Office.Excel.Server.WebServices	Microsoft.SharePoint.Portal.Administration
Microsoft.Office.Excel.WebUI	Microsoft.SharePoint.Portal.Analytics
Microsoft.Office.RecordsManagement.Holds	Microsoft.SharePoint.Portal.Analytics.Processing

Microsoft.Office.RecordsManagement.InformationPolicy	Microsoft.SharePoint.Portal.Audience
Microsoft.Office.RecordsManagement.PolicyFeatures	Microsoft.SharePoint.Portal.Search.Admin.WebControls
Microsoft.Office.RecordsManagement.RecordsRepository	Microsoft.SharePoint.Portal.Search.PortalCrawl
Microsoft.Office.RecordsManagement.Reporting	Microsoft.SharePoint.Portal.Security
Microsoft.Office.RecordsManagement.SearchAndProcess	Microsoft.SharePoint.Portal.ServerAdmin
Microsoft.Office.Server	Microsoft.SharePoint.Portal.SingleSignon
Microsoft.Office.Server.Administration	Microsoft.SharePoint.Portal.SingleSignon.Security
Microsoft.Office.Server.ApplicationRegistry.Administration	Microsoft.SharePoint.Portal.SingleSignonAdministration
Microsoft.Office.Server.ApplicationRegistry.Infrastructure	Microsoft.SharePoint.Portal.SiteAdmin
Microsoft.Office.Server.ApplicationRegistry.MetadataModel	Microsoft.SharePoint.Portal.SiteAdmin.General
Microsoft.Office.Server.ApplicationRegistry.Runtime	Microsoft.SharePoint.Portal.SiteData
Microsoft.Office.Server.ApplicationRegistry.Search	Microsoft.SharePoint.Portal.SiteDirectory
Microsoft.Office.Server.ApplicationRegistry.SystemSpecific.Db	Microsoft.SharePoint.Portal.Topology
Microsoft.Office.Server.ApplicationRegistry.SystemSpecific.WebService	Microsoft.SharePoint.Portal.UserProfiles
Microsoft.Office.Server.ApplicationRegistry.WebService	Microsoft.SharePoint.Portal.UserProfiles.AdminUI
Microsoft.Office.Server.Audience	Microsoft.SharePoint.Portal.WebControls
Microsoft.Office.Server.Auditing	Microsoft.SharePoint.Portal.WebControls.Alerts
Microsoft.Office.Server.EvaluatorModeProvisioning	Microsoft.SharePoint.Portal.WebControls.WSRPWebService
Microsoft.Office.Server.Infrastructure	Microsoft.SharePoint.Publishing
Microsoft.Office.Server.Search.Administration	Microsoft.SharePoint.Publishing.Administration
Microsoft.Office.Server.Search.Administration.Security	Microsoft.SharePoint.Publishing.Administration.WebServices
Microsoft.Office.Server.Search.Query	Microsoft.SharePoint.Publishing.Design.WebControls

Microsoft.Office.Server.Search.WebControls	Microsoft.SharePoint.Publishing.WebControls
Microsoft.Office.Server.Security	.EditingMenuActions
Microsoft.Office.Server.UserProfiles	Area Web Service
Microsoft.Office.Server.Utilities	Official File Web Service
Microsoft.Office.Server.WebControls	Published Links Web Service
Microsoft.Office.Server.WebControls.FieldTypes	Search Web Service
Microsoft.SharePoint.Publishing.Fields	User Profile Change Web Service
Microsoft.SharePoint.Publishing.Navigation	User Profile Web Service
Microsoft.SharePoint.Publishing.WebControls	Workflow Web Service

For more information about these namespaces and references, refer to *http://msdn2.microsoft .com/en-us/library/ms577961.aspx.*

By exposing these services, the Office server platform empowers developers to start building their own custom solutions with rich Office features and functionality. For example, let's drill down into Excel Services found in MOSS. In Figure 4-2, you can see the ExcelService class found in the Microsoft.Office.Excel.Server.WebServices namespace and all of its public methods.

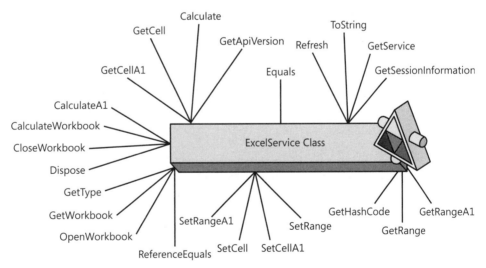

FIGURE 4-2 Public methods of the ExcelService class found in the Microsoft.Office.Excel.Server .WebServices namespace; Excel Services is a new feature in Office SharePoint Server 2007

Excel Services has full calculation fidelity with the client, so if you consume its Web services, you are getting the full power of Excel right within your custom application. Excel Services has two front ends: the Web services and also the Excel Web Access, which is really the

Web part feature in WSS. The back end is the Excel Calculation Services on the Application Server where any user-defined functions can be deployed. More information about Excel Services is available further on in the chapter.

Presentation Layer for Services in the Office 2007 Client

Whether you want to use Office 2007 Web services or you want to consume custom or third-party services, Office 2007 can become the host application for bringing in the data from all your services. Between the flexible development tools and the new user interface it offers, developers can customize the look and feel of the application-use services in ways that appear natural, seamless, and integrated.

There is a whole chapter in this book on customizing the UI (see Chapter 2, "Creating a Smart Client for Your Office Business Application by Using VSTO"), so we will not get into detail on this. Keep in mind that customizing the UI means both client and server and that the server can also be quite richly customized. This is true especially with technologies such as AJAX and Silverlight, which can be applied to SharePoint, and with tools such as SharePoint Designer for the design of master pages. Silverlight is a cross-browser, cross-platform plug-in for delivering next-generation media experiences and rich interactive applications for the Web. It has a flexible programming model that supports JavaScript, Visual C#, Visual Basic, and other languages.

Job Candidate Recruiting Interview Feedback Solution

In this human resources solution, Christoph is a recruiter whose main job function is to fill open positions in the company by searching for candidates in the software industry, recruiting them, interviewing them, negotiating with them, and then finally either offering them a position or giving them the bad news. This solution focuses on gathering feedback during an interview but also incorporates many other aspects of the recruiter's job.

Scenario Overview

The recruiter, Christoph, has opened the Interview Feedback document template that the Wide World Importers human resources department provides for its recruiters to take notes in when interviewing job candidates. As shown in Figure 4-3, the template has a header with information such as the recruiter name, candidate name, interview date, hiring manager, and a link to the résumé stored in a SharePoint list in the Recruiting site.

The Ribbon is customized so that the Home tab has a button on it in the Recruiting Tools group to show or hide the task pane, depending on whether the task pane is toggled to be visible or not. The custom task pane is actually a Document Actions Pane, which means that it is a document-level task pane and shows up only for this template and not for all instances of a Word document, and it allows Christoph to find everything he needs in the context of the application, even though the information he needs may exist in SharePoint or other applications. The first tab in the multi-tab control allows Christoph to search for Interview

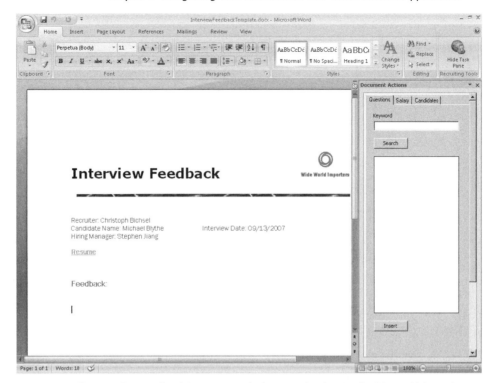

FIGURE 4-3 The Interview Feedback Document solution contains the Word Add-In, which consists of a customized Ribbon and task pane. The Home tab contains a button that toggles the task pane, and the latter is the heart of the solution.

Questions in the repository of best-practice interview questions stored in the Recruiting SharePoint site. This makes use of the SharePoint Lists Web service, which allows users to retrieve items in custom applications. When Christoph selects one he likes, he can insert it into the document with the click of a button, without any copying and pasting.

The second tab allows Christoph to negotiate the salary with the candidate by entering in information such as the candidate's job category, title, location, and education. Clicking Calculate makes use of the Excel Services Web service to use a calculation model stored in a spreadsheet uploaded in a document library in the Recruiting site. This returns a salary range that Christoph can refer to when negotiating with the candidate. The third tab allows Christoph to search for candidates and to see the list of candidates in the LOB system that is being surfaced through SharePoint. As a result, Christoph is able to do all of his research efficiently right within Word while interviewing the candidate.

A Possible End-To-End Solution

This solution starts in the Word document where it focuses on the actual interviewing process. An interesting way to have this scenario extend into an end-to-end scenario would be to have it start off when the recruiter schedules a meeting request in Outlook. Since not all meetings are interviews, the Ribbon could be customized to include an option in which the recruiter could check a checkbox if the meeting request is an interview. When it is time for the meeting, another button launches Word and opens the Interview Feedback Document, where the recruiter can see the custom Ribbon and task pane. This document can be hooked up to SharePoint as a Content Type and therefore be tied to a workflow. When it is time for the interview, the recruiter can seamlessly enter into the document from the meeting request and automatically save the document to the appropriate SharePoint document library, which kicks off a workflow immediately routing the document to the next interviewer or to the hiring manager, depending on the process of the organization and the step that the interviewee is in.

Retrieving Best-Practice Interview Questions

Windows SharePoint Services 3.0 provides Web services so that you can manipulate the items in your lists by doing things such as retrieving and deleting items or attachments. In this scenario, we are using the Lists Web service to retrieve interview questions stored in a WSS list when a user types a keyword into a search box. Figure 4-4 shows the experience presented to the user.

FIGURE 4-4 When the recruiter searches for best-practice interview questions in the custom task pane, the code uses the SharePoint Lists Web service to retrieve list items from a SharePoint list, which acts as a repository containing best-practice interview questions. The user can then insert these questions into the document.

You can see that the recruiter can then also select an interview question and insert it into the document, a functionality that we'll go over later.

Using the SharePoint List Web Service to Retrieve List Items

To hook up the WSS list Web service to the custom task pane in Word, we need to add the Web reference to our add-in project. To do this, in Solution Explorer you right-click on References, click Add Web Reference, enter in **http://<servername>/_vti_bin/lists.asmx**, and click Go. At this point you will see all of the available Web methods in this service, such as AddAttachment, AddList, and GetListItemChanges. You can change the Web Reference name to whatever you like and then click Add Reference.

Now we are ready to start instantiating the service object and calling the methods. Behind the Search button, we need to declare and initialize a variable for the Lists Web service and then authenticate the current user. We do this by passing the default credentials from the system credential cache to the Web service. We then set the URL property of the service for the path to the subsite that we are targeting. Here you can use either the GUID or the URL.

```
ListService.Lists listService = new ListService.Lists();
listService.Credentials = System.Net.CredentialCache.DefaultCredentials;

listService.Url =
"http://moss/SiteDirectory/Human%20Resources/Recruiting/_vti_bin/lists.asmx";
```

We need to formulate a CAML query in order to filter our results, which we will pass in as a parameter of type XML string into the GetListItems method.

```
string qry =
"<Query><Where><Contains><FieldRef Name='Title'/><Value Type='Text'>" +
            txtKeyword.Text + "</Value></Contains></Where></Query>";
string flds = "<ViewFields><FieldRef Name='Title'><FieldRef Name='Body'>" +
            "</FieldRef></FieldRef></ViewFields>";

XmlDocument doc1 = new XmlDocument();
doc1.LoadXml(qry);

XmlDocument doc2 = new XmlDocument();
doc2.LoadXml(flds);
```

From the GetListItems method, we will receive an XML string with all of our information, which we will then need to parse. An interesting thing is when you retrieve the list of titles from SharePoint lists, they are all preceded with the string ows_ so you need to strip that out.

```
try
{
    //bind to the gridview
    System.Xml.XmlNode oNode = listService.GetListItems(listName.ToString(),
        null, doc1.DocumentElement, doc2.DocumentElement, null, null, null);
    XmlNodeReader rd = new XmlNodeReader(oNode);
    DataSet ds = new DataSet();
    ds.ReadXml(rd);
```

```
        rd.Close();
        ResultsGridView.DataSource = ds.Tables[1];

        //add only the first column and remove the "ows_" that is at the
        //beginning of the string
        ResultsGridView.Columns.Clear();
        ResultsGridView.Columns.Add("ows_Title", "Interview Questions");
        ResultsGridView.Columns["ows_Title"].DataPropertyName = "ows_Title";

ResultsGridView.AutoResizeColumns(DataGridViewAutoSizeColumnsMode.AllCells);
    }
    catch (SoapException ex)
    {
        MessageBox.Show("Message:\n" + ex.Message + "\nDetail:\n" +
            ex.Detail.InnerText + "\nStackTrace:\n" + ex.StackTrace);
    }
}
```

Inserting an Interview Question

This part is simple and just deals with working with the Word object model. The trick is to Activate the document. Because the gridView always has at least one item selected, we don't need to verify that there is an item selected in the control. This code only inserts at the end of the document for simplicity.

```
private void btnInsert_Click(object sender, EventArgs e)
{
    string txtQuestion = ResultsGridView.CurrentCell.Value.ToString();
    Globals.ThisDocument.Activate();
    Globals.ThisDocument.Paragraphs[Globals.ThisDocument.Paragraphs.Count].Range.Text
        = txtQuestion;
}
```

Verifying a Candidate's Salary Using the Recruiting Salary Model

As we briefly described earlier, Office SharePoint Server has a new feature called Excel Services, which allows developers to use the Excel calculation engine as a service. In this scenario, as shown in Figure 4-5, the recruiter is able to get a quick salary estimate by entering the candidate's information in the Salary tab in the Word task pane. A general salary range is then calculated and retrieved based on the company's salary model.

Overview of Excel Services

Excel Services is a MOSS Enterprise edition offering that publishes Excel Workbooks to the server and exposes Web service interfaces that enable developers to access the Excel Calculation engine so that they can create custom applications.

Excel Services is built on the SharePoint Products and Technologies platform. As shown in Figure 4-6, at a high level it is made up of three core components: Excel Web Access (EWA), Excel Web Services (EWS), and Excel Calculation Services (ECS).

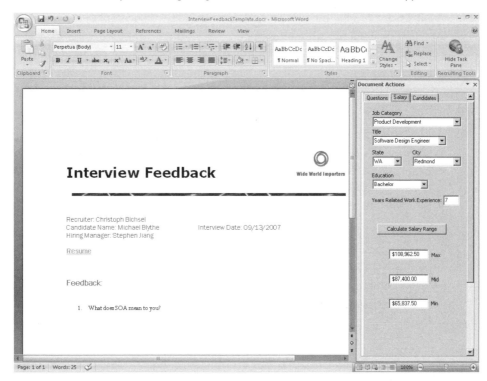

FIGURE 4-5 The Salary tab allows the recruiter to bring up a quick salary range as specified by the company's salary model. This is calculated server-side using Excel Services Web Services after the recruiter enters in the interviewee's pertinent information.

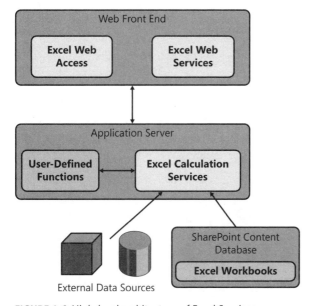

FIGURE 4-6 High-level architecture of Excel Services

On the front end, based on the WSS user interface, we have the EWA, which is a Web part that enables a thin browsing experience. This is where users can interact with Excel spreadsheets that have been published to the server, sort and filter tables, and drill up and drill down on pivotTables without requiring end users to have Excel on their machines. In fact, there is zero footprint here since this is just HTML and JavaScript and the end user doesn't need to install any ActiveX controls either in order to use the EWA.

Also on the front end is the EWS, which is the programmatic interface to server calculations. It is a Web service hosted in SharePoint. Developers can build custom applications—for example, those reliant on calculation-intensive financial models—by consuming these Web services with methods that perform actions like setting cells, calculating ranges in the workbook, and refreshing the workbook.

On the back end or application server, we have the ECS, which loads the published spread-sheet, calculates it, refreshes the external data, and maintains the session state for interactivity. It is the engine of Excel Services. The ECS also maintains the caching of the file itself, the results within the file, and the location of the file. All the cache settings are controllable by the administrator. If any user-defined functions are used, these are also deployed to the application server.

Performing Calculations Server-Side in Word Using the Excel Calculation Engine

In this Recruiting Scenario, as shown in Figure 4-7, the simple business logic of the salary calculator is stored in an Excel spreadsheet, which is uploaded to a SharePoint document library.

Each "field" is a Named Range in the spreadsheet. This is important because we need to know the cell range to perform the calculation via the Web services. If we pass in a literal range and at some point we change this spreadsheet around, the formulas will break. On the other hand, if we use Named Ranges, the formulas will remain tied to our new ranges.

So the spreadsheet is uploaded in a document library in SharePoint, and the services in Office SharePoint Service, specifically Excel Services, allow us to set the fields in the salary calculator, which causes the Min, Mid, and Max Salary values to calculate, which we can then access using another Excel Service method.

Let's start to build this. First we need to add the Web reference to the project. In Solution Explorer, right-click References, click Add Web Reference, enter **http://<servername>/_ vti_bin/ExcelService.asmx**, and click Go. At this point, you will see all of the available Web methods in this service, such as OpenWorkbook, SetRange, and CalculateWorkbook. You can change the Web Reference name to whatever you like and then click Add Reference.

Behind the Calculate Salary Range button, we first initialize the Web service, set variables, and pass in the default credentials in the system credential cache.

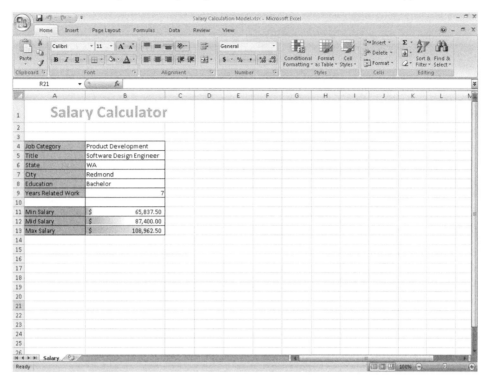

FIGURE 4-7 The salary model, which calculates server-side, is stored in a workbook in a SharePoint document library. The custom task pane in the Word Add-In accesses the named ranges in the workbook, using the Excel Services Web services to write the text from the selected fields in the task pane to the cells in the workbook and returning the calculated results from the named ranges in the workbook to display in the task pane.

```
ExcelService es = new ExcelService();
Status[] outStatus;
string sheetName = "Salary";
string targetWorkbookPath = "http://moss/HR/Recruiting/Recruiting%20Tools/Salary%20
                            Calculation%20Model.xlsx";
es.Credentials = System.Net.CredentialCache.DefaultCredentials;
```

Next we call the OpenWorkbook method from the Excel Services. This loads our Salary Calculation Workbook that was published to SharePoint and returns a sessionID that can be used to perform further operations.

```
try
{
    string sessionId = es.OpenWorkbook(targetWorkbookPath, "en-us", "en-us",
                                        out outStatus);
```

Now we link what the user selected in the drop-down box to the values in the cells in the spreadsheet so that we can calculate the salary range. After that, we retrieve the calculated values where Min_Salary, Mid_Salary, and Max_Salary are the Named Ranges containing the formulas.

```
es.SetCellA1(sessionId, sheetName, "Job_Category", comboJobCategory.Text);
es.SetCellA1(sessionId, sheetName, "Title", comboJobTitle.Text);
es.SetCellA1(sessionId, sheetName, "State", comboState.Text);
es.SetCellA1(sessionId, sheetName, "City", comboCity.Text);
es.SetCellA1(sessionId, sheetName, "Education", comboEducation.Text);

object oMin = es.GetCellA1(sessionId, sheetName, "Min_Salary", true, out outStatus);
object oMid = es.GetCellA1(sessionId, sheetName, "Mid_Salary", true, out outStatus);
object oMax = es.GetCellA1(sessionId, sheetName, "Max_Salary", true, out outStatus);

if (oMin != null)
{
    txtMinSalary.Text = Convert.ToString(oMin);
    txtMidSalary.Text = Convert.ToString(oMid);
    txtMaxSalary.Text = Convert.ToString(oMax);
}
else
{
MessageBox.Show("Error retrieving salary values");
return;
}
    es.CloseWorkbook(sessionId);
}

catch (SoapException ex)
{
    MessageBox.Show("SOAP Exception Message: {0}", ex.Message);
}
```

Retrieving Candidate Data from the LOB System from the Custom Task Pane

In this section, we'll learn how to create and consume custom Web services, which wrap the Business Data Catalog functionality in MOSS, that define the LOB entity. In the Candidate tab, the recruiter is able to search for candidates and to see the list of candidates in the LOB system that is being surfaced through SharePoint. The recruiter can also query based on a specific candidate ID. This data is pulled in through the use of custom Web services, which access the Business Data Catalog in MOSS through which we surface our LOB entities. Since these entities are surfaced through MOSS, the recruiter is able to click on the link in the Profile column in the task pane and view the metadata about the candidate in SharePoint, a feature that comes out of the box with the BDC. Figure 4-8 shows what the user experience looks like for the Candidate tab.

Since this LOB data is surfaced through the Business Data Catalog in MOSS, the recruiter is able to take advantage of the SharePoint integration and click on the link in the Profile column in the gridView control. This launches the browser showing the candidate's profile in SharePoint, as displayed in a dynamic Web part page (see Figure 4-9).

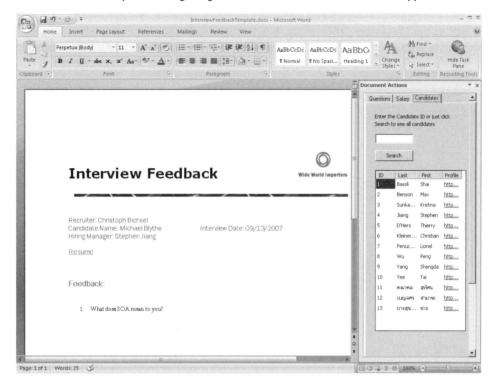

FIGURE 4-8 In the Candidate tab, the recruiter can pull up lists of candidates from the LOB system.

Overview of the Business Data Catalog

The Business Data Catalog (BDC) is a new feature in Office SharePoint Server 2007; it surfaces data from any line-of-business application, such as SAP or Siebel, into SharePoint without writing any code. As a result, this rich data is available through Web parts, is indexed as part of the Enterprise Search in your portal, and is available through lists and user profiles. Furthermore, developers can use it to create custom applications.

For information workers who often need to access LOB data, this means that they no longer need to go into separate applications to retrieve data from applications that are not intuitive or often require a lot of training, and as a result are usually limited to specific roles. MOSS, with the addition of the BDC, allows all users to view data from traditional LOB systems easily from a familiar interface.

For developers, the great advantage is that you can surface your LOB data into SharePoint without writing any code. The BDC makes use of standard .NET classes to interface with LOB systems, connecting with OLEDB and ODBC data sources using an ADO.NET interface, or to any other data source using a SOAP interface. In this recruiting example, the BDC is connecting to the AdventureWorks sample database through its ADO.NET interface. Figure 4-10 gives a high-level architecture view of the BDC. For more detailed

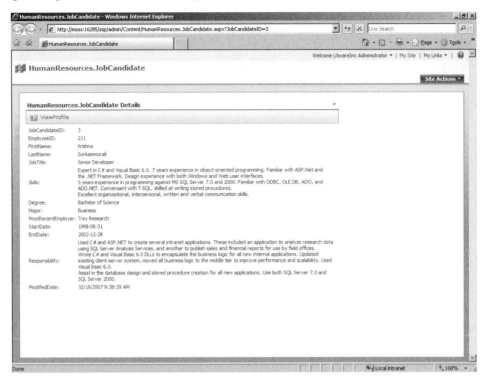

FIGURE 4-9 The SharePoint Profile page of the candidate that the recruiter sees when he or she clicks on the Profile link in the custom task pane of the solution

information on the architecture of the BDC, go to *http://msdn2.microsoft.com/en-us/ library/ms499729.aspx.*

To make this connection, you need to describe the data source using an XML metadata file, called an application definition file (ADF), and define your business entities. The ADF contains all of the necessary information to connect to the LOB data and return the requested data. Here, you define your business entities, which are like business objects with properties, methods, and actions. Application definitions follow the schemas defined in the BDCMetaData.xsd file located under the Program Files\Microsoft Office Servers\12.0\Bin directory.

You do not need to author the ADF from scratch. If you download the SDK for Office SharePoint Server 2007, there is a tool called the Microsoft Business Data Catalog Definition Editor where you can create the XML using a UI.

Once you have created the ADF, you go to SharePoint 3.0 Central Administration, click Shared Services Administration on the left-hand navigation panel, and then pick your Shared Service Provider. As shown in Figure 4-11, you have a Business Data Catalog section where you can manage all the entities you have uploaded from the various LOB systems you have connected to SharePoint.

Features and applications

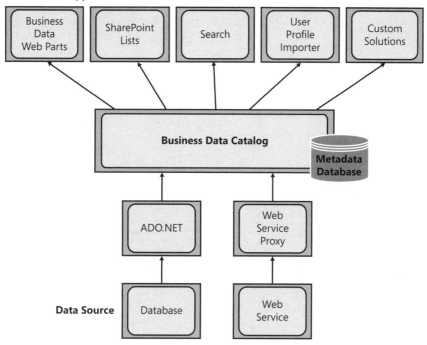

FIGURE 4-10 High-level architecture of the Business Data Catalog

To upload your ADF, just click Import Application Definition, which validates the file.

Creating the Application Definition File

In our example, we are using the AdventureWorks SQL Server database as our LOB system, which therefore interfaces with an ADO.NET connection to the BDC. The first thing we need to do is create an ADF file, which defines all this connection information, plus all the entities we want to define, in this case, JobCandidates. Off of these entities, we'll have properties, methods, and actions. Figure 4-12 shows what the ADF looked like for the Recruiting solution when loaded into the Business Data Catalog Definition Editor.

We have an instance of the AdventureWorks database called AdventureWorksRecruiting and one Entity called HumanResources.JobCandidate with several methods. These methods execute SQL queries against the LOB system since it is based on a SQL Server database. You won't see the View Profile action in the BDC Definition Editor, but it gets created by default when you upload the ADF into SharePoint so you don't need to create an action where you see all the metadata about your entity.

In our Recruiting scenario, we make use of the methods GetJobCandidate and GetJobCandidateSpecificFinder. Let's dive deeper into how we built the method GetJobCandidate.

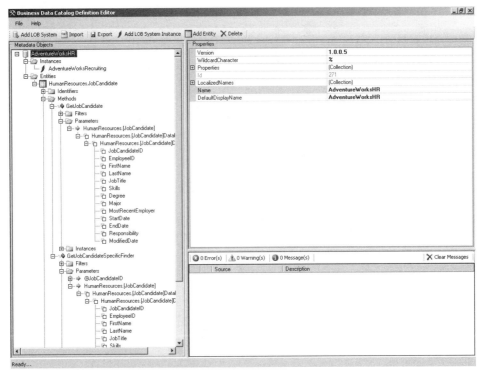

FIGURE 4-12 View of the Interview Feedback Document solution ADF as uploaded in the Business Data Catalog Definition Editor, which ships with the MOSS SDK

```
<Method Name="GetJobCandidate">
  <Properties>
    <Property Name="RdbCommandType" Type="System.Data.CommandType, System.Data,
      Version=2.0.0.0, Culture=neutral, PublicKeyToken=b77a5c561934e089">Text</Property>
          <Property Name="RdbCommandText" Type="System.String">SELECT
[JobCandidateID],[EmployeeID],Resume.value('declare namespace
r="http://schemas.microsoft.com/sqlserver/2004/07/adventure-
works/Resume";(r:Resume/r:Name/r:Name.First)[1]', 'nvarchar(100)') as
[FirstName],Resume.value('declare namespace
r="http://schemas.microsoft.com/sqlserver/2004/07/adventure-
works/Resume";(r:Resume/r:Name/r:Name.Last)[1]', 'nvarchar(100)') as
[LastName],Resume.value('declare namespace
r="http://schemas.microsoft.com/sqlserver/2004/07/adventure-
works/Resume";(r:Resume/r:Employment/r:Emp.JobTitle)[1]', 'nvarchar(100)') as
[JobTitle],Resume.value('declare namespace
r="http://schemas.microsoft.com/sqlserver/2004/07/adventure-
works/Resume";(r:Resume/r:Skills)[1]', 'nvarchar(1000)') as
[Skills],Resume.value('declare namespace
r="http://schemas.microsoft.com/sqlserver/2004/07/adventure-works/Resume";(r:Resume/
r:Education/r:Edu.Degree)[1]', 'nvarchar(100)') as
[Degree],Resume.value('declare namespace
r="http://schemas.microsoft.com/sqlserver/2004/07/adventure-
works/Resume";(r:Resume/r:Education/r:Edu.Major)[1]', 'nvarchar(100)') as
[Major],Resume.value('declare namespace
```

```
r="http://schemas.microsoft.com/sqlserver/2004/07/adventure-
works/Resume";(r:Resume/r:Employment/r:Emp.OrgName)[1]', 'nvarchar(100)') as
[MostRecentEmployer],Resume.value('declare namespace
r="http://schemas.microsoft.com/sqlserver/2004/07/adventure-
works/Resume";(r:Resume/r:Employment/r:Emp.StartDate)[1]', 'nvarchar(10)') as
[StartDate],Resume.value('declare namespace
r="http://schemas.microsoft.com/sqlserver/2004/07/adventure-
works/Resume";(r:Resume/r:Employment/r:Emp.EndDate)[1]', 'nvarchar(10)') as
[EndDate],Resume.value('declare namespace
r="http://schemas.microsoft.com/sqlserver/2004/07/adventure-
works/Resume";(r:Resume/r:Employment/r:Emp.Responsibility)[1]', 'nvarchar(1500)') as
[Responsibility],[ModifiedDate]FROM
[AdventureWorks].[HumanResources].[JobCandidate]</Property>
        </Properties>
        <Parameters>
          <Parameter Direction="Return" Name="HumanResources.[JobCandidate]">
            <TypeDescriptor TypeName="System.Data.IDataReader, System.Data,
            Version=2.0.3600.0,
                    Culture=neutral, PublicKeyToken=b77a5c561934e089"
            IsCollection="true"
                    Name="HumanResources.[JobCandidate]DataReader">
              <TypeDescriptors>
                <TypeDescriptor TypeName="System.Data.IDataRecord, System.Data,
                    Version=2.0.3600.0, Culture=neutral,
                    PublicKeyToken=b77a5c561934e089"
                    Name="HumanResources.[JobCandidate]DataRecord">
                  <TypeDescriptors>
                    <TypeDescriptor TypeName="System.Int32"
                    IdentifierName="[JobCandidateID]"
                      Name="JobCandidateID"/>
                    <TypeDescriptor TypeName="System.Int32" Name="EmployeeID"/>
                    <TypeDescriptor TypeName="System.String" Name="FirstName"/>
                    <TypeDescriptor TypeName="System.String" Name="LastName"/>
                    <TypeDescriptor TypeName="System.String" Name="JobTitle"/>
                    <TypeDescriptor TypeName="System.String" Name="Skills"/>
                    <TypeDescriptor TypeName="System.String" Name="Degree"/>
                    <TypeDescriptor TypeName="System.String" Name="Major"/>
                    <TypeDescriptor TypeName="System.String" Name="MostRecentEmployer"/>
                    <TypeDescriptor TypeName="System.String" Name="StartDate"/>
                    <TypeDescriptor TypeName="System.String" Name="EndDate"/>
                    <TypeDescriptor TypeName="System.String" Name="Responsibility"/>
                    <TypeDescriptor TypeName="System.String" Name="ModifiedDate"/>
                  </TypeDescriptors>
                </TypeDescriptor>
              </TypeDescriptors>
            </TypeDescriptor>
          </Parameter>
        </Parameters>
        <MethodInstances>
          <MethodInstance Type="Finder"
ReturnParameterName="HumanResources.[JobCandidate]"
                ReturnTypeDescriptorName="HumanResources.[JobCandidate]DataReader"
                ReturnTypeDescriptorLevel="0"
Name="HumanResources.[JobCandidate]Finder"/>
        </MethodInstances>
        </Method>
```

You can see that we've specificed that the SQL query return several values of data for the candidate from the table, such as JobCandidateID, EmployeeID, and tagged sections of the Resume field such as Skills. For the Resume field, the values are of type XML containing custom XML, which will display in the SharePoint profile page as one long XML string if we return the data as is. As a result, we need to create a query string, which navigates to the location in the XML string and parses out the data.

Next we define our parameters. Since this is just a Finder Method method, which does not take in a query parameter, we will only have parameters of the direction "return" defined and not of the direction "in," as we would with the SpecificFinder method. Off of our return parameter, we create a Root TypeDescriptor, an object of the type IDataReader, which will basically read data from the returned recordset. From the Root TypeDescriptor you create a TypeDescriptor, which is a Data Record, which holds the columns for all the parameters that you want to return. This is where we define all our out parameters as TypeDescriptors, JobCandidateID of type System.Int32, for example. Finally, we need to have at least one instance of our method to have a valid ADF.

Developing the Custom Web Service

While the BDC does have an object model for extensibility, it does not provide Web services if you would like to access the LOB data from a client application remotely. In the recruiting scenario, a custom Web service was built to access the LOB system through the BDC, access the HumanResources.JobCandidate entity, and then wrap the methods off of that entity.

Let's take a look at code, specifically the GetJobCandidate method in the JobCandidate Web service. The first thing we need to do is set application information so that we can retrieve the data.

```
[WebMethod]
public XmlNode GetJobCandidate(string SSPName, string
LobInstanceName, string EntityName, string MethodName, string SearchTerm, string
ActionName)
{
   try
   {
      if (SSPName != null)
        SqlSessionProvider.Instance().SetSharedResourceProviderToUse(SSPName);

        NamedLobSystemInstanceDictionary lobInstances =
            ApplicationRegistry.GetLobSystemInstances();
        LobSystemInstance lobInstance = lobInstances[LobInstanceName];
        Entity entity = lobInstance.GetEntities()[EntityName];
        MethodInstance methodInstance =
            entity.GetMethodInstances()[MethodName];
      Microsoft.Office.Server.ApplicationRegistry.MetadataModel.Action action =
            entity.GetActions()[ActionName];
```

We set up the filter for searching and then pass that filter's collection and our lobInstance into the FindFiltered method of the entity object to return the data we want.

```
FilterCollection filters = entity.GetFinderFilters();
DbEntityInstanceEnumerator records =
        (DbEntityInstanceEnumerator)entity.FindFiltered(filters, lobInstance);
```

We load the results into a data table so that we can include the Action URL from the View Profile action defined in the ADF.

```
DataTable entitiesTable = new DataTable();

while (records.MoveNext())
{
    //Load each entity and include the Action URL
    DbEntityInstance record = (DbEntityInstance)records.Current;
    DataTable entityTable = record.EntityAsDataTable;
    entityTable.Columns.Add("ActionURL", typeof(string));
    try { entityTable.Rows[0]["ActionURL"] = record.GetActionUrl(action); }
    catch { entityTable.Rows[0]["ActionURL"] = ""; }
    entityTable.AcceptChanges();
    entitiesTable.Merge(entityTable);
}
```

We return the results as the expected XML document.

```
XmlElement entitiesElement = document.CreateElement("bdc", "Entities", bdcSpace);
    document.AppendChild(entitiesElement);

    foreach (DataRow entityRow in entitiesTable.Rows)
    {
        XmlElement entityElement = document.CreateElement("bdc","Entity",bdcSpace);
        entitiesElement.AppendChild(entityElement);

        foreach (DataColumn entityColumn in entitiesTable.Columns)
        {
            try
            {
                XmlAttribute valueAttribute = document.CreateAttribute("bdc",
                entityColumn.ColumnName, bdcSpace);
                valueAttribute.Value = entityRow[entityColumn.ColumnName].ToString();

                entityElement.Attributes.Append(valueAttribute);
            }
            catch { }
        }
    }
return document;
}
catch (Exception x)
{
    XmlDocument document = new XmlDocument();
    XmlElement errorElement = document.CreateElement("bdc", "Error", bdcSpace);
        document.AppendChild(errorElement);
    XmlNode messageNode = document.CreateNode(XmlNodeType.Text, "bdc", "Message", bdcSpace);
```

```
messageNode.Value = x.Message;
errorElement.AppendChild(messageNode);
return null;
    }
}
```

The GetJobCandidateSpecificFinder method varies in that it calls the method FindSpecific off the Entity object rather than FindFiltered and passes in an identifier that is the JobCandidateID.

```
DbEntityInstance record = (DbEntityInstance)entity.FindSpecific(Identifier,lobInstance);
```

Consuming the Custom Web Service in the Client Application

Once the Web service is deployed, you can add it as a Web reference to your Word add-in project, instatiate, and use the methods.

```
private void btnSearchCandidates_Click(object sender, EventArgs e)
{
RecruitingService.JobCandidate jobCandidateService = new RecruitingService.JobCandidate();
    jobCandidateService.Url = "http://localhost:2223/JobCandidate.asmx";
    jobCandidateService.Credentials = System.Net.CredentialCache.DefaultCredentials;
```

Recall the way the Candidate search tab worked. If the text box was empty, then all the candidates were returned. If a candidate ID was entered in the search box, then a query went out to search for that candidate. Technically, in the former case, the Finder method was called, and in the latter case, the SpecificFinder method was called. The difference in the parameters of the two methods is that for GetJobCandidate, which returns all the candidates, you pass in the value of the search textbox, and for GetJobCandidateSpecificFinder, which returns only one candidate, you pass in the ID of the candidate.

```
XmlNode jobCandidateNode;

if (txtCandidateSearch.Text == "")

{

    jobCandidateNode =

jobCandidateService.GetJobCandidate("SharedServices1", "AdventureWorksRecruiting",
"HumanResources.JobCandidate", "HumanResources.[JobCandidate]Finder", txtCandidateSearch.
Text, "View Profile");

}

else

{

    int jobCandidateID = Convert.ToInt32(txtCandidateSearch.Text);

    jobCandidateNode = jobCandidateService.GetJobCandidateSpecificFinder
("SharedServices1", "AdventureWorksRecruiting", "HumanResources.JobCandidate",
"HumanResources.[JobCandidate]SpecificFinder", jobCandidateID, "View Profile");

}
```

Because these methods return XML strings, we need to parse them. Here, the results are bound to the gridView control in the CTP. The results show the candidate's ID, last name, and first name.

```
XmlNodeReader rd = new XmlNodeReader(jobCandidateNode);
DataSet ds = new DataSet();
ds.ReadXml(rd);
rd.Close();
gridViewRecruits.DataSource = ds.Tables[0];

gridViewRecruits.Columns.Clear();
gridViewRecruits.Columns.Add("JobCandidateID", "ID");
gridViewRecruits.Columns["JobCandidateID"].DataPropertyName = "JobCandidateID";
gridViewRecruits.Columns.Add("LastName", "Last Name");
gridViewRecruits.Columns["LastName"].DataPropertyName = "LastName";
gridViewRecruits.Columns.Add("FirstName", "First Name");
gridViewRecruits.Columns["FirstName"].DataPropertyName = "FirstName";

gridViewRecruits.AutoResizeColumns(DataGridViewAutoSizeColumnsMode.AllCells);
}
```

Summary

This Recruiting scenario shows how the services offered by the 2007 Office System platform enable developers to build S+S-rich OBAs. A custom task pane, built using VSTO in VS 2008, hosted our solution, enabling the recruiter to live in the Word application while accessing different systems and performing multiple tasks. From a development perspective, we were able to pull data from SharePoint lists using the lists Web service so that the end user could access best practices from the enterprise portal. We used Excel Services Web services to calculate a candidate's salary range based on a model that was created in a spreadsheet, published, and calculated on the server. The recruiter was also able to retrieve specific candidates or a list of candidates from the LOB system through custom Web services that accessed the Business Data Catalog, which exposes LOB entities in SharePoint. The BDC allows you to surface any LOB system into SharePoint through lists, Web parts, Enterprise Search, and custom applications. Using the richness of the Office Web services APIs coupled with the ability for rapid development enabled by tools such as VSTO in VS 2008, Office 2007 allows developers to build enterprise-ready solutions that are built around information worker processes and bring value to IT investments.

Further Reading and Resources

Office Business Applications

- OBA Web site: *www.obacentral.com*

- Office Business Applications Developer Portal: *http://msdn.microsoft.com/oba*

- MSDN Architecture Center: *http://msdn2.microsoft.com/en-us/architecture*

- Steve Ballmer talks about S+S in Office 2007:
  http://www.news.com/1606-2_3-6182663.html

General Office Development

- MSDN Office Developer How-To Center:
  http://msdn2.microsoft.com/en-us/office/bb266408.aspx

- Office Developer Webcasts:
  http://www.microsoft.com/events/series/officedeveloperlive.mspx

- How Do I? Screencasts: *http://msdn.microsoft.com/office/learn/screencasts/*

Office SharePoint Server

General

- Office SharePoint Server SDK (download; contains the Microsoft Business
  Data Catalog Definition Editor): *http://www.microsoft.com/downloads/
  details.aspx?FamilyId=6D94E307-67D9-41AC-B2D6-0074D6286FA9&displaylang=en*

- *Inside Microsoft Office SharePoint Server 2007* by Patrick Tisseghem (Microsoft Press)

Excel Services

- Excel Services Information Center Portal on MSDN: *http://msdn2.microsoft.com/en-us/
  office/bb203828.aspx*

- Architecture of Excel Services: *http://msdn2.microsoft.com/en-us/library/ms499729.aspx*

Business Data Catalog

- BDC SDK: *http://msdn2.microsoft.com/en-us/library/ms563661.aspx*

- BDC Information Center: *http://msdn2.microsoft.com/en-us/office/bb251754.aspx*

- Using the Business Data Catalog and Smart Tags with the 2007 Microsoft Office System
  (article, white paper, and code sample): *http://msdn2.microsoft.com/en-us/library/
  bb608684.aspx*

- MSDN/TechNET BDC Forum: *http://mssharepointforums.com*

Windows SharePoint Services

- *Inside Microsoft Windows SharePoint Services 3.0* by Ted Pattison and Daniel Larson
  (Microsoft Press)

- *Microsoft SharePoint: Building Office 2007 Solutions in C# 2005* by Scot Hillier (APress)

- Office SharePoint Server SDK (contains the WSS 3.0 SDK): *http://www.microsoft.com/
  downloads/details.aspx?FamilyId=6D94E307-67D9-41AC-B2D6-0074D6286FA9&displaylang=en*

Visual Studio Tools for Office

- *VSTO for Mere Mortals: A VBA Developer's Guide to Microsoft Office Development Using Visual Studio 2005 Tools for Office* by Paul Stubbs and Kathleen McGrath (Addison-Wesley Professional)

- VSTO Developer Portal: *http://msdn2.microsoft.com/en-us/office/aa905533.aspx*

Blogs
Office Business Applications

- OBA team: *http://blogs.msdn.com/oba*

- Joanna Bichsel: *http://blogs.msdn.com/Joanna_Bichsel/*

- Javeds: *http://blogs.msdn.com/javeds/*

Visual Studio Tools for Office

- Microsoft Visual Studio Tools for the Microsoft Office System: *http://blogs.msdn.com/vsto/*

SharePoint Products and Technologies

- SharePoint team: *http://blogs.msdn.com/sharepoint/*

- Patrick Tisseghem: *http://www.u2u.info/Blogs/Patrick/default.aspx*

Excel Services

- Cum Grano Salis: *http://blogs.msdn.com/cumgranosalis/default.aspx*

- Luis Bitencourt-Emilio: *http://blogs.msdn.com/luisbeonservices/*

- Excel team: *http://blogs.msdn.com/excel/*

ECM and Business Data Catalog

- ECM team: *http://blogs.msdn.com/ecm/*

- Sahil Malik: *http://blah.winsmarts.com/2007-4-SharePoint_2007__BDC_-_The_Business_Data_Catalog.aspx*

Chapter 5
Building Social Networking into Your Office Business Application

What Is Social Networking?

Roughly defined, social networking is the process of developing relationships across and within a group of people. What defines the links amongst the group of people is the social network, which is a structure made up of nodes tied together through various interdependencies; it is essentially a map that defines how people in a network are connected. You might sometimes hear people also refer to social networking as social computing, though these are two distinctly different things.

While the *social* might connote nonbusiness networking, many people use social networking as an extension of the workplace to build their interpersonal and business networks. The Internet has in some sense revolutionized the ways in which we build these networks, providing virtual environments for our networks to grow and flourish. For example, recent examples of social networking environments on the Internet are Flickr, MySpace, LinkedIn, and Facebook. If we take a look at how social networking has evolved, you can see that there are many common technologies (for example, e-mail) we've probably all been using that fit within this general heading of social networking. Figure 5-1 provides an overview of some key social networking technology advancements over the past couple of decades.

Many companies are taking a keen interest in these social networking environments (as evidenced by the stake Microsoft recently bought in Facebook) because they provide an organic way to extend and build not only your social but also your business network, to communicate, and, what some might argue is most important, to share knowledge. (In some cases, they also represent platforms on which you can build interesting applications or mash-ups, as we'll see later in this chapter.) And at the end of the day, developing and sustaining key relationships is paramount to doing good business in today's competitive environment. And social networking is integral to this relationship management.

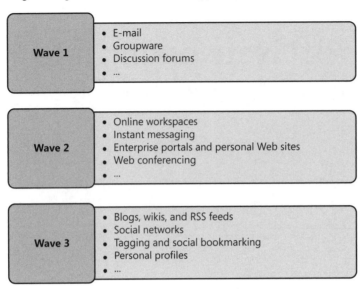

FIGURE 5-1 Evolution of social networking technologies

Applying Social Networking to OBAs

By now you should have a pretty good understanding of what an Office Business Application is, and you're probably beginning to understand how you go about building one. Your next question, then, is probably how does social networking apply to OBAs? The answer is an important one. OBAs are primarily about bringing business data within key line-of-business (LOB) systems closer to the information worker (IW), and while that's all good, we can't treat the IW as an isolated individual within the modern organization, or else we're really right back where we started, with the results gap existing across *people* as opposed to *the business data and the people*. Thus, part of the critical ingredient to our OBAs is the ability to bring other IWs into our knowledge paradigm, creating social networks around specific areas within the organization. This means that we need to have the ability to invite, manage, and evolve networks around, for example, our SharePoint sites and portals (which would be developed as part of our OBA) so other IWs can be armed with similar information that can help them make strong and qualified business decisions. Figure 5-2 illustrates this by extending the simple OBA pie chart (representing the three high-level pieces of an OBA) with a more detailed representation of some of the core social networking features within SharePoint. In this representation, we're leveraging features such as My Site (or indeed wider team sites through SharePoint sites), My Profile, blogs, wikis, RSS, and so on, to extend the reach of our OBA into the enterprise—or conversely to enable access to our personal project information or profiles through SharePoint search or our blogs through RSS feeds. Either way, the goal is to extend the reach of your OBA through the mechanism of social networking, and each one of the SharePoint technologies in Figure 5-2 can help achieve this. (Note: In Figure 5-2, "SharePoint Server++" indicates that while SharePoint is a key part of OBAs, you can also use other servers in the Office platform, like Exchange Server, to build your OBA.)

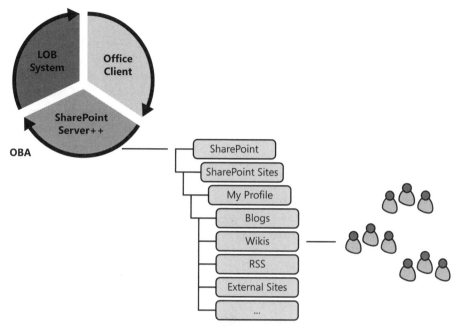

FIGURE 5-2 OBA social networking with SharePoint

As you saw earlier in Figure 5-1, there are many different types of technologies that we can classify as being a part of the social networking paradigm. However, the social networking technologies this chapter discusses are predominantly Microsoft Office SharePoint Server (MOSS) 2007-centric, and thus will cover the following:

- My Site and My Profile
- Blogs
- Wikis
- RSS
- Third-party social networking environments

And while we'll discuss the development of social networking customizations within your OBA, we'll predominantly be talking about higher-level development within SharePoint (for example, creation and configuration of Web parts) as opposed to lower-level coding (for example, adding C# code to a VSTO client-side customization). That said, let's now turn to a deeper discussion on each of these.

My Site and My Profile

My Site and My Profile are two key elements in building social networking capabilities into your OBA. They do this by providing first an individual page that you can build to contain information specific to you and your projects, and second, by providing a place where you can add profile information that people can search against or be attached to. Let's first discuss My Site and then turn to discussing My Profile.

My Site

The SharePoint site is the point of entry for not only you to view, edit, and manage information on your projects, but also a point of entry for others in your team and wider organization to be connected to you (for example, through the Colleague Tracker Web part), the project information you want to expose to them, and information you may be an expert in that you also want to expose to them. It is this collaborative annex that provides a key social networking piece to the OBAs that you build. More specific than the SharePoint Team Site is this idea of My Site, or a personalized site that you can build and deploy on your team site that provides personal information about you and the projects you may be working on. Figure 5-3 illustrates a sample My Site and shows that there are different things that you can do with it. For example, you can connect your Outlook calendar to your site so you can view your appointments, you can have a Colleague Tracker, which provides links to colleagues who may serve as experts in other related areas in which you may be interested, as well as other Web parts that are more general, like house links to documents. You can also create links to membership DLs, connect to Outlook and expose your contacts and mail, as well as a host of other interesting Web parts.

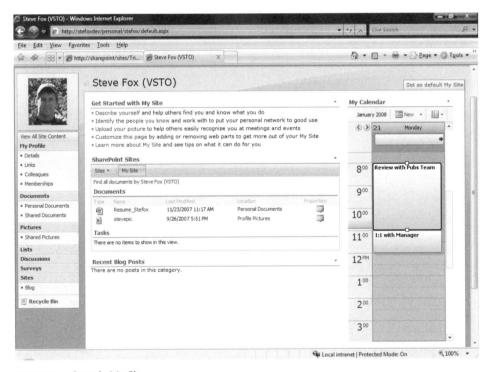

FIGURE 5-3 Sample My Site

The nice thing about My Site is that you can assess permissions to expose the information to specific people, so if there is confidential information on your site (for example, budget information), then you can expose that information only to specific people in your organization.

Setting up your own My Site is straightforward. To do so, you click the My Site link in the upper right-hand portion of your SharePoint site. If you have not done this before, SharePoint will prompt you to answer some configuration questions and then create the default My Site for you, which you can then go ahead and customize. For example, if you click the Describe Yourself link, this opens a page where you can provide personal information about yourself, as seen in Figure 5-4. Note that on this page, you have the option to display the properties that you enter into the page to specific people in your organization, for example, Only Me, Everyone, My Manager, My Colleagues, and so on.

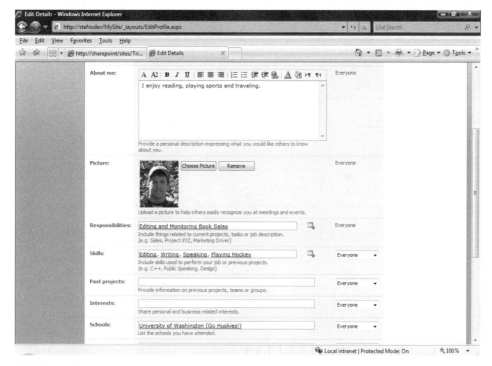

FIGURE 5-4 Personal description

One of the key social networking elements, as mentioned above, is the Colleague Tracker. This is where you can add colleagues to your site, thus creating an organic social/business network through attaching others to your My Site. Colleagues are a list of friends (within your organization), team members, and co-workers who are related to a specific person in an organization through one's user profile and are presented to users through My Site. The colleagues list (or Colleague Tracker Web part), presented through a Web part on the personal profile page of My Site, lists these related individuals and provides contact, presence, and organizational information to other users. This aspect of social networking enables broader communication and information exchange across the organization and is thus a key pillar for supporting social networking.

You can add colleagues to your My Site by clicking the Colleague Tracker link. After you click the link, SharePoint opens the Add Colleagues page. Use the Identify Colleagues section to find and add colleagues to your list. You can then select who to expose within this list of colleagues in the Show These Colleagues list box. You can then add the colleagues to an existing workgroup or create a new workgroup. In the next example (Figure 5-5), we've created a new workgroup called OBA Working Group and added the aforementioned colleagues to that workgroup.

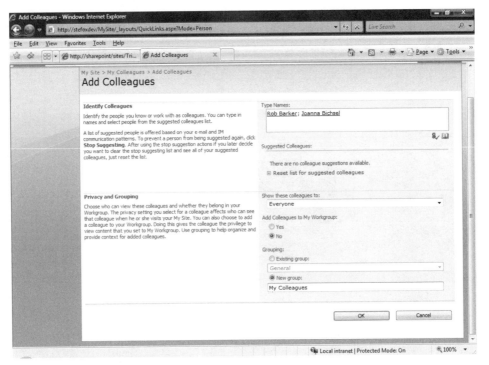

FIGURE 5-5 Adding a colleague

As mentioned earlier, you can also manage a subset of your Outlook calendar functionality through the My Calendar Web part, which loads a view of your calendar into the Web part. For example, if you click the New drop-down button, you'll be presented with a number of options, such as Appointment, Meeting, Message, etc. (see Figure 5-6). Clicking on any one of these loads Outlook Web Access (OWA), which is essentially a thin client layer that enables Outlook access through your browser.

We've shown you just a couple of things that you can do with your My Site. Note that you can take other actions, such as adding links to your favorite sites by clicking My Links (in the upper right-hand corner of the page), adding personal documents to your site, and adding

FIGURE 5-6 Accessing Calendar functionality in My Site

additional Web parts to your site (for example, a Business Data Catalog Web part that loads project information into My Site). You can also add other sites to your My Site by clicking Site Actions and Create Page. This will invoke the New SharePoint Site page, where you can select a specific site type under the Template Selection area of the page. And lastly, similar to other pages on SharePoint, you can adjust the settings for your individual page. To access the settings, click Site Actions and Site Settings. Here you can do things like alter the look and feel of your page and edit the permissions for the site.

While My Sites are often not thought about in the context of extending OBAs, we encourage you to think about how you can leverage them when designing and deploying your OBA to your own organization. That is, an important element in the context of building OBAs is the collaborative and social aspect, so leveraging the core SharePoint features is something organizations should definitely take advantage of.

My Profile

In MOSS 2007, one of the key strengths is the collaboration features that are built into the product. Within the area of collaboration, MOSS provides a framework for the creation and management of user profiles as well as the ability to understand the relationship between those profiles. And while user profiles may not be sexy, it is important when we want to connect IWs with and to one another; it is the user profile that provides that object, if you will, that helps us represent ourselves at our most metadata level within SharePoint.

The user profile essentially collects and stores data on users and also contains a set of fields that can be extended and/or customized. You can also import or manually enter data into a user profile. For example, if you wanted to map the fields to an organizational data source, you could connect the fields to that source or you could tie the user profile data to Active Directory (AD) or Lightweight Directory Access Protocol (LDAP) compliant directory services, or through the Business Data Catalog (BDC). One of the major value-adds for the user profile is the fact that IWs can use existing social relationships in order to quickly find resources or subject-matter experts (SMEs) for a particular area or project. The ability to search for specific experts (that is, search against the user profiles) is primarily facilitated through the use of colleagues.

The goal for many organizations is to optimize their social networking experience by combining heterogeneous personnel information into an Office SharePoint Server user profile. By combining this information and modifying user profile properties, organizations can enrich the presentation of team and colleague information to organization members. In order to accomplish this goal, organizations require a carefully planned strategy when combining multiple sources of personnel information to provide a rich user profile for social networking using SharePoint Products and Technologies.

You can create and manage user profiles either programmatically or through your SharePoint site. In this chapter, we'll focus on creating and managing user profiles via your SharePoint site. While the discussion on programmatically creating a user profile is interesting, this chapter can't possibly cover all of the discussion. Besides, there are books out there that already cover the programmatic side in fairly good detail. (See the Further Reading section in this chapter for recommendations.)

To edit your profile from your SharePoint site, click My Site and then click the My Profile link at the top left-hand side of the page. This invokes your profile page. Figure 5-7 illustrates a sample profile page that I built using a demo SharePoint site. You can see in the profile I've set up that I've added a picture with some personal details, some of the common links I use, as well as a couple of sample files in my Documents Web part. Note that there are also pieces of the profile page that are linked to our internal Microsoft system—for example, my title, organization, office information, and organizational hierarchy. This type of "inherited" data is noneditable on your Profile Details page.

You can edit each of the parts of your personal profile by clicking the links underneath My Profile in the left-hand launch bar. This invokes the Edit Details page (see Figure 5-4), in which you can edit and set permissions against your personal information. Figure 5-8 illustrates the fact that I have set some personal information on My Profile to be viewable by different people who are looking at my site. For example, my birthday is set to be viewed by Only Me, and my mobile and home phone numbers to be viewable by My Colleagues, and my fax by Everyone.

After you've created your profile page, others in the enterprise will be able to search against you (for example, "Steve Fox") as the search criteria, and your profile page will be indexed

FIGURE 5-7 Sample profile page

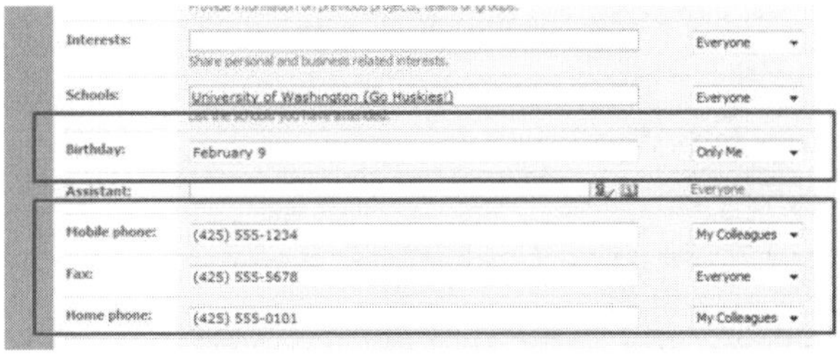

FIGURE 5-8 Setting permissions on shared profile information

and exposed as part of the search results. Those searching on you can subsequently add you to their Colleague Tracker, and then attach you to their social network, thus building a network around a specific knowledge space.

Beyond the details of your profile, you can also edit other information from your profile page, such as links, colleagues, memberships, and documents. For example, to edit the links you want to expose on your site, click the Links link and SharePoint opens the My Links page (see Figure 5-9). Click Add Link and provide a title, URL address, permissions for the link, and grouping.

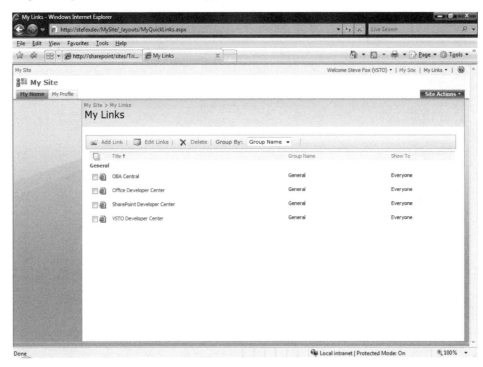

FIGURE 5-9 Adding links to your profile page

Note you can also access the links directly from your My Profile page by clicking the My Links link in the upper right-hand corner of the page (see Figure 5-10). You can also access the My Links page from here as well to add and manage the links you have associated with your profile.

FIGURE 5-10 Accessing links from My Links

We discussed adding colleagues earlier; adding documents is similar to adding documents in a document library.

Memberships are similar to the Colleague Tracker in that they provide relationships between and among people in the enterprise and the content that is generated by those people.

Memberships can either relate to Active Directory (for example, distribution lists) or they can be generated within SharePoint, thus becoming a custom object within and consumed by SharePoint—specifically Windows SharePoint Services 3.0. To edit memberships, click the Memberships link underneath My Profile. This launches the Edit Memberships page, in which you can click Edit Memberships to edit information about your memberships. (Note that if you're editing memberships for the first time, you'll need to make sure you have a membership group to which you attach your members.)

Now that we've discussed My Sites and My Profile, let's now turn to talking about other SharePoint features to further integrate social networking into your OBA.

Integrating Blogs into Your OBA

Of growing use and importance for communication are blogs. A straightforward technology, essentially a Web-based diary in reverse chronological order, blogs provide users with a) an additional way to publish information outside of normal publication channels (such as documents, formal Web sites, etc.), b) a way to get information out to a specific audience (either by virtue of topic or through RSS subscription to the blogs), and c) a way to publish information in a more personable and unstructured fashion. In the IT world, blogs often provide ways for SMEs to post information about specific facets of the area in which they're experts. Indeed, many experts—Microsoft technology guru and long-time developer (not to mention Microsoft General Manager) Scott Guthrie, for one—have strong followings through their informative blogs, which contain a wealth of technical information.

In the context of OBAs, blogs aid in the collaboration of teams around specific project or technical areas. This collaboration provides a voice for experts or important information that is delivered to (or subscribed to) teams and groups within your organization from your SharePoint site. Thus, SharePoint blogs allow for an informational exchange from and by SMEs. And similar to Internet-facing blogs, internal (to the organization) consumers of SharePoint blogs can subscribe to these blogs as well. The supplemental importance to OBAs, then, is to provide an additional communication avenue that helps inform individuals, teams, and the wider organization on particular areas of a technology or project.

Let's take a look at how you can create your own blog for your SharePoint site.

The first thing you need to do is navigate to your site. After you've done this, click Site Actions and Create Site. This will invoke the New SharePoint Site page, where you can provide properties (for example, Title, Description, and URL) for your new site. Provide these properties, but then make sure that in the Template Selection area you select the Collaboration tab and then select the Blog template and click Create. Figure 5-11 illustrates this page.

After you've done this, SharePoint will create your blog site for you and open the default page. It is here where you can, for example, add/configure categories for your blog, add links to other related blogs or sites, and manage the blog as the administrator for the blog. For

FIGURE 5-11 Creating a blog

example, if you want to provide specific categories for your blog, click the Categories link on your default blog site. This will open the Categories page, on which you can edit or add the categories. By default, you have three categories that can be edited (that is, *Category 1*, *Category 2*, and *Category 3*); however, more than likely you'll want to provide more intuitive ways of classifying your blog postings. In Figure 5-12, I have created five different categories for my new blog that I'll then use to categorize postings to my blog. When I go ahead and create my blogs, this will help me classify the blogs into different categories.

That said, let's go ahead and create a new blog post. If you return to your default view, not only should you now see your new categories, but you should also see a link to the right that reads Create a Post. Click this link, and SharePoint will open the New Item page, as shown in Figure 5-13. On the New Item page, you can enter a title for your blog, type some text for the content of the blog, and then provide a category (from the ones you just created). You can then provide a Published time, which will be set to the current date as the default (you can select an alternate date if desired). You can then select Save as Draft, if you're not completely finished with the blog post, or click Publish if you're ready to publish the blog to your SharePoint site.

After you click Publish, SharePoint will publish your post to the site and then take you to the default blog view, as shown in Figure 5-14.

Note that there are also other functions that as the administrator you have access to on your blog site. For example, you might want to edit or delete certain postings, change the look

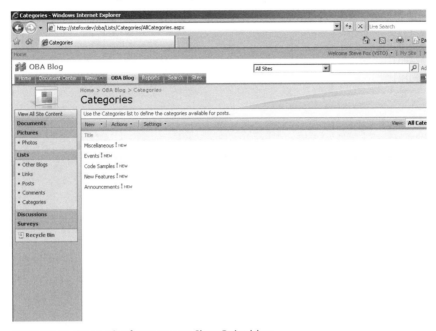

FIGURE 5-12 Categories for your new SharePoint blog

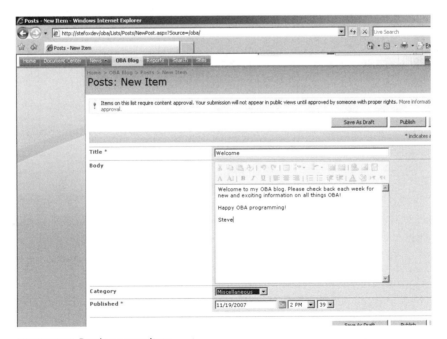

FIGURE 5-13 Posting a new item

FIGURE 5-14 New blog post

and feel of your blog site, or provide special permissions for others to either access or post to your blog site. If you look on the right-hand side of the default blog site page, there are a number of Admin links that provide different types of functionality for you, which are listed as follows:

- Create a post—creates a new blog post

- Manage posts—supports management functions around posts such as view, edit, and delete specific blog posts (see Figure 5-15)

- Manage comments—supports management functions around comments such as view, edit, and delete

- All content—lists all of the site content

- Set blog permissions—enables you to edit site permissions and parent site permissions

- Launch blog program to post—enables you to publish blog postings from client-side applications such as Microsoft Word 2007 (see Figure 5-16)

Beyond these links, you can also configure different settings within your blog site. To do this, click Site Actions and then select Site Settings. This invokes the Site Settings page (see Figure 5-17), where you can edit or configure different parts of your blog site. For example, you can edit the Title, Description, and icon from this page, change the look and feel of your blog site through the Site theme link, and add users to your site by clicking the Advanced permissions link.

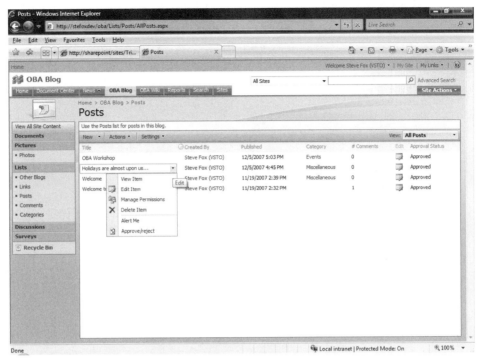

FIGURE 5-15 Managing blog posts

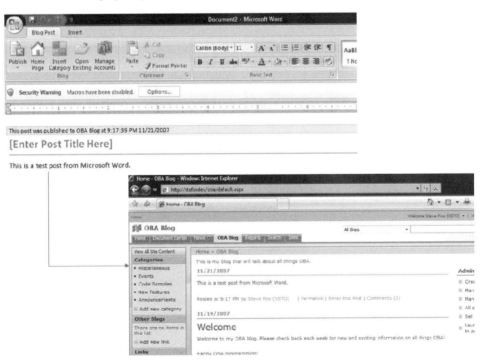

FIGURE 5-16 Posting blog from Word to SharePoint

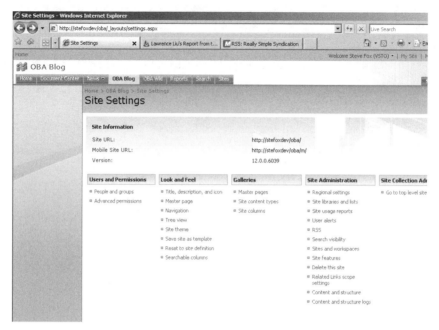

FIGURE 5-17 Site Settings page

Overall, blogs are a great way to publish additional information about a specific topic, be it technical or otherwise. They provide a collaborative way for teams and organizations to not only push information to SharePoint sites, but they also provide a way for people to subscribe to them. Beyond the blog, another type of SharePoint communication feature that provides cross-team, collaborative discussion is the wiki, which we'll discuss next.

Integrating Wikis into Your OBA

As we've seen in the preceding sections (and in the preceding chapters), collaboration is important. I would argue that in the context of OBAs, collaboration not only means proximity and interaction with other people, but also proximity to the business data and information that other people in the organization generate and store. This chapter thus far has discussed SharePoint profiles, sites, and blogs, but another interesting type of interactive and collaborative communication is the often underused wiki.

A wiki is essentially a type of Web site that allows multiple authors to interact with the same document, so those who have permissions for a specific wiki can edit and update the content for that wiki. What results is a constantly changing and interactive platform for content exchange. Using a wiki, multiple people can edit the content on the page, add new content to the page, add new pages to the wiki, and add links to other sites within the organization. Interestingly, in a corporate environment where our conversations often happen in e-mail, around the "water cooler," on whiteboards, in the halls, and so on, the wiki provides an alternative way to record these conversations in a way that not only makes them part of the organic knowledge of the organization, but also makes them centrally accessible. And if you remember back to earlier in the book, it is this idea of centrally accessible data (and in our case here, centrally accessible information exchange) that lies at the heart of a successful OBA.

Creating a wiki is straightforward. First, you navigate to your SharePoint site, click Site Actions, and then click Site Settings and Modify All Site Settings. In the Site Administration section, click the Sites and Workspaces link, and then click Create. This will open a page where you can provide properties for your new Wiki page (see Figure 5-18). Now fill in the Title and Description fields and complete the URL address for your wiki. Next, select the Wiki template from within the Collaboration tab within the Template Selection section. Set the permissions for your wiki (inheriting the parent site permissions or providing unique permissions for your specific wiki site), select where you want the wiki to be displayed (for example, Quick Launch bar), and then click OK.

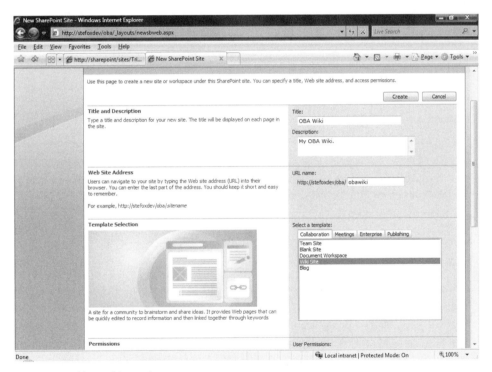

FIGURE 5-18 New wiki creation process

After you've created your wiki, SharePoint opens the default wiki site. This is essentially the collaborative space within which you can edit team-contributed content. To do so, click Edit and edit the page. After you've finished your editing, click OK to publish. You can also view the history of the wiki, which provides a strikethrough history of what has been added or removed to the wiki, and view any incoming links to the page. Figure 5-19 provides a screenshot of a newly published wiki page.

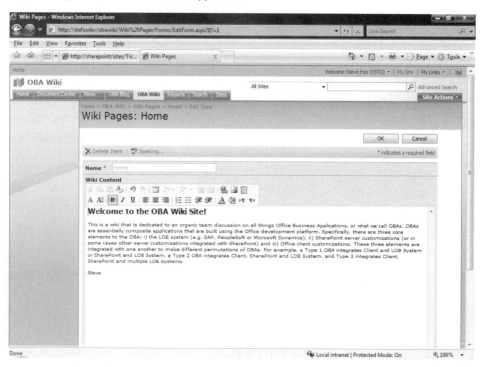

FIGURE 5-19 New wiki page

Similar to other SharePoint sites, you can edit the settings for your Wiki pages. To do this, click Site Actions and Settings, and SharePoint opens the Site Settings page. For example, to change the theme of the wiki site, click Site Theme under Look and Feel and select one of the templates from the list.

RSS

We've discussed how you can create blogs to record and publish information and data that is specific to your area in the organization; however, is it reasonable to assume that someone in the organization is going to be checking back to review your blog on a regular basis? Probably not. The way in which many people automate the process of having information delivered to them is through RSS. RSS, or Really Simple Syndication, is essentially a news feed that provides a way for data from one source to be exposed to other tools. At its core, RSS is an XML document specification that provides the mechanism to deliver content like blogs and search, and it's a great way to have information pushed directly to your desktop. In the Further Reading section of this chapter are some links to XML examples of RSS feeds and additional resources on more general RSS reading.

When you develop your OBAs, RSS feeds may integrate in a couple of different areas. For instance, Outlook ships with the ability to connect RSS feeds to specific folders within your

RSS Feeds folder. For example, Figure 5-20 illustrates the fact that in my mailbox, one of the blogs I subscribe to is Lawrence Liu's social networking blog (which I highly recommend if you're interested in being part of a wider social networking discussion).

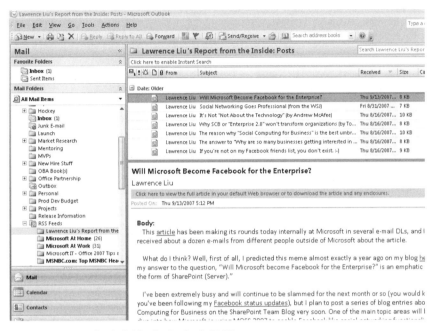

FIGURE 5-20 RSS feeds folder in Outlook 2007

Interestingly, while Figure 5-20 shows the feed being displayed in the reading pane, you can also display feed displays for those RSS feeds where the feed only provides a headline and a link out to an external source—many Microsoft sites do this to optimize the display of information in your feed. To do this, you first create a new Outlook form region in a VSTO Outlook add-in project and then add a Web browser control to the default design surface (see Further Reading for additional references on the Outlook Form Region). You then add the code in the FormRegionShowing event (which invokes whenever the form region displays) and the ParseURL method to the code behind the Outlook form region (in this case I added it to the RSSFeed class), and your form region will now display the Web page from the RSS feed (see Listing 5-1).

LISTING 5-1 RSS feed that displays Web page from feed

```
using System;
using System.Collections.Generic;
using System.Linq;
using System.Text;
using Office = Microsoft.Office.Core;
using Outlook = Microsoft.Office.Interop.Outlook;

namespace CustomOFR
{
    partial class RSSFeed
```

```
    {
        ...
        private void RSSFeed_FormRegionShowing(object sender, System.EventArgs e)
        {
            Outlook.PostItem rssItem = (Outlook.PostItem)this.OutlookItem;
            this.RSSWebBrowser.Navigate(ParseUrl(rssItem));
        }
        private void RSSFeed_FormRegionClosed(object sender, System.EventArgs e)
        {
        }
            private void RSSWebBrowser_DocumentCompleted(object sender, System.Windows.Forms
            .WebBrowserDocumentCompletedEventArgs e)
        {

        }
// Return the url of the 'View article' link that appears in the headline of the RSS item.
        public static string ParseUrl(Outlook.PostItem item)
        {
            string lookUpText = "HYPERLINK";
            string articleStr = "View article";
            string body = item.Body;

            int index = body.IndexOf(lookUpText, 0, body.Length);
            int end = 0;
            // Look through body for 'HYPERLINKS' and narrow down to 'View article...' link.
            while (true)
            {
                end = body.IndexOf(articleStr, index, body.Length - index);
                int nextIndex = body.IndexOf(lookUpText, index + 1, body.Length - (index + 1));

                if (nextIndex > index && nextIndex < end)
                {
                    index = nextIndex;
                }
                else
                    break;
            }
            // Get the Link to the article.
            string url = body.Substring(index + lookUpText.Length + 1, end - index -
            (lookUpText.Length + 1));
            url = url.Trim('"');
            return url;
        }
    }
}
```

What the implementation of this code results in is a custom Outlook form region with the article displayed in the Web browser control you added to the form region designer, as shown in Figure 5-21. The thing to note here is that the RSSFeed form region now displays the page behind the "View Article" link. For more information on the previous customer Outlook RSS form region sample, you can download the sample solution and the code from MSDN here: *http://msdn2.microsoft.com/en-us/library/bb157881(VS.90).aspx.*

The second way of integrating RSS feeds into your OBA is SharePoint-based and specifically addresses enabling the RSS feed on your SharePoint blog or creating a Web part where you

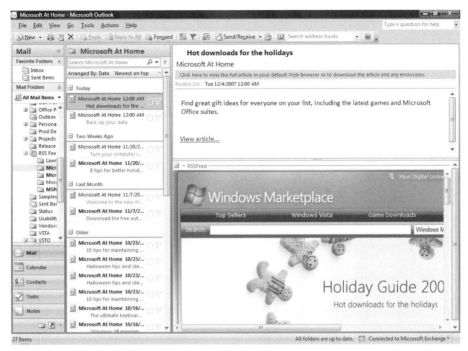

FIGURE 5-21 Custom Outlook form region RSS feed display

can display content from either internal (that is, SharePoint blogs that are internal to your organization) or external (i.e., publicly facing blogs that you can integrate into your internal SharePoint sites).

We discussed the creation of a blog to integrate social networking into your OBA earlier in the chapter. However, we again run into this problem of the connectivity of the content that you publish making its way to the people who care about that content. The subscription-based model of RSS is a great and simple answer to this problem. That is, have users subscribe to your blog so that the content is pushed to them when you update it. So, let's talk about how you do this.

After you've created your blog, you can enable RSS feeds from your blog so other people can subscribe to it. To do this, click Site Actions, Site Settings, and under the Site Administration section, click RSS. This invokes the RSS page (see Figure 5-22), on which you check the Allow RSS feeds in this site and add information in the Advanced Settings section (for example, copyright, editor, etc.).

When you enable the RSS feeds for your blog, you enable other people to subscribe to your blog. You will know RSS is enabled on your blog because you will have the RSS Feed standard image when you load your blog site, as shown in Figure 5-23.

Now that we've enabled the RSS feed on the blog that we created earlier in the chapter, let's now create a Web part on another SharePoint page that then points to this blog. Again,

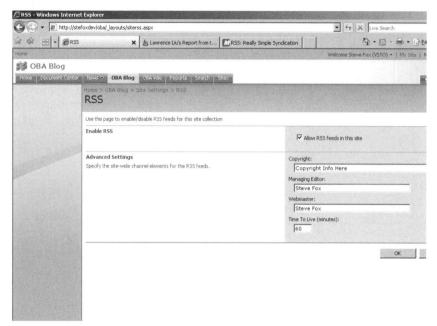

FIGURE 5-22 Enabling RSS feed for blog

FIGURE 5-23 RSS Feed image

the goal of doing this is to more tightly couple SMEs and the content they create to information workers across the organization. To create a Web part, navigate to the page where you want to add the Web part and click Site Actions and Edit Page. Click Add a Web Part (in the area of the page you want to edit) and then check the RSS Viewer Web part and click Add. When the Web part has been added to the page, click the Open the Tool Pane link to edit the properties of the Web part. You add the RSS Feed URL to the RSS Feed URL field. If you don't want to edit any of the other properties, click OK. SharePoint will then load the blog postings into your new RSS Viewer Web part, as shown in Figure 5-24.

You may be asking yourself where you actually get the RSS Feed URL that I added when I had the tool pane open, and the answer is it depends on where your feed comes from. If it's an internal blog (meaning intranet blog on SharePoint), you navigate to that blog, click the RSS Feed link (beside the image, as shown in Figure 5-23) and then click the View feed properties link. This invokes the Feed Properties dialog box (see Figure 5-25), where you can copy the RSS URL out of the Address field and into the RSS Feed URL field in the RSS Viewer Web part tool pane.

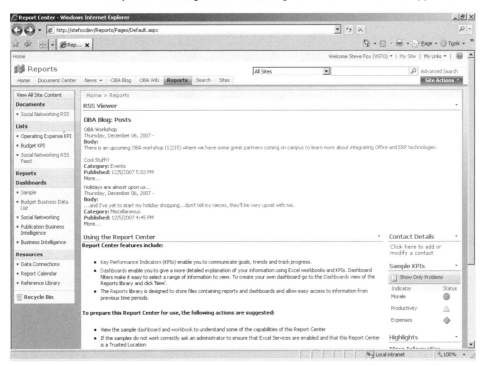

FIGURE 5-24 RSS Viewer Web part showing blog

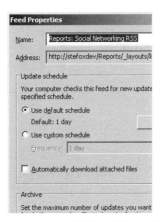

FIGURE 5-25 RSS Feed Properties

To add an RSS feed to an external blog is similar to the process just described; the only major difference would be that you'd get the RSS URL from the public blog. For example, in the case of Lawrence Liu's social networking blog, I clicked on the Feed link for the posts on his blog site and then retrieved the feed from the View Feed XML link. I then added that URL in the same way I added my internally facing blog—to the RSS Feed URL field in the RSS Viewer Web part tool pane.

With regard to RSS, I'll lastly mention that you need to be wary of the information that you're exposing through your RSS feeds. If there's any chance of exposing sensitive data or information, then your organizational security policy will likely restrict you from revealing that blog content. If this is the case, you can disallow RSS feeds for specific objects (for example, lists, libraries, etc.). To do this, navigate to the list where you do not want RSS feeds to be allowed and click Settings and then List Settings (or Document Library Settings in the case of a document library). Under Communications, click the RSS Settings, and this will invoke the Modify List RSS Settings page (see Figure 5-26). Here you can change whether the list allows or disallows RSS by clicking Allow RSS for this list.

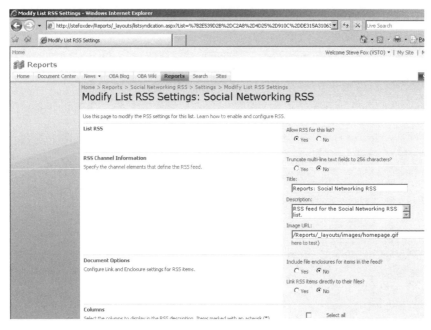

FIGURE 5-26 Modify List RSS Settings

Thus far, we've discussed My Sites, user profiles, blogs, wikis, and RSS feeds—all important aspects of integrating social networking with your OBA. Lastly, we'll discuss the use of SharePoint to integrate with third-party social networking applications. Specifically, we'll explore how you can integrate a Facebook mash-up into your OBA.

Third-Party Social Networking Applications and OBAs

Facebook, among many other types of social networking environments, is being used more frequently not only in a social context, but also in a business context. The result of this is that our organic social networks not only include our friends from high school, girlfriends/boyfriends, and college roommates, but also our colleagues and, in some cases, our managers. The blurring distinction between work and home notwithstanding (that you *do* need to manage), this can be a very powerful network to harness and integrate within your OBA. For example, think of a scenario in which you want to integrate a list of contacts from different regions in the world that specialize in, say, biophysics into your SharePoint site. By doing this, you've now extended your professional contacts for a specific area quite a distance—all through social networking. You can do this in a number of ways, but let's look at the inclusion of a Popfly Facebook mash-up in your SharePoint site as one way of integrating Facebook into your OBA.

Popfly is a recent technology that allows both developers and nondevelopers to build mash-ups, gadgets, blocks, or Web pages that can be shared with other Web sites and applications (for example, gadgets for Vista). At the time of this writing, Popfly is in beta and requires a Windows Live ID to use it. However, once you get your Windows Live ID (which you would have if you have a Windows Live e-mail account) and you have a Facebook account, you can begin. What we're going to do here is create a mash-up that connects to my Facebook account and displays information about my Facebook friends list. I'm then going to take the mash-up code and add that to a Web part in my SharePoint site, which will then connect to my Facebook account and render photos and information about my friends in the Web part. Essentially, this is a fairly simple example that illustrates an integration with Facebook.

To begin, navigate to the Popfly site and then log in. After you log in, you have a number of different options. Select Create Stuff, and then choose Mashup. This will launch the Mashup designer, where you can drag and drop existing "blocks" onto the designer surface. Figure 5-27 illustrates the Popfly designer with the Facebook block on the designer. [Note

FIGURE 5-27 Popfly tool

that in order to implement the block, you'll need to obtain a Facebook developer key—that is, a key that is specific to your account that allows you to develop against your Facebook account. To get this key, go to *www.facebook.com*, sign up for an account (if you don't have one already), and go to the Developers area of the site and click the Get Started link, which will walk you through the process of getting a key.]

After you've added the Facebook block, there are a number of preconfigured functions that you can implement. To view these options, click the small wrench. This will enlarge the block and display a drop-down list with a number of options on it (for example, getFriends, getMyInfo, and so on). Each of these predefined options enables you to implement event calls against your Facebook account. Click the drop-down list and select getFriends. This is a method call that will retrieve the list of friends you currently have associated with your Facebook account.

After you've selected getFriends, click Display in the left-hand navigation and select the PhotoFlip block. This is a block that will show images passed to it in a flip-chart format. Figure 5-28 illustrates how the photo flip renders the photos. Note that in Popfly you can preview your mash-ups; however, it typically will not render the specific data from Facebook, but it will render mock data just to show you what the mash-ups will look like. With your simple mash-up created, click Save, provide a name and description for your mash-up, and click Accept and Save.

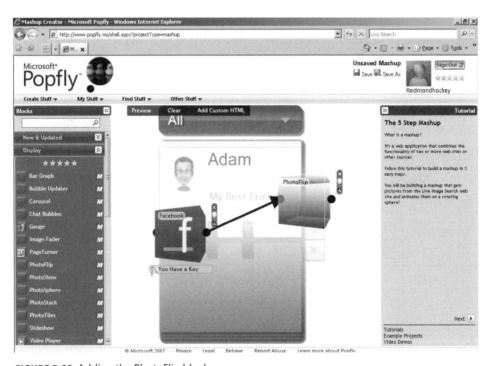

FIGURE 5-28 Adding the PhotoFlip block

At this point, you've created a mash-up, but you will now want to embed the mash-up within a SharePoint site. To do this, you need to click My Stuff and then select Projects. This will list any active (in other words, saved) projects in your Popfly account. In your project options, click Share. This will add another option to your project options called MashOut. Click MashOut and then select Embed It. This will open a small window with some embeddable code that was generated by your mash-up (see Listing 5-2).

LISTING 5-2 Mash-up embedded code reference

```
<iframe style='width:100%; height:100%;' src='http://www.popfly.ms/users/Redmondhockey/
MyFacebookPhotoFlip.small'

frameborder='no'>

</iframe>
```

This code snippet can then be copied and pasted into a Web page, and the mash-up you created will be rendered—assuming no connectivity issues with Facebook exist. Copy the code out of the Embed It text box and then open up your SharePoint site. Navigate to where you want to add the mash-up and click Site Actions and Edit Page. In Edit mode, click Add a Web Part and select the Content Editor Web Part and click Add. Once added, you'll need to click the Open the Tool Pane link. In the tool pane, click Source Editor, which will open up a window in which you can paste the mash-up Embed It code. Click OK after you've done this, and SharePoint will load and display the embedded mash-up in the published page (see Figure 5-29).

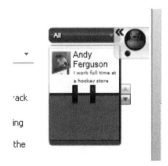

FIGURE 5-29 Embedded Facebook mash-up in SharePoint site

The interesting thing about mash-ups, specifically the social networking Popfly blocks, is that there are many different types of mash-ups you can create and add to your SharePoint site. For example, you can take your Facebook friend information and create Virtual Earth mappings of where they're located, or display their contact information. Each action, of course, is going to have varying degrees of usefulness in your OBA, and this is something you'll surely work through as you explore this technology. Note that you can also create your own custom blocks in Popfly as well; it's a little more involved than what we've explored thus far, but it certainly can be done.

Summary

Many organizations may not see social networking as a core feature of the OBA, so hopefully this chapter has relayed the importance of integrating SharePoint's social networking features (and indeed external social networking sites) into your OBA solution. Remember that people today are constantly looking for more information, and they will search through many different mechanisms to find that information. This is something that should certainly be considered when designing and building your OBAs. We encourage you to check out some of the references added to the Further Reading section to obtain more information around what you've seen in this chapter.

Further Reading

Here are some references that I have used in the past, and in some cases use on a regular basis. I hope they'll help you as well in your quest to integrate social networking into your OBA.

- *Inside Microsoft Office SharePoint Server 2007* by Patrick Tisseghem (Microsoft Press)

- *6 Microsoft Office Business Applications for Office SharePoint Server 2007* by Rob Barker, Steve Fox, Bhushan Nene, Joanna Bichsel, John Holliday, Adam Buenz, and Karthik Ravindran (Microsoft Press)

- *Professional SharePoint 2007 Development* by John Holliday, John Alexander, Jeff Julian, Eli Robillard, Brendon Schwartz, Matt Ranlett, J. Dan Attis, Adam Buenz, and Tom Rizzo (Wrox)

- Office Developer Portal: *http://msdn2.microsoft.com/en-us/office/default.aspx*

- VSTO Developer Portal: *http://msdn2.microsoft.com/en-us/office/aa905533.aspx*

- SharePoint Server 2007 Developer Portal: *http://msdn2.microsoft.com/en-us/office/aa905503.aspx*

- OBA Central: *www.obacentral.com*

- Popfly: *www.popfly.com*

- Information on RSS XML Documents: *http://cyber.law.harvard.edu/rss/rss.html*

- Lawrence Liu's social networking blog: *http://sharepoint.microsoft.com/blogs/lliu/default.aspx*

Chapter 6
SharePoint and Developing Office Business Applications

SharePoint is the fastest-growing product in Microsoft's history and also has a tremendous following in the developer community, which means more innovative solutions are being created every day. This chapter will help define and position the role that SharePoint plays in developing OBA solutions. In this chapter, you will learn about the different components and services of Windows SharePoint Services (WSS) version 3.0 and Microsoft Office SharePoint Server (MOSS) 2007 and how they can be leveraged, customized, and extended by developers to build Office Business Application (OBA) solutions. An OBA would not be an OBA without SharePoint.

Where to Start?

There is so much information when it comes to SharePoint Products and Technologies. It is sometimes a daunting task to figure out where to start because of all the possibilities that are enabled with the underlying platform and technologies. So before we begin diving into some of the details about SharePoint development it is important to first define what the role of SharePoint is within an OBA. As discussed in Chapter 1, OBAs provide a comprehensive solution for information workers that integrates the client, the server, and line-of-business (LOB) systems to provide business information in the context of their current activity.

Two great examples of this can be seen in Figures 6-1, 6-2, and 6-3. The first example shows how an information worker using Microsoft Office Outlook 2007 can work directly in Outlook to view the sales forecasts from individual sales persons using a custom Outlook form region (discussed in Chapter 2) that accesses business data directly from his LOB system. The most important point to make about this first example is the fact that the information worker never left Outlook to accomplish his work. This is one of the most powerful aspects of using Microsoft Office and the SharePoint platform to build OBA solutions.

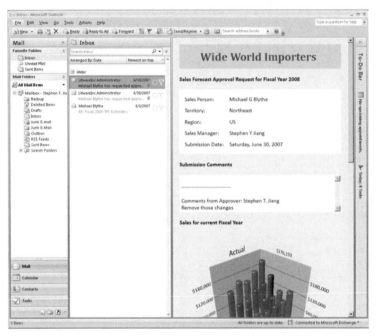

FIGURE 6-1 An example of working in business context using Microsoft Office Outlook 2007

Figure 6-2 showcases integration between Microsoft Office Word 2007 and Microsoft Office SharePoint Server 2007 through the use of the Business Data Catalog (BDC) to create quotes and invoices. As in the earlier example, the individual working on this document is able to stay within the context of her business activity, creating a quote, without having to switch back and forth between different applications. This is all accomplished through the use of smart tags that expose the information worker to custom actions to quickly query the BDC to retrieve product information directly from an LOB system and incorporate those details in the document.

> *What are smart tags?* They provide information workers with the ability to access different actions that are linked to keywords that are recognized by a Smart Tag Recognizer. In Figure 6-2, the keyword in the document that is recognized is the part number, CL-9009, which then displays the available custom actions to the end users.

Figure 6-3 represents an alternative way of displaying data from the previous example. Instead of the information worker using a smart tag action from a recognized keyword in the document, a custom task pane (discussed in Chapter 2) is used as an alternative way to display the very same data from the LOB using the BDC.

I think these examples should provide you with enough background on how to think about providing OBA solutions that focus on delivering data to information workers in the applications that they use every day. In the second example cited, MOSS 2007 plays a central role in being

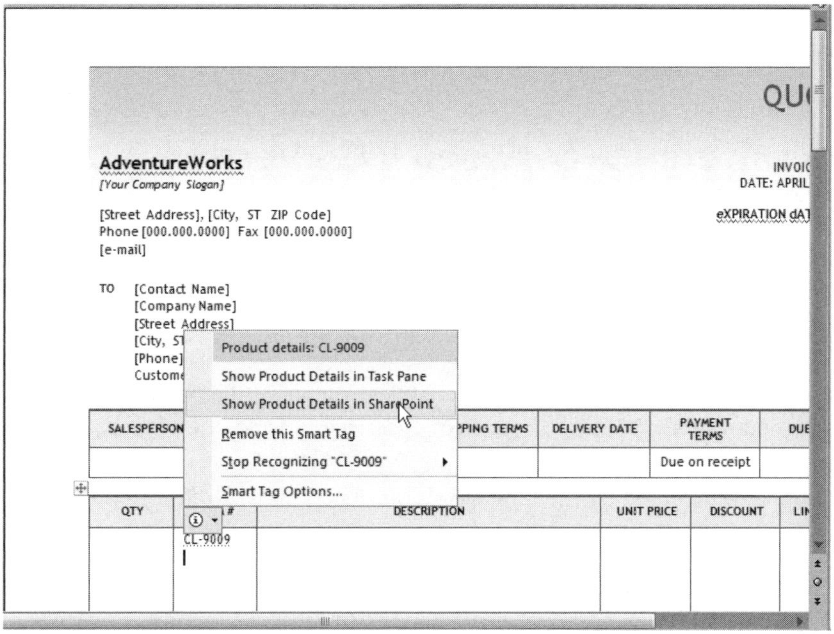

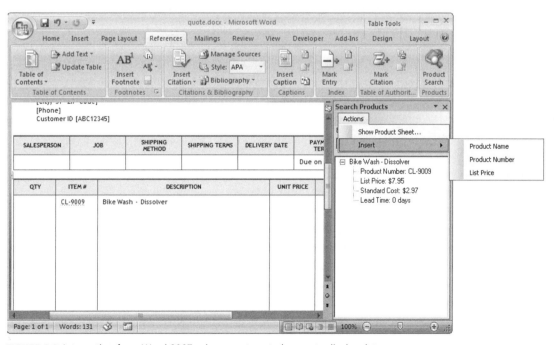

FIGURE 6-2 Integration from Word 2007 using smart tags to insert product data surfaced via the BDC

FIGURE 6-3 Integration from Word 2007 using a custom task pane to display data

able to deliver a contextual business solution. This example also provides an end-to-end view of connecting the desktop, server, and LOB system.

What's the Difference between WSS Version 3.0 and MOSS 2007?

The simplest way to explain the difference between WSS and MOSS is platform and services, respectively. WSS provides the core platform services that include security, Web parts, master pages, lists, Web services, and a site-provisioning framework.

WSS is part of the Windows Server 2003 core infrastructure and is based on the Windows Server licensing model. MOSS provides a set of services and solutions that are built on the WSS platform. Figure 6-4 illustrates a layered view of the different platform services and solutions that are provided by each individual product. This illustration should help address any confusion regarding the differences between Windows Server, WSS, and MOSS.

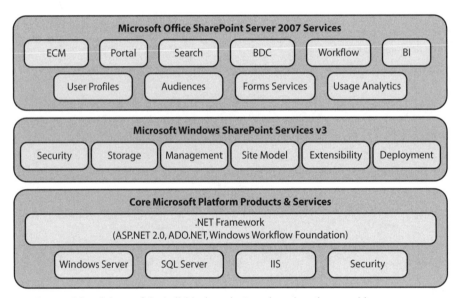

FIGURE 6-4 A breakdown of the individual products and services they provide

Regardless of whether you are developing a solution for Windows SharePoint Services version 3.0 or Microsoft Office SharePoint Server 2007, the same development skills and extensibility points are available. Figure 6-5 illustrates in great detail the logical architecture for the 2007 Microsoft Office system platform and the different components, interfaces, and tools that can be consumed, extended, and used to develop OBAs.

Just about every part of the Microsoft Office system platform is accessible via Web services or the object model. So regardless of whether you are writing a completely custom application

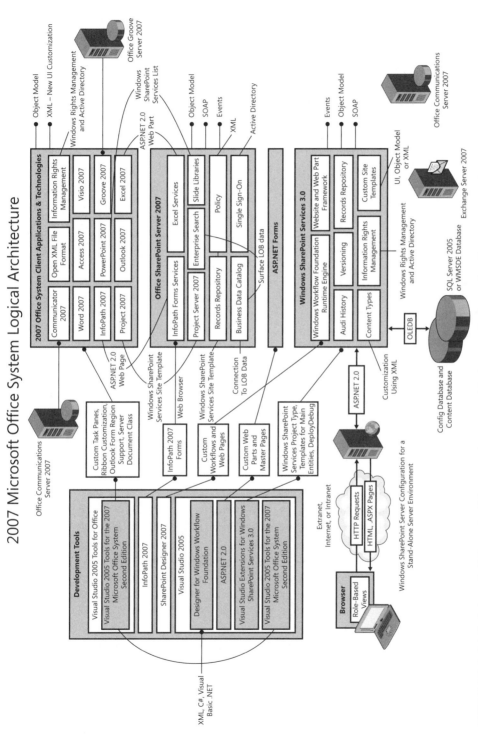

FIGURE 6-5 A detailed view of all the potential ways to integrate with the overall Microsoft Office system platform

based on Windows Forms, Windows Presentation Foundation (WPF) technology, or Microsoft Office itself, the level of integration is unprecendented to deliver both a compelling user experience and integration with LOB data.

When we refer to the Microsoft Office system platform, most developers only think of Microsoft Office as a set of client technologies like Word, PowerPoint, Excel, InfoPath, etc., but in fact, the Office platform includes both client and server products that enable the building of robust business applications. This is also an important point to make because when developing OBAs, it is the combination of all of these products and services that make up an end-to-end solution. When discussing OBAs we believe that there are different levels of an OBA, depending on the type of solution you are developing; Figure 6-6 helps to visualize the different levels of an OBA.

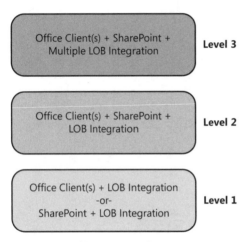

FIGURE 6-6 Different levels of an OBA

You can see from the different levels in Figure 6-6 that each one builds on top of the next, with each level providing deeper integration across the Office platform and LOBs. You will also notice that within each level there is always some type of LOB system integration, and this is a key element for an application to be considered a true Office Business Application. When integrating with an LOB system you should always be thinking about doing this through the use of Web services, either directly connected to the LOBs or through the use of the Business Data Catalog (BDC).

In many situations, OBAs will need to integrate with a multitude of end points to make the overall solution valuable to businesses and information workers. In the next section, we will briefly discuss OBA Reference Application Packs (RAPs), which all use Microsoft Office SharePoint Server 2007. RAPs provide a great starting point to understand the different types of architectures, integration mechanisms, and overall approach to building OBAs for specific industries.

OBA Reference Application Packs

The Solutions Architecture team in the Microsoft Developer and Platform Evangelism group has developed a set of reference applications that illustrate how to build several OBAs using the Microsoft Office platform. Each of the RAPs focuses on providing architectural and developer guidance for various industry solutions. The RAPs are a great way to not only start learning how to build OBAs, but they also provide an excellent starting point to see what is involved in an end-to-end solution. Even if you may not be building an industry-specific OBA (for example, financial services), the concepts within each of the RAPs should provide you with enough reference information and sample code to begin creating your solution.

The following list provides all of the currently released RAPs that are available for download from MSDN.

- OBA RAP for loan origination systems: *http://msdn2.microsoft.com/en-us/architecture/ bb265266.aspx*

- Consumer engagement reference architecture (CERA) for health plans: *http://msdn2.microsoft.com/en-us/architecture/bb530326.aspx*

- OBA RAP for supply chain management: *http://msdn2.microsoft.com/en-us/architecture/aa702528.aspx*

- OBA RAP for price management: *http://msdn2.microsoft.com/en-us/architecture/bb467601.aspx*

- OBA RAP for manufacturing plant floor analytics: *http://msdn2.microsoft.com/en-us/architecture/bb643797.aspx*

- OBA RAP for e-forms processing in the public sector: *http://msdn2.microsoft.com/en-us/architecture/bb643796.aspx*

In the following sections, we will explore the various tools that enable you as a developer to customize and extend both WSS and MOSS. The same tools that will be discussed were used to develop the OBA RAPs.

What Tools Are Available?

In this next section, I will provide an overview of the various development tools that can be used to create OBA solutions, as well as simply customize and develop SharePoint solutions. In reading previous chapters, you may have noticed that this book is heavily focused on showcasing the power of Microsoft Visual Studio 2008 and its many new features for developing Office solutions for both Microsoft Office 2007 and 2003. It is important to mention from a developer standpoint that when developing solutions on SharePoint you will need to have several tools in your arsenal, and all of them offer different approaches and capabilities. In the next several sections, I will dig into some of the details.

Visual Studio 2008

The latest release of Microsoft Visual Studio 2008 has many new capabilities added for developing Office solutions. Chapter 2 discussed the use of the Visual Ribbon Designer, building custom task panes, and creating various Office application add-ins, all key elements of extending the client capabilities of Office. Visual Studio 2008 also provides two new project types for creating Sequential and State Machine Workflows. Figure 6-7 illustrates the different project types provided by Visual Studio 2008, of which you can see the two new SharePoint 2007 workflow types. It is important to mention that these new workflow project types require Microsoft Office SharePoint Server 2007.

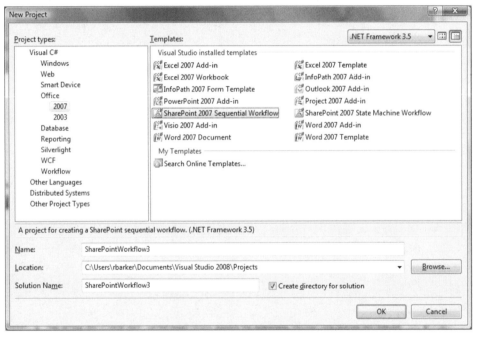

FIGURE 6-7 Two SharePoint 2007 template projects for workflow, Sequential, and State Machine

The next two sections describe the different capabilities that these two workflow types provide to OBAs. It is also important to mention that the Sequential and State Machine Workflows are included with Windows SharePoint Services version 3.0 out of the box.

Sequential Workflow

A Sequential Workflow represents a workflow as a procession of steps that execute in order until the last activity completes. A good example of this would be routing around an expense report for approval. However, Sequential Workflows are not purely sequential in their execution. Because they can receive external events, and include parallel logic flows, the exact order of activity execution can vary somewhat. Figure 6-8 illustrates the design time environment provided by Visual Studio for setting up a Sequential Workflow.

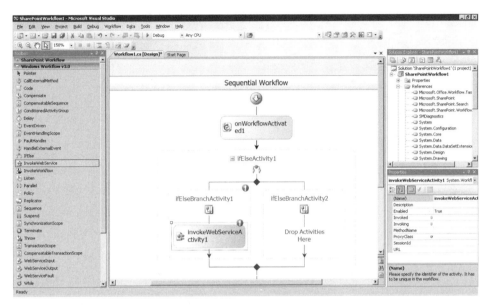

FIGURE 6-8 Setting up a Sequential Workflow with Visual Studio 2008

State Machine Workflow

A State Machine Workflow represents a set of states, transitions, and actions. One state is denoted as the start state, and then, based on an event, a transition can be made to another state. The State Machine can have a final state that determines the end of the workflow. Figure 6-9 illustrates a State Machine Workflow.

These new workflow capabilities added to Visual Studio 2008 allow for the development of customized workflows that you can build to address whatever business requirements you may have when developing OBAs and integrating with various LOBs. But don't think that you have to develop all your workflows custom. Both WSS version 3.0 and MOSS 2007 come with out-of-the-box workflows that you can immediately leverage in building OBAs.

MOSS 2007 Out-of-the-Box Workflows

The following workflows are provided after installation of MOSS 2007. Each of these workflows can be associated with a document library or list. It is also important to mention that the State Machine and Sequential Workflows are included in the installation of Windows SharePoint Services version 3.0.

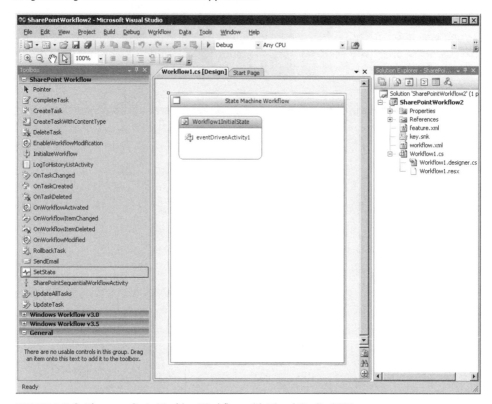

FIGURE 6-9 Setting up a State Machine Workflow with Visual Studio 2008

Approval Workflow

The Approval Workflow is one of the most important and most used workflows that come with MOSS 2007. The Approval Workflow is primarily used for routing documents around to colleagues; these could be simple or complex documents ranging from a product data sheet to an expense report. The Approval Workflow provides the ability to handle either serial or parallel processing. We can use the two examples of the data sheet and expense report to explain this further; in the scenario of routing the data sheet around, this could go to several people in parallel, therefore not causing a potential bottleneck if a reviewer is out of the office. In the case of the expense report, this would most likely be a serial approval, requiring each level of management in an organization to approve before proceeding to the next. Another great example of using the Approval Workflow is with the Web content management capabilities of MOSS 2007. Again referring back to the product data sheet example, once the document is approved you can automatically publish this content to your Web site with major and minor versioning.

Collect Feedback Workflow

The Collect Feedback Workflow is all about collaboration. Given the worldwide distribution of teams in today's business world, an effective way to collect others' feedback is needed.

The Collect Feedback Workflow provides an information worker with the ability to route around a document to a set of people to request their individual feedback. As the workflow progresses from person to person, the feedback is collected until it is complete. After completion, the collective feedback is then available to the feedback requestor for review. An example of how you could use this workflow within an OBA is to make it part of an overall business process.

Collect Signatures Workflow

The Collect Signatures Workflow is provided to do exactly as it states—collect digital signatures. Unlike the other workflows, the Collect Signatures can be started only from one of the Microsoft Office 2007 client programs, such as Microsoft Office Word 2007, Microsoft Office Excel 2007, or Microsoft Office PowerPoint 2007. In order to start this workflow, it must be saved to a document library that has the workflow associated; next you click on the Microsoft Office Button and choose the Workflows option to initiate. OBA scenarios in which you would use the Collect Signatures Workflow could involve capturing digital signatures for releasing documentation for products, vacation requests, personnel reviews, financial statements, business and sales contracts, and medical documents, to name a few.

Disposition Approval Workflow

The Disposition Approval Workflow is best used to manage the expiration and retention of documents within a document library. This workflow provides a process flow that allows information workers to decide whether or not to retain or delete documents. This workflow is well suited for use with the MOSS 2007 Records Center. Now you may be asking, "Why would I use this workflow and the Records Center in an OBA solution?" OBAs are all about integrating data into the Microsoft Office 2007 clients and server products in order to produce additional content that is of some business value to an organization. The combination of the workflow and Records Center is the *vault* to store business contracts, legal documents, and the like to ensure compliance with the many regulations all businesses are bound by in today's business world.

You'll find a more in-depth discussion of workflow in Chapter 7, "Managing Complex Business Processes with Custom SharePoint Workflow."

Windows SharePoint Services 3.0 Tools: Visual Studio 2005 Extensions

You may be wondering why we are talking about Visual Studio 2005 when this book is focused on Visual Studio 2008. The simple answer to that question is that, when developing SharePoint solutions, you currently need an arsenal of tools, not just one. It's unfortunate, and we have received a lot of feedback on the topic, so understand that we are listening and the future looks very promising for SharePoint development; by the time you start reading this book, the next version of Extensions for Windows SharePoint Services version 3.0 may be available for Visual Studio 2008, but until that new version is released we need to use the tools that are available today. With that said, let's discuss one of the most powerful tools, Visual Studio 2005 extensions for Windows SharePoint Server (VSeWSS) version 3.0 for developing SharePoint components, especially Web parts, team and blank site definitions, and list definitions. Figure 6-10 illustrates the SharePoint project types.

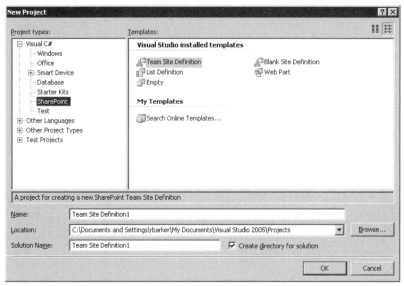

FIGURE 6-10 Project templates for SharePoint provided by VSeWSS

Web Parts Template

With VSeWSS the Web part template provides you, the developer, the ability to generate a basic Web part that you can immediately begin customizing with your own custom code and user interface design. Figure 6-11 illustrates the project that is generated after choosing the Web part project template, and Figure 6-12 shows the actual project running inside of MOSS.

Using the stubbed-out Web part project and simply changing the output text, and then hitting F5, you end up with Figure 6-12—all within just a few moments after installing VSeWSS on either your WSS version 3.0 or MOSS 2007 developer machine. When developing OBAs that utilize SharePoint (WSS version 3.0 or MOSS 2007), Web parts will be the predominant method for you to build custom integration with a LOB system. Web parts will allow you to present to information workers a custom user experience that provides integration with an LOB without having that information worker actually need to use the LOB user interface.

SharePoint Solution Generator

The SharePoint Solution Generator (SSG) is a handy utility that allows you to take a site "instance" that has been customized with Microsoft Office SharePoint Designer 2007 or with

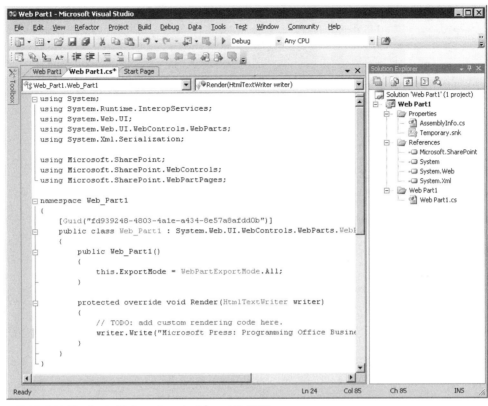

FIGURE 6-11 The basic Web part project from VSeWSS

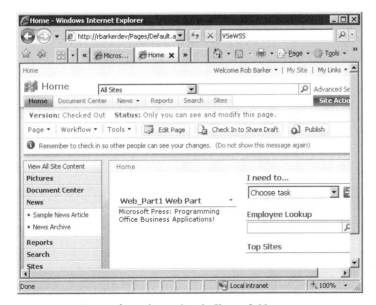

FIGURE 6-12 Output from the project in Figure 6-11

the browser, and convert it into a *site definition*, which we discussed earlier. The extra value added is that after the conversion, the developer can further edit that definition in Visual Studio 2005. Figures 6-13, 6-14, 6-15, and 6-16 illustrate the SSG wizard, and Figure 6-17 illustrates the converted site definition opened in Visual Studio 2005 for further customization.

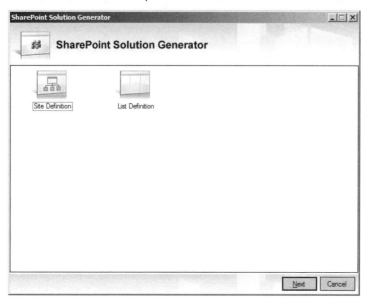

FIGURE 6-13 Starting screen for the SSG wizard

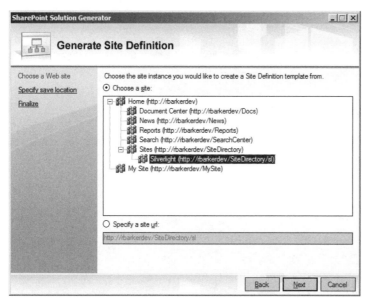

FIGURE 6-14 Enumerated view of sites that are available from the SharePoint instance

The SSG provides the ability to generate (or convert) an existing site definition or list definition.

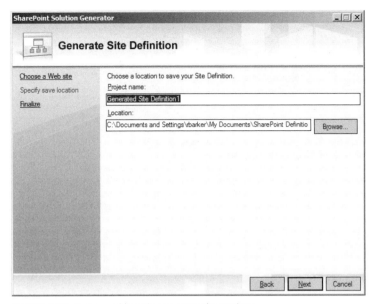

FIGURE 6-15 Name and location to store the project

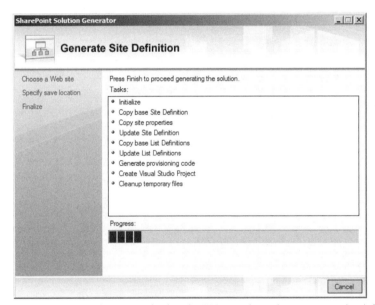

FIGURE 6-16 Step-by-step tasks that the SSG runs through to generate the definition

You can run the SSG on the machine that contains the instance of SharePoint or you can choose a specific URL. Figure 6-14 shows the SSG running locally on a development machine.

When developing OBA solutions and custom site and list definitions for SharePoint, the SSG will provide you with a great tool to help build up a library of definitions that can be used for other projects. Keep your eye on the MSDN Office Developer Center for version 1.1 of Visual Studio extensions for Windows SharePoint Services!

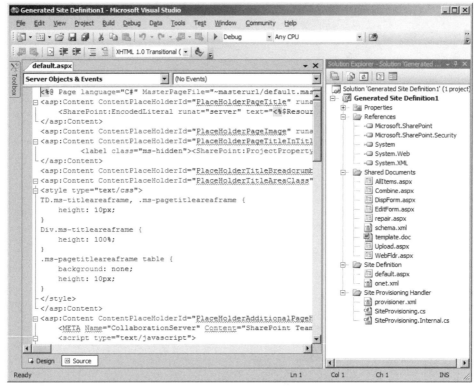

FIGURE 6-17 Generated site definition opened in Visual Studio 2005

Microsoft Office SharePoint Designer 2007

SharePoint Designer (SPD), previously known to everyone as Microsoft FrontPage, is the tool of choice for customizing SharePoint, both WSS and MOSS. SharePoint Designer has many capabilities that most developers are not aware of because many developers see SPD as a toy and not a professional development tool. However, if you spend a little time using SPD you will quickly see its power and how easy it makes customizing a SharePoint site. Because Microsoft Visual Studio 2005 and 2008 do not provide detailed management of SharePoint sites, SPD is the best tool to work with your content, folders, Web parts, and more. Figure 6-18 illustrates all of the various management panes provided by SPD that are connected to a Microsoft Office SharePoint Server 2007 implementation. You can manage the folder structure, get an almost 100 percent WYSIWYG view of a Web part page, view the styles of the page, and have the ability to add components from the Web parts gallery.

When you install Windows SharePoint Services, a single default master page is applied to all the pages in a site. You can, however, create your own master pages for a site and make them available to the site and any sites beneath it.

There are two supported scenarios for customizing master pages in Windows SharePoint Services:

- Copy the default.master file that is installed with Windows SharePoint Services to another file and make your changes to your renamed file.

FIGURE 6-18 Editing a master page in MOSS 2007

- Edit the default.master page in Microsoft Office SharePoint Designer 2007, where you can edit master pages, view master pages, create content pages, and view content pages with the master pages marked as masters and read-only.

Office SharePoint Designer 2007 is the only application in which you can see a master page preview.

Figure 6-19 provides a view of the toolbox in SPD for the various SharePoint controls that are provided.

The use of the term *designer* in the product name can be somewhat misleading because you can do much more than simply design pieces of your SharePoint site. SPD provides the ability to customize workflows that are based on the Windows Workflow Foundation and are a key component for task automation when working with documents within an OBA solution.

Microsoft Business Data Catalog Definition Editor

The BDC Definition Editor, shown in Figure 6-20, is included with the latest release of the Microsoft Office SharePoint Server 2007 Software Development Kit available on MSDN. The BDC Definition Editor provides developers the ability to author application definition files and edit metdata for OBAs for use with the Business Data Catalog in Microsoft Office SharePoint Server 2007. The BDC is included as a feature of MOSS and is not available in WSS.

Note   Metadata is data about the business applications' APIs. For each business application, metadata defines the business entities that the business application interacts with and the methods available in the business application. Metadata authors define metadata by using XML. The Business Data Catalog stores the metadata in the metadata repository.

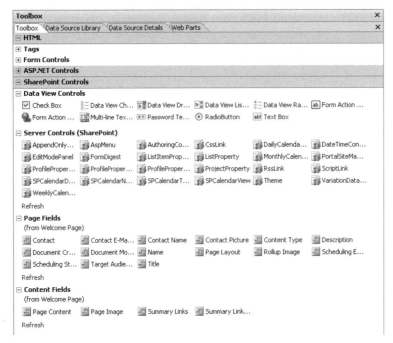

FIGURE 6-19 Toolbox showing the different SharePoint controls that can be used in SPD

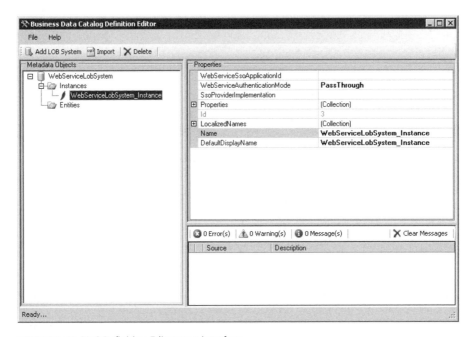

FIGURE 6-20 BDC Definition Editor user interface

The BDC Definition Editor helps developers save a huge amount of time when creating application definitions, which previously had to be done through hand-coding XML—a lot of XML. For those not familiar with what an application definition looks like, Listing 6-1 illustrates what is required for creating a single business entity.

LISTING 6-1 AdventureWorks sample application definition XML showing one business entity.

```xml
<Entity EstimatedInstanceCount="10000" Name="SalesOrder">
   <LocalizedDisplayNames>
      <LocalizedDisplayName LCID="1033">Sales Order</LocalizedDisplayName>
   </LocalizedDisplayNames>
   <Identifiers>
      <Identifier Name="SalesOrderID" TypeName="System.Int32"/>
   </Identifiers>
   <Methods>
      <Method Name="GetSalesOrders">
         <Properties>
            <Property Name="RdbCommandText" Type="System.String">
               SELECT SalesOrderID, OrderDate, SubTotal, IndividualID
               FROM SalesOrderHeader, Individual WHERE (SalesOrderID &gt;= @MinSalesOrderID)
               AND (SalesOrderID &lt;= @MaxSalesOrderID) AND (SalesOrderNumber LIKE
               @SalesOrderNumber) AND SalesOrderHeader.CustomerID = Individual.CustomerID
            </Property>
            <Property Name="RdbCommandType" Type="System.String">Text</Property>
         </Properties>
         <FilterDescriptors>
            <FilterDescriptor Type="Comparison" Name="ID" >
               <Properties>
                  <Property Name="Comparator" Type="System.String">Equals</Property>
               </Properties>
            </FilterDescriptor>
            <FilterDescriptor Type="Wildcard" Name="SalesOrderNumber"/>
         </FilterDescriptors>
         <Parameters>
            <Parameter Direction="In"  Name="@MinSalesOrderID">
               <TypeDescriptor TypeName ="System.Int32" IdentifierName="SalesOrderID"
                                  AssociatedFilter="ID" Name="MinSalesOrderID">
                  <DefaultValues>
                  <DefaultValue MethodInstanceName="SalesOrderFinderInstance"
                                       Type="System.Int32">0</DefaultValue>
                  </DefaultValues>
               </TypeDescriptor>
            </Parameter>
            <Parameter Direction="In"  Name="@MaxSalesOrderID">
               <TypeDescriptor TypeName="System.Int32" IdentifierName="SalesOrderID"
                                  AssociatedFilter="ID" Name="MaxSalesOrderID">
                  <DefaultValues>
                     <DefaultValue MethodInstanceName="SalesOrderFinderInstance"
                                          Type="System.Int32">99999999</DefaultValue>
                  </DefaultValues>
               </TypeDescriptor>
            </Parameter>
            <Parameter Direction="In"  Name="@SalesOrderNumber">
               <TypeDescriptor TypeName="System.String" AssociatedFilter="SalesOrderNumber"
                                  Name="SalesOrderNumber">
```

```xml
              <DefaultValues>
              <DefaultValue MethodInstanceName="SalesOrderFinderInstance"
                                    Type="System.String">%</DefaultValue>
              <DefaultValue MethodInstanceName="SalesOrderSpecificFinderInstance"
                                    Type="System.String">%</DefaultValue>
              </DefaultValues>
            </TypeDescriptor>
          </Parameter>
          <Parameter Direction="Return"  Name="SalesOrders">
              <TypeDescriptor TypeName="System.Data.IDataReader, System.Data,
                  Version=2.0.3600.0, Culture=neutral,
                  PublicKeyToken=b77a5c561934e089" IsCollection="true"
                  Name="SalesOrderDataReader">
            <TypeDescriptors>
              <TypeDescriptor TypeName="System.Data.IDataRecord, System.Data,
                  Version=2.0.3600.0, Culture=neutral,
                  PublicKeyToken=b77a5c561934e089"
                  Name="SalesOrderDataRecord">
            <TypeDescriptors>
              <TypeDescriptor TypeName="System.Int32"
                  IdentifierName="SalesOrderID" Name="SalesOrderID">
                  <LocalizedDisplayNames>
                    <LocalizedDisplayName LCID="1033">ID</LocalizedDisplayName>
                   </LocalizedDisplayNames>
              </TypeDescriptor>
              <TypeDescriptor TypeName="System.DateTime" Name="OrderDate">
                <LocalizedDisplayNames>
                  <LocalizedDisplayName LCID="1033">Order Date
                  </LocalizedDisplayName>
                </LocalizedDisplayNames>
                  <Properties>
                    <Property Name="DisplayByDefault"
                      Type="System.Boolean">true</Property>
                  </Properties>
                  </TypeDescriptor>
                    <TypeDescriptor TypeName="System.Int32" Name="IndividualID">
                      <LocalizedDisplayNames>
                        <LocalizedDisplayName LCID="1033">IndividualID
                        </LocalizedDisplayName>
                      </LocalizedDisplayNames>
                      <Properties>
                        <Property Name="DisplayByDefault" Type="System.
                        Boolean">true
                        </Property>
                      </Properties>
                    </TypeDescriptor>
                    <TypeDescriptor TypeName="System.Decimal" Name="SubTotal">
                      <LocalizedDisplayNames>
                        <LocalizedDisplayName LCID="1033">SubTotal
                        </LocalizedDisplayName>
                      </LocalizedDisplayNames>
                      <Properties>
                      <Property Name="DisplayByDefault"
                                    Type="System.Boolean">true
                        </Property>
                      </Properties>
```

```
                      </TypeDescriptor>
                    </TypeDescriptors>
                  </TypeDescriptor>
                </TypeDescriptors>
              </TypeDescriptor>
            </Parameter>
          </Parameters>
        <MethodInstances>
        <MethodInstance Name="SalesOrderFinderInstance" Type="Finder"
                        ReturnParameterName="SalesOrders" />
        <MethodInstance Name="SalesOrderSpecificFinderInstance" Type="SpecificFinder"
                        ReturnParameterName="SalesOrders" />
      </MethodInstances>
    </Method>
  </Methods>
</Entity>
```

You can use the BDC Definition Editor to connect to your LOB system through Web services or a direct database connection to create and configure an instance of that LOB sytem. Once you have created and configured your LOB instance, you then can export the generated XML for that specific instance's application definition. Once you have an application definition file, you can then add that to the BDC for use with Microsoft Office SharePoint Server 2007. Another advantage of the tool is the ability to import an existing application definition file and edit the details. The BDC Definition Editor is far from perfect, but it definitely alleviates a lot of the detailed work involved in creating application definition files.

An important point to note is that if you download and install the Microsoft Office SharePoint Server 2007 Software Development Kit (SDK), you will notice that the BDC Definition Editor is not installed by default. You will need to navigate to wherever you installed the SDK and open the Tools folder to install the tool.

Summary

The innovations and extensibility points delivered in Windows SharePoint Services version 3.0 make it a true solutions platform for developers. Coupled with the investments made in WSS, the extended set of services in Microsoft Office SharePoint Server 2007—one example being the Business Data Catalog discussed earlier in Chapter 4—make for even greater OBA solution opportunities when integrating with LOB systems. From a developer's perspective, it should be easy to see that SharePoint Products and Technologies are continually evolving and offer a solid foundation to continue to invest in learning and leveraging as a core part of your OBA solution.

The context of this book is about building Office Business Applications. When you couple MOSS with integration of LOB system data that then can be surfaced inside the 2007 Microsoft Office system, clients' developers have an incredible breadth of solution opportunities. The ability to deliver a wide range of integrated solutions that can offer integrated experiences that millions of information workers are familiar with today is a huge advantage for both developers and, more importantly, businesses.

This chapter provided an overview of the different ways Windows SharePoint Services version 3.0 and Microsoft Office SharePoint Server 2007 can be extended and customized by developers when creating OBAs. There is so much content to cover on this topic, and I know I missed some of the finer details, so I encourage you to review the SDK in depth to uncover even more information on the topics covered in this chapter. Enjoy the closing chapters; they showcase even more of the solution possibilities that can be delivered with the Office system.

Further Reading and Related Technologies

As mentioned previously, SharePoint is the fastest-growing product in Microsoft's history, which also means that information, opportunities, and innovations are becoming more and more abundant. Each of the preceding chapters has provided resources for you to learn more about the various technologies introduced within each chapter. The resources included below are all targeted at SharePoint. I encourage you to review as many, if not all, of the resources outlined here to learn as much as you can about the features and developer extensibility points for creating SharePoint solutions, features, Web parts, and more. When you think about building an Office Business Application, know that SharePoint, whether it be Windows SharePoint Services version 3.0 or Microsoft Office SharePoint Server 2007, plays a critical role as the centerpiece of the solution.

- Microsoft Office SharePoint Server 2007 SDK: Software Development Kit: *http://www.microsoft.com/downloads/details.aspx?familyid=6D94E307-67D9-41AC-B2D6-0074D6286FA9&displaylang=en*

- Windows SharePoint Services 3.0: Software Development Kit: *http://www.microsoft.com/downloads/details.aspx?FamilyId=05E0DD12-8394-402B-8936-A07FE8AFAFFD&displaylang=en*

- *Inside Microsoft Windows SharePoint Services 3.0* by Ted Pattison and Daniel Larson (Microsoft Press)

- *Inside Microsoft Office SharePoint Server 2007* by Patrick Tisseghem (Microsoft Press)

- *Windows SharePoint Services 3.0 Inside Out* by Errin O'Connor (Microsoft Press)

- Microsoft Office SharePoint Server 2007 Developer Center: *http://msdn2.microsoft.com/en-us/office/aa905503.aspx*

- Microsoft Windows SharePoint Services Developer Center: *http://msdn2.microsoft.com/en-us/sharepoint/default.aspx*

- Microsoft Office Visual How-to Center: *http://msdn2.microsoft.com/en-us/office/bb266408.aspx*

Chapter 7

Managing Complex Business Processes with Custom SharePoint Workflow

Workflow Processes in the Real World

Take a moment to think about all the things you do every day in your work. You may come up with a huge list of individual tasks that are directly related to your organizational responsibilities and accountabilities. You will also come to realize that you interact extensively with your peers and direct managers. If you work in a medium- or large-size company, you may also cross-collaborate with departments or groups outside of your own. All this interaction happens in many different ways. It can happen in the many e-mails you send and receive every day, in phone calls, during the frequent knock-on-someone-else's door, in meetings, and in chat messages. Even when we do not realize we're doing it, we all play roles in different business processes. We all interact and need these frequent small communication exchanges to get things done and to make the necessary decisions that keep our businesses working. However, in many cases, coordinating business processes is complicated, and employees do not collaborate in the most efficient way. Also, some business processes are quite complex in the sense that they require interaction between multiple actors and systems.

There is more to all these challenges and opportunities. While all of this out-of-band interaction takes place, we fail to update back-end systems that exist to help store information related to a business process. Sometimes we do not update systems because of all the overhead and increased work that they bring. We either get the work done or spend our time tracking metadata. Back-end systems represent a huge investment for companies, and sadly, they may be seen as overhead since they do not map to the real way that people work. In many cases, back-end systems require end users to log on to other systems to copy and paste data. The consequence: frustrated employees and slow business productivity.

Fortunately, new workflow technologies provide the option to automate and coordinate business processes. Workflows help bring together the power of human collaboration with the power of software to improve communication and task management. Workflows allow you to route specific tasks to different actors and systems. Therefore, you can streamline business processes while greatly increasing business efficiency. Additionally, workflows provide end users the ability to work productively by not requiring them to log on to all the systems in which the enterprise has invested.

The goal of this chapter is to introduce you to a new set of workflow capabilities offered by the 2007 Microsoft Office system. You will explore different Microsoft products and technologies that you can use to build custom OBA workflow solutions. Hopefully, this chapter can help you understand how to leverage your current technology investments and think about the wide variety of custom workflow solutions and architectures that you can use to optimize the efficiency of your business processes.

Introduction to Workflow in the 2007 Microsoft Office System

A workflow can be defined as a set of related tasks or activities that form an executable representation of a business process. Workflows help improve human interaction by automating individual tasks and streamlining processes.

The 2007 Microsoft Office system includes a set of applications, servers, services, and tools designed to work together to build and deploy custom workflow solutions. Additionally, you can use the Microsoft .NET Framework Windows Workflow Foundation (WF) and Microsoft Visual Studio 2008 to build powerful workflow solutions that integrate with the 2007 Microsoft Office system. Depending on your business needs, you can use different combinations of these tools and technologies to create workflow solutions that connect line-of-business (LOB) information with Office client applications. Therefore, you can provide end users with a simplified and well-known set of programs to interact with LOB data and reduce the complexity of business workflows. Figure 7-1 shows a roadmap of key developer tools and technologies you can use to create custom workflow solutions.

As a developer, you face a common question: Which set of tools and technologies should I use to build a custom solution workflow? The following sections of this chapter provide a high-level overview of the different key developer tools and technologies that you can use to build workflow-enabled applications. It also discusses advantages and disadvantages of each one to guide you to a better informed technology decision.

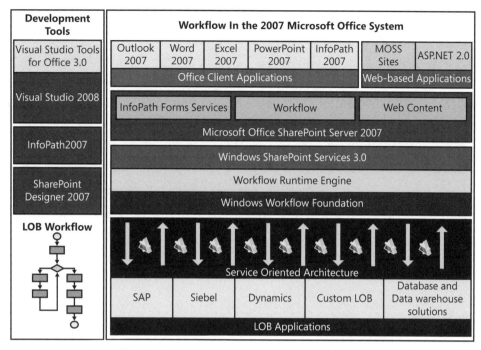

FIGURE 7-1 Roadmap of key developer tools and technologies that help create custom workflow solutions

Windows Workflow Foundation

Windows Workflow Foundation (WF) is a platform component of the Microsoft .NET Framework 3.5. WF provides a workflow run-time engine, an extensible programming model, and tools that help build and execute workflow-enabled applications. WF allows asynchronous programming to help define persistent workflow applications. That is, you can define long-running workflows that preserve state and wait indefinitely until a user or application executes the next activity. Additionally, WF allows you to build applications that consist of one or more workflows. The workflow run-time engine executes individual activities that compose workflows one at a time and hosts the execution inside any Windows process, including console applications, Windows forms applications, Windows Services, ASP.NET Web sites, and Web services. For more information about the WF programming model, visit *http://msdn2 .microsoft.com/en-us/library/ms734702.aspx*.

You can use Visual Studio 2008 to create workflow solutions using a graphic workflow designer or you can create entire workflow solutions programmatically. Since workflows are based on activities, WF provides a Base Activity Library (BAL) that includes a set of general purpose activities that are common to workflow solutions. They include *Code, Sequence, While, IFElse*, and other activities that help model primitive operations that exist in different programming languages. Additionally, you can define custom activities and create custom activity libraries (CAL).

There are three main namespaces you can use to create workflows programmatically using WF:

- **System.Workflow.Activities**   Defines activities that can be added to workflows to create and run an executable representation of a work process

- **System.Workflow.ComponentModel**   Provides the base classes, interfaces, and core modeling constructs used to create activities and workflows

- **System.Workflow.Runtime**   Contains classes and interfaces you can use to control the workflow runtime engine and the execution of a workflow instance

Figure 7-2 shows the WF components: activities, workflows, custom activity libraries, the WF runtime engine, the WF services, and the WF BAL. They are all hosted in a process that executes a workflow-enabled application.

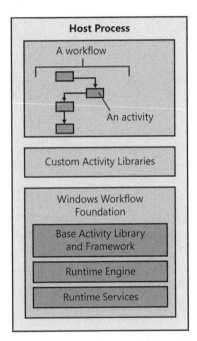

FIGURE 7-2 A workflow-enabled application running on the Windows Workflow Foundation platform

Workflow Authoring Styles

The WF supports two main authoring styles of workflow programs:

- **Sequential workflow**   Executes activities in a predefined pattern and represents a workflow as a procession of steps that must be executed in order until the last activity is completed. This type of workflow can be modeled as a flowchart. Therefore, to design a graphical representation of a workflow, you can use flowchart structures such as start, activity, repetition, loops, and finish. A good example to explain a sequential workflow is a simple notification system. Imagine that you need to build a vacation leave notification system for your company. In this solution, the workflow starts when Valeria, an employee, opens the vacation leave notification form to define the days she plans to be away for the holidays. Once the form is complete, the employee submits the form and the system sends a notification to her manager, Monica, who reviews the summary document, assessing the number of days the employee is planning on being away. If the manager approves the document, the document is moved to an "approved document library" that backups all time-off summary documents. Next, the system will notify the rest of the team that Valeria plans to be on vacation for the holidays. However, if the manager rejects the document, the system will notify Valeria, and she will have to review the manager's comments attached in the form. In either case, the workflow reaches an end and terminates the execution.

- **State machine workflow**   Responds to external events as they occur and represents a group of states, transitions, and events, which trigger transitions between these states. We will use a document publishing process to explain state machine workflow. Imagine that you work for an editorial company that publishes technical articles for software developers and you are asked to build an article publishing workflow application. In this solution, the workflow starts when Hubert, a well-known contributor, submits a technical article using a Web-based publishing system. Submitting an article triggers a *OnDocumentCreated* event. This event calls a Web service that stores the technical article in a Microsoft Office SharePoint 2007 document library and sends an e-mail to the corresponding subject-matter experts to ask for a technical review. The technical article will remain in a *DocumentCreated* state until all approvers review and approve the technical article. Once this step is completed, the system will trigger an *OnDocumentApproved* event. This event changes the status of the technical article to *DocumentApproved* and sends an e-mail to the publisher to notify him that this particular technical article is ready for publishing. Carlos, the publisher, fills out a form specifying that this document is ready for publishing and submits the form to the printer. This will trigger an *OnDocumentPublished* event that changes the status of the article to *DocumentPublished*, after which an e-mail is sent to the contributor notifying him that his technical article was sent to the printer. Finally, the printer logs on to the publishing system and marks the technical article as completed. This launches an *OnDocumentCompleted* event that changes the status of the document to *DocumentCompleted* and sends an e-mail notifying all the participants in the workflow that the technical article was printed. The workflow reaches an end and terminates the execution.

Figure 7-3 shows a sequential workflow and a state machine workflow diagram.

As we explained earlier, the WF provides a workflow run-time engine, an extensible programming model, and tools that help build and execute workflow-enabled applications. However, if you want to build custom workflow solutions that integrate seamlessly with the

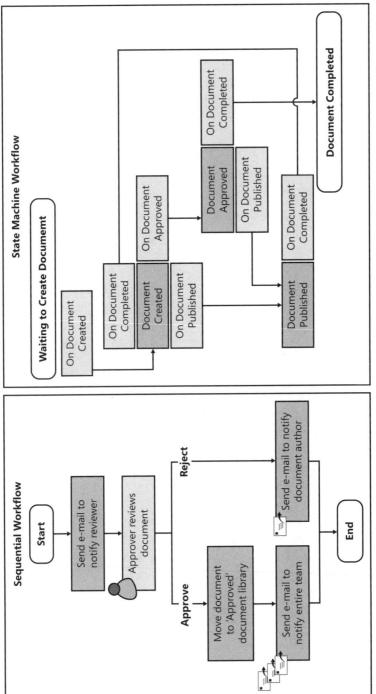

FIGURE 7-3 Sequential and state machine workflow diagrams

2007 Microsoft Office system, you can consider using the workflow services provided by Windows SharePoint Services 3.0 and Microsoft Office SharePoint Server 2007.

Windows SharePoint Services 3.0

Windows SharePoint Services 3.0 provides enhanced support to create document-oriented features and helps integrate a human dimension to custom workflow solutions. Windows SharePoint Services workflows can assign tasks to users and allow users to see status on any workflow instance. Windows SharePoint Services workflows can be added to documents, list items, or content types and are made available to users at the document library or list level.

We explained earlier that the WF run-time engine executes individual activities that compose workflows one at a time and hosts the execution inside any Windows process. In the same way, Windows SharePoint Services can also act as a host for the WF runtime engine. Windows SharePoint Services supports the WF run-time engine and WF services. However, it provides a different programming model. The *Microsoft.SharePoint.Workflow* namespace inherits many of the classes from the *System.Workflow* namespace and provides a new set of classes, interfaces, and enumerations that represent the workflow functionality contained in Windows SharePoint Services. For more information, visit *http://msdn2.microsoft.com/en-us/ library/microsoft.sharepoint.workflow.aspx*.

An important item to consider while designing workflow OBAs is the tools you can use to create them. You can create custom workflow OBA solutions using Microsoft SharePoint Designer 2007 or the workflow designer in Visual Studio 2008. The last section of this chapter explains how to create custom workflow OBAs using these tools.

In Windows SharePoint Services, a workflow running on a specific item is a workflow instance, and workflow templates are workflow programs that are available on a site, list, or content type. Association is the process of binding a workflow template to a site, list, or content type. Workflows can be associated to servers or Web forms running Windows SharePoint Services.

Figure 7-4 shows the workflow architecture in Windows SharePoint Services 3.0.

Workflow templates may or may not have workflow input forms. These forms allow end users to interact with workflows and can be of four different kinds.

- **Association form**   Allows site administrators to capture general parameter settings for a workflow, such as the name of the workflow and the association of the workflow with a specific list, document library, or content type.

- **Initiation form**   Allows end users to specify or override options when a workflow instance starts. A workflow can be initiated either as the result of a manual action by the end user or triggered from an event. This form is presented to the user only when a workflow is started manually.

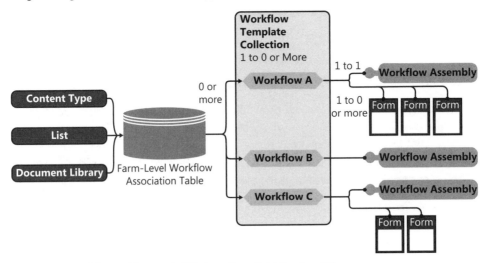

FIGURE 7-4 Workflow architecture in Windows SharePoint Services 3.0

- **Task form**   Allows end users to specify the details of tasks assigned to them.
- **Modification form**   Allows users to define new tasks or delegate the task to a different end user.

Windows SharePoint Services defines the previous forms as ASP.NET 2.0 pages. While designing OBAs, you have the option to create custom ASP.NET 2.0 Web forms to define the behavior you need for association, initiation, task, and modification forms. Additionally, you can use custom forms to control the Web design of the forms. For example, you can configure a set of forms using your company logo and Web site stylesheets. You can use master pages in custom association, initiation, task, and modification forms to display the same user interface you use for your internal Web sites.

Windows SharePoint Services provides a set of definition and configuration files that contain the information necessary to create a workflow template and instantiate workflows. These files can be represented by different combinations of files, including an XML markup file that includes the declarative metadata of the workflow, in combination with a code-behind file that contains custom code representing the properties and behavior of the workflow.

The workflow definition schema allows you to define multiple settings such as the name, GUID, description, and URLS for custom forms, the name of the workflow assembly and class, and custom metadata of the workflow. Listing 7-1 shows a sample XML markup file for an Expense reporting solution. Note how the *AssociationURL, InititiationURL,* and *ModificationURL* attributes of the workflow element define the custom forms that this workflow solution uses for association, instantiation, and modification, respectively.

LISTING 7-1   This is an example of an XML markup file for an expense report solution.

```
[XML]
<?xml version="1.0" encoding="utf-8" ?>
<Elements xmlns="http://schemas.microsoft.com/sharepoint/">
   <Workflow
      Name="ExpenseReportWorkflow"
      Description="Use this workflow to track expense report status."
      Id="C6964BFF-BG8D-41ac-AC5E-B61EC111731C"
      CodeBesideClass="OBAExpenseReport.Workflow1"
      CodeBesideAssembly="OBAExpenseReport, Version=12.0.0.0, Culture=neutral,
      PublicKeyToken=71e3bce121e9429c"
      TaskListContentTypeId="0x01080100C9C9515DE4E24001905074F980F93160"
      AssociationUrl="_layouts/expenseReportAssociationPage.aspx"
      InstantiationUrl="_layouts/expenseReportInitiationPage.aspx"
      ModificationUrl="_layouts/expenseReportModificationPage.aspx">
   <Categories/>
   <AssociationData>
   …
   </AssociationData>
   <MetaData>
   …
   </MetaData>
   </Workflow>
</Elements>
```

 Note   This sample has been edited for clarity.

Keep in mind that Windows SharePoint Services must use ASP.NET 2.0 to define input forms for workflow solutions. InfoPath Forms cannot be used for Windows SharePoint Services workflows. If you have an existing ASP.NET 2.0 application and want to take advantage of workflows in SharePoint, you can use Windows SharePoint Services workflows. On the other hand, Windows SharePoint Services workflow solutions can't use Office client applications to interact with end users. That includes InfoPath forms. If you want seamless support for 2007 Microsoft Office system clients in custom OBA workflow solutions, Microsoft Office SharePoint Server 2007 is the better option.

Microsoft Office SharePoint Server 2007

Microsoft Office SharePoint Server 2007 provides a true enterprise portal platform and builds upon the Windows SharePoint Services 3.0 infrastructure. In the context of OBA workflow solutions, Office SharePoint Server 2007 provides the following capabilities:

- Hosting of InfoPath forms thanks to the integration with InfoPath Forms Services
- Integration with 2007 Microsoft Office system client applications such as Outlook 2007, Word 2007, PowerPoint 2007, and Excel 2007
- Customization of out-of-the-box (OOB) workflows
- Customization of workflows

Support for InfoPath Forms

Office SharePoint Server 2007 allows users to interact with workflows using InfoPath forms in the same way that users interact with ASP.NET 2.0 Web forms for Windows SharePoint Services workflows. Some developers prefer InfoPath forms over ASP.NET 2.0 forms for a couple of reasons:

- InfoPath forms can be displayed by the 2007 Microsoft Office system clients. For example, you can host an InfoPath form in Word 2007, Excel 2007, PowerPoint 2007, or Outlook 2007.

- InfoPath forms are easier to create. InfoPath 2007 provides a designer experience that helps you create forms faster and with less code. Also, InfoPath forms provide built-in validation and data proofing.

You can use a workflow definition schema file to define InfoPath forms for association, initiation, tasks, and modification that integrate with Office SharePoint Server 2007 workflows solutions. To define the custom forms you want to use in a workflow template definition, you must set the form URLs of each specific process (association, initiation, modification, edit task) to the appropriate ASP.NET 2.0 predefined page of an Office SharePoint Server 2007 instance as shown in Listing 7-2. Next, you add an element that specifies the URN for the custom InfoPath form you built for each type of process. Listing 7-2 shows a sample XML markup file for an expense reporting solution that uses InfoPath forms.

LISTING 7-2   Example of XML markup file for an expense report solution using InfoPath forms

```
[XML]
<?xml version="1.0" encoding="utf-8" ?>
<Elements xmlns="http://schemas.microsoft.com/sharepoint/">
   <Workflow
        Name="ExpenseReportWorkflow"
        Description="Use this workflow to track expense report status."
        Id="C6964BFF-BG8D-41ac-AC5E-B61EC111731C"
        CodeBesideClass="OBAExpenseReport.Workflow1"
        CodeBesideAssembly="OBAExpenseReport, Version=12.0.0.0, Culture=neutral,
                    PublicKeyToken=71e3bce121e9429c"
        TaskListContentTypeId="0x01080100C9C9515DE4E24001905074F980F93160"
        AssociationUrl="_layouts/CstWrkflIP.aspx"
        InstantiationUrl="_layouts/IniWrkflIP.aspx"
        ModificationUrl="_layouts/ModWrkflIP.aspx"
        StatusUrl="_layouts/WrkStat.aspx">
   <Categories/>
   <!-- Tags to specify InfoPath forms for the workflow; delete
   tags for forms that you do not have -->
   <MetaData>
     <Association_FormURN>
       urn:schemas-OBAExpenseReport-com:workflow:ReviewRouting-Assoc
     </Association_FormURN>
     <Instantiation_FormURN>
       urn:schemas-OBAExpenseReport-com:workflow:ReviewRouting-Init
     </Instantiation_FormURN>
```

```
<Task0_FormURN>
    urn:schemas-OBAExpenseReport-com:workflow:ReviewRouting-Review
</Task0_FormURN>
<Task1_FormURN>
    urn:schemas-OBAExpenseReport-com:workflow:ReviewRouting-Review
</Task1_FormURN>
<AssociateOnActivation>false</AssociateOnActivation>
        </MetaData>
      </Workflow>
</Elements>
```

To design an InfoPath form for a workflow in Office SharePoint Server 2007, you use InfoPath 2007 and start designing a custom form the same way you would with any other InfoPath 2007 form. In general, to create InfoPath forms for workflow solutions, you start by adding controls on your form. Next, you data bind the controls so that the form can send and receive data to Office SharePoint Server 2007 and the workflow instance. Next, you add and customize a button that submits your form data to Office SharePoint Server 2007. Finally, you set the forms security level to Domain and publish the form. For more information about creating InfoPath forms, visit *http://office.microsoft.com/en-us/infopath/HA012111841033.aspx*.

Figure 7-5 shows an InfoPath form used as an initiation form for an expense reporting workflow solution.

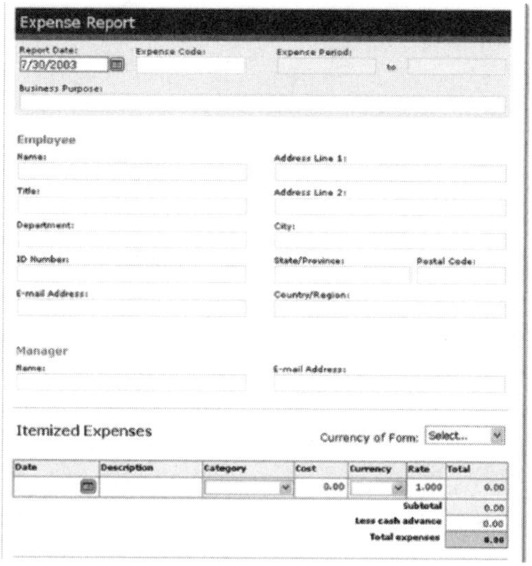

FIGURE 7-5 Sample InfoPath form for expense reporting workflow solution

Integration into 2007 Microsoft Office System Client Applications

One of the most powerful features offered by Office SharePoint Server 2007 is the ability to connect custom workflow solutions with Office Client applications. This allows end users to interact in a natural way with OBA workflow solutions. End users can interact with workflows directly from Word 2007, Excel 2007, PowerPoint 2007, and Outlook 2007. As mentioned in the previous section of this chapter, Office client applications can host InfoPath forms.

 Note   This option is available for users that installed InfoPath 2007.

For example, you can open, fill out, and submit InfoPath forms from Outlook 2007. InfoPath e-mail forms help streamline workflow processes that you use to collaborate and share data using well-known applications and, therefore, reduce the need for training. Figure 7-6 shows how you can open InfoPath forms in Outlook 2007.

FIGURE 7-6 Open InfoPath forms in Outlook 2007

Another powerful possibility offered by Office SharePoint Server 2007 is the ability for end users to initiate a workflow from Word 2007. You can open a Word 2007 document and create a running workflow instance using the *Start New Workflow* option. This greatly simplifies the process of starting workflows involving document approval. Earlier in this chapter, we explored a state machine workflow document publishing scenario in which you work for an editorial company that publishes technical articles for software developers and you are asked to build an article publishing workflow application. In this scenario, contributors can use Word 2007 to initiate a document approval workflow right after they finish writing an article. Figure 7-7 shows how a contributor can initiate a document approval workflow instance from Word 2007.

Another integration possibility includes reporting tools that provide an aggregate analysis of workflow history. You may be interested in analyzing workflow processes to identify problems, bottlenecks, and the performance of your organization. Office SharePoint Server 2007 includes several predefined Excel 2007 reports that provide aggregate analysis of workflow history. Additionally, you can use Visio 2007, Access 2007, or custom monitoring solutions to analyze workflow history information stored in SharePoint lists.

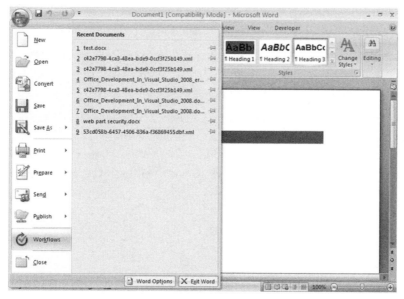

FIGURE 7-7 Initiate a document approval workflow from Word 2007

Out-of-the-Box Workflows

Office SharePoint Server provides a set of out-of-the-box (OOB) workflow solutions. Information workers (IWs) can use these workflow templates with no developer intervention. However, you can customize predefined workflows based on your business needs. The predefined workflows templates in Office SharePoint Server 2007 include the following:

- **Approval** Provides business logic and predefined settings that help you route documents for approval. When the workflow is initiated, the end user defines a list of approvers.

- **Collect feedback** Provides business logic and predefined settings that help you route documents for review. This workflow is similar to the previous one. However, this workflow allows end users to provide feedback.

- **Collect signatures** Provides business logic and predefined settings that help you collect signatures for a document. This workflow works like the previous ones, but requires end users to provide a signature to complete a workflow. This workflow can be started only in Office client programs.

- **Disposition approval** Provides business logic and predefined settings that help users decide whether to retain or delete expired documents.

- **Three-state workflow** Provides business logic and predefined settings that help users track the status of a list item through three states. It can be used to manage business processes that require organizations to track a high volume of issues or items, such as customer support issues, sales leads, or project tasks.

■ **Translation management workflow**   Provides business logic and predefined settings that help manage document translation. This workflow allows users to assign tasks and track the status of translated documents.

To create OOB workflow solutions, you start by opening a document library, list, or content type. Next, you select Settings, Document Library Settings, and then Workflow. This opens an Add Workflow page that allows you to configure an OOB workflow. Figure 7-8 shows how you can create an OOB workflow in a preexisting workflow document library in Office SharePoint Server 2007.

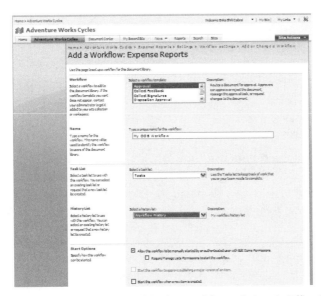

FIGURE 7-8 Creating out-of-the-box workflow solutions in Office SharePoint Server 2007

For more information, visit *http://office.microsoft.com/en-us/sharepointserver/ CH101782961033.aspx.*

Customization of Workflows

In many cases, you may want to create a custom workflow solution that is specific to your business needs. Office SharePoint Server 2007 and Windows SharePoint Services allow you to build custom workflow solutions using Office SharePoint Designer 2007 or Visual Studio 2008. The next section walks you through the process of building custom workflows using both tools.

Creating Custom Workflows

You can create custom OBA workflow solutions for Windows SharePoint Services and for Office SharePoint Server 2007 using either Office SharePoint Designer 2007 or Visual Studio 2008. Both tools provide design templates that help you build workflow solutions. However, each authoring tool provides different capabilities.

Overview of Creating Custom Workflows in SharePoint Designer

Office SharePoint Designer 2007 provides a simple rules-based approach that enables you to create workflow solutions based on preexisting activities and to associate workflows directly to lists or document libraries. This authoring tool allows you to define workflows with no custom code. Office SharePoint Designer also simplifies the deployment process, since workflow markup, rules, and supporting files are stored in a specific document library. For those reasons, it is a tool commonly used by information workers and Web designers. You can use this authoring tool to build simple OBA workflow solutions that automate business processes in your enterprise such as document approval, document review, task management, and more. Figure 7-9 shows how you can create new workflows or open existing ones using Office SharePoint Designer as an authoring tool for workflows.

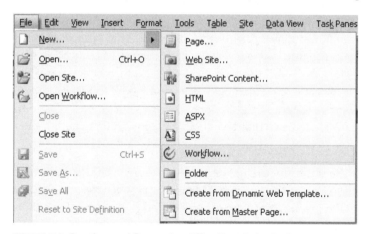

FIGURE 7-9 Creating workflows using Office SharePoint Designer 2007 as an authoring tool

Office SharePoint Designer 2007 provides a wizard-like designer that enables you to define workflow solutions that use a set of business rules and predefined rules, for example, sending notifications via e-mail. This greatly simplifies the process of building workflows. However, when you are making a technology decision, there are some considerations you should keep in mind if you plan to use Office SharePoint Designer 2007:

- **Workflow association**   You can associate workflows to lists or document libraries, but you cannot associate workflows to content types. Once you associate a workflow, you cannot change which list or document library a workflow is attached to. Instead, you must create a new workflow and attach it to the list that you want.

■ **Forms support** You can design custom ASP.NET 2.0 forms, but SharePoint Designer does not provide support for InfoPath forms. Something else to consider is that workflows authored from Office SharePoint Designer 2007 only support initiation and task completion forms. This is because workflows designed in SharePoint designer cannot be modified while running. Therefore, you cannot define modification forms. As explained earlier, you associate workflows directly to lists or document libraries, meaning the association process happens in design time. Therefore, you cannot define association forms.

■ **Workflow authoring styles** You can create sequential workflows, but SharePoint Designer does not support state machine workflows.

Expense Report Scenario

Imagine that you work for Adventure Works Cycles, a sports store franchise that sells bicycles worldwide. This company has sales representatives that visit different countries to help new franchisees open new sports stores. You are asked to build a simple Expense Reporting OBA workflow solution. In this solution, sales representatives will start by filling out a simple expense report form that provides their name, the expense purpose, the expense total, and their direct manager's name and e-mail address. When sales representatives submit the expense report, the workflow business rules need to verify that the expense total does not exceed $5,000. If the expense total exceeds $5,000, the workflow will submit an e-mail to the direct manager asking for approval. If the expense total is less than or equal to $5,000 the system will send an e-mail to the accounting department asking it to reimburse the sales representative with the expense total amount. Since this is a simple scenario that needs no coding, you decide to use Office SharePoint Designer 2007 to author this OBA workflow solution.

To create this workflow solution, first create a document library in Office SharePoint Server 2007. For this scenario, you name the document library Expense Reports. You must add an Expense Total column of type number to the document library. Once that is configured, use Office SharePoint Designer 2007 to associate the OBA workflow solution you are creating. Figure 7-10 shows the document library you use for the expense reporting solution.

To create the workflow solution, you open Office SharePoint Designer 2007. Next you select the Open Site option from the File menu to select the SharePoint site where you want to create the workflow. Next, in the File menu, select New and click Workflow. This step will launch the Workflow Designer window, as shown in Figure 7-11.

The Workflow Designer window allows you to configure the name of the workflow. In this case, you will name the workflow ExpenseReport. Site visitors see this name when they view the Workflow pages and Workflow status in the Web browser. The Workflow Designer

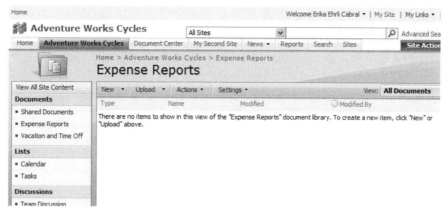

FIGURE 7-10 Microsoft Office SharePoint Server 2007 document library for the expense reporting solution

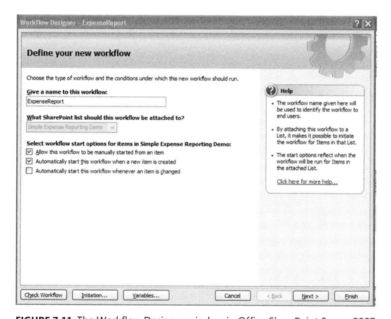

FIGURE 7-11 The Workflow Designer window in Office SharePoint Server 2007

window enables you to select the SharePoint list or document that you want to use and associates it with the workflow. In this case, you will select the Simple Expense Reporting Demo document library that you created previously. Finally, the Workflow Designer window provides three checkboxes that enable you to select whether you want to:

■ Allow the workflow to be started manually from an item.

■ Automatically start the workflow when a new item is created.

■ Automatically start the workflow whenever an item is changed.

For the expense reporting solution, you must select the first two checkboxes, as shown in Figure 7-11.

The Workflow Designer also provides an Initiation button that enables you to define the workflow parameters to collect data from participants who manually start workflows. In this case, you can define parameter values for the employee name, the expense purpose, the expense total, the manager's name, and the manager's e-mail address. Figure 7-12 shows the workflow initiation parameters for the expense reporting workflow scenario.

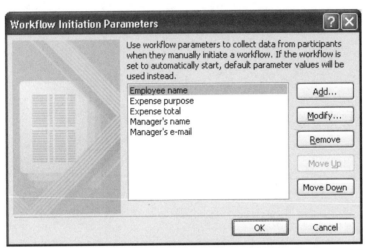

FIGURE 7-12 Workflow initiation parameters for the Expense reporting workflow scenario

Once you are done defining the workflow initiation parameters, you can define the set of business rules for the workflow. The requirements of the OBA workflow solution define business rules that are specific for this scenario. We explained earlier that when sales representatives submit an expense report, the workflow business rules need to verify that the expense total does not exceed $5,000. If the expense total exceeds $5,000, the workflow submits an e-mail to the direct manager asking for approval. If the expense total is less than or equal to $5,000 the system sends an e-mail to the accounting department asking it to reimburse the sales representative with the expense total amount. The Workflow Designer window enables you to define business rules by using a set of predefined conditions that apply to your scenario. You can compare fields in a current list and perform actions based on satisfied conditions. For this solution, you need to define an if-then-else condition to compare if the expense total field is greater than $5,000. If this condition is satisfied, the manager will receive an e-mail notification, else the accounting department will receive an e-mail notification. Figure 7-13 shows the business rules definition process.

Once you click the Finish button in the Workflow Designer window, the workflow is saved and attached to the list you specified. Each time a sales representative submits an expense report, Office SharePoint Server 2007 launches a workflow instance and validates the business rules.

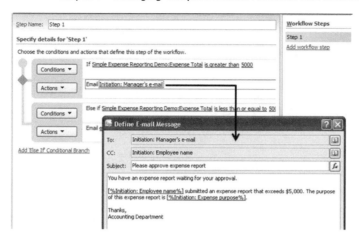

FIGURE 7-13 Business rules definition process

Workflow Project Templates in Visual Studio Tools for Office

At the beginning of this chapter, we discussed the challenges and opportunities that modern enterprises currently face when creating solutions that better integrate back-end systems and LOB information with commonly used information worker applications. Today, developers have in their hands a new set of developer tools and technologies that simplify the process of building solutions that connect back-end systems with Office client applications. As discussed in Chapter 4, you can define Software + Services (S+S) to build services that connect to LOB systems. The Office platform simplifies the integration between software services and software to simplify the consumption of these services.

In addition, Microsoft provides Visual Studio 2008 and Visual Studio Tools for Office (VSTO) as authoring tools that greatly simplify the development of elaborate OBA workflow solutions. Visual Studio Tools for Office 3.0 is a component that ships with Visual Studio 2008. Chapter 2 explains how you can build custom smart client solutions for your OBAs using VSTO. In addition, VSTO has an improved set of workflow project templates that support Rapid Application Development (RAD) of custom workflow SharePoint Solutions. Together, Visual Studio 2008 and VSTO provide tools that help you create custom workflow templates that manage the life cycle of documents and list items in a SharePoint Web site. Some of these tools include a graphic designer, a complete set of drag-and-drop activity controls, and the necessary assembly references you need to build a workflow solution. VSTO also includes the New Office SharePoint Workflow wizard, which greatly simplifies the configuration process and steps for creating workflow templates in Visual Studio. Figure 7-14 shows the different Visual Studio installed templates for Office 2007. These templates include a SharePoint Sequential Workflow template and a SharePoint State Machine Workflow template.

Workflow solutions in Visual Studio 2008 allow a greater level of customization than workflow solutions authored in Office SharePoint Designer 2007. Not only can you

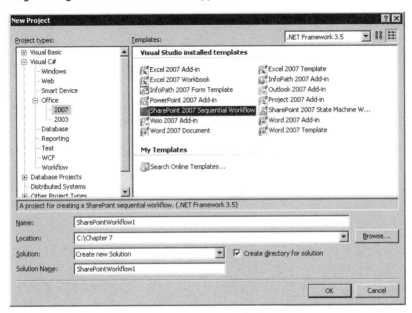

FIGURE 7-14 SharePoint Sequential Workflow and SharePoint State Machine Workflow templates in Visual Studio 2008

use a predefined set of activities, but you can create new activities for use as workflow components. Additionally you can define forms for association, initiation, modification, and task editing using either ASP.NET 2.0 Web forms or InfoPath forms. Visual Studio 2008 provides support to design, code, and publish the forms to the server.

As explained earlier, you can use Visual Studio 2008 to build workflow solutions for either Windows SharePoint Services or Office SharePoint Server 2007. Once compiled, workflow solutions are packaged as templates that can later be associated to different lists, document libraries, and content types. This provides another great advantage with respect to workflow solutions built with Office SharePoint Designer 2007. Another great advantage is that Visual Studio 2008 allows you to build workflow solutions and custom activities that you can reuse in different workflow solutions. You can, for example, create a custom activity that adds workflow steps as tasks in Outlook.

Finally, since you are using Visual Studio 2008, you are given all the advantages provided by Visual Studio as an authoring tool for developer solutions. Some of these advantages include the use of code-behind files, intellisense, debugging, use of the different workflow object models that enable workflow extensibility, and support for building custom classes and Web services that can bring LOB data.

Note: You can build workflow solutions with Visual Studio 2005 using the Visual Studio 2005 Designer for Windows Workflow Foundation add-in. This add-in is available as part of the Microsoft Windows Workflow Foundation Runtime Components and Visual Studio 2005 Extensions for Windows Workflow Foundation. However, Visual Studio 2008 reduces complexity and greatly speeds development of SharePoint workflow OBA solutions. For that reason, this book chapter focuses on showing the latest workflow enhancements added to Visual Studio 2008 and Visual Studio Tools for Office. For more information about the Visual Studio 2005 Designer for Windows Workflow Foundation, visit *http://www.microsoft.com/downloads/details.aspx?familyid=5c080096-f3a0-4ce4-8830-1489d0215877&displaylang=en*. For more information about the Visual Studio 2005 extensions for the .NET Framework 3.0 (Windows Workflow Foundation), visit *http://www.microsoft.com/downloads/details.aspx?familyid=5D61409E-1FA3-48CF-8023-E8F38E709BA6&displaylang=en*.

Visual Studio 2008 offers a basic activity library (BAL) that provides a set of predefined activities you can use to define a workflow template. An activity is a step or task that performs an action in a workflow—for example, sending an e-mail, adding tasks to Outlook 2007, adding items to SharePoint lists, or connecting to an LOB database to retrieve or save information. While designing workflows, you can use the toolbox in Visual Studio 2008 to drag and drop activities to your workflow solution. Activities are built as classes, and therefore, have properties, events, and methods as any other class. You can use activities from either the Windows Workflow tab or the SharePoint Workflow tab. The Windows Workflow tab provides a set of activities provided by the Windows Workflow Foundation, while the SharePoint Workflow tab provides a set of activities that are specific to Windows SharePoint Services and Office SharePoint Server 2007. Some of these activities include OnWorkflowActivated, CreateTask, DeleteTask, SendEmail, and CompleteTask. Additionally, you can build your own custom activities by creating a class that implements the SequentialWorkflowActivity class if you need a sequential activity or the StateMachineWorkflowActivity if you need a state machine activity. Figure 7-15 shows the Windows Workflow 3.0 and the SharePoint Workflow toolbox tabs in Visual Studio 2008.

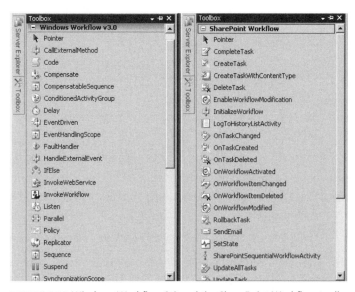

FIGURE 7-15 Windows Workflow 3.0 and the SharePoint Workflow toolbox tabs in Visual Studio 2008

For more information about creating custom activities, visit *http://msdn2.microsoft.com/ en-us/library/ms734563(VS.90).aspx*.

The next section of this chapter provides a high-level overview of and guidance for creating sequential workflows and state machine workflows using Visual Studio 2008 as an authoring tool.

Sequential Workflows

As we explained earlier, sequential workflows execute activities in a predefined pattern and represent a workflow as a procession of steps that must be executed in order until the last activity is completed. As shown in Figure 7-14 Visual Studio 2008 has a new SharePoint Sequential Workflow project template that provides a graphic workflow designer, a complete set of drag-and-drop activity controls, and the necessary assembly references you need to build a sequential workflow solution.

Previously, we talked about a scenario in which you have to build a vacation leave notification system for your company. When an employee saves a document, the direct manager receives an e-mail notification to let her know that she has to approve vacation time for an employee. If the manager approves the document, the system sends an e-mail to the employee. If the manager rejects the vacation request, the employee receives an e-mail with comments from the manager. In either case, the workflow reaches an end and terminates the execution. Because you want to add more customization and use debugging, you decide to use Visual Studio 2008.

To create this solution, you start by creating a simple "Vacation and Time Off" document library. You should add the following four columns to the document library, as shown in Figure 7-16:

- **Employee Name:**   Create this column as Single line of text.

- **Manager's Name:**   Create this column as Single line of text.

- **Planned days off:**   Create this column as Number.

- **Notes:**   Create this column as Multiple line of text.

Workflow participants will use this document library to store vacation approval forms. Next, in Visual Studio 2008, you start by opening the New Project dialog box and selecting the SharePoint 2007 Sequential Workflow project located under the Office node. In the name box, you type **OBAVacationApprovalDemo**. This last step opens the New Office SharePoint Workflow wizard, as shown in Figure 7-17.

The next window prompts for a workflow name and a site for debugging the page. Click Next to accept the default settings. The next step requires that you select the document library, task list, and history list you want to use when debugging. In this case, you accept

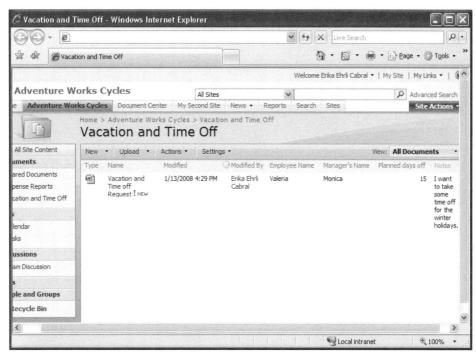

FIGURE 7-16 "Vacation and Time Off" document library

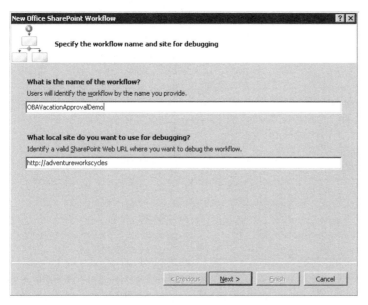

FIGURE 7-17 New Office SharePoint Workflow wizard

the default settings. The last step of the wizard requires you to define the conditions for how your workflow is started. Visual Studio 2008 allows you to automatically associate a workflow to a document library or list. Additionally, you can choose to handle the association step manually. In this case, you will associate the workflow with the "Vacation and Time Off" document library you created previously. Finally, the wizard asks for the conditions for how your workflow is started. In this case, you choose "Manually by users" and "When an item is created."

Next, you open the Windows Workflow activities and the SharePoint Workflow activities in the toolbox to drag and drop activities to the Visual Studio 2008 design surface. Visual Studio 2008 enables you to create workflow diagrams just as you can create flowchart diagrams using Visio 2007. Figure 7-18 shows a completed sequential workflow diagram for the vacation leave notification system.

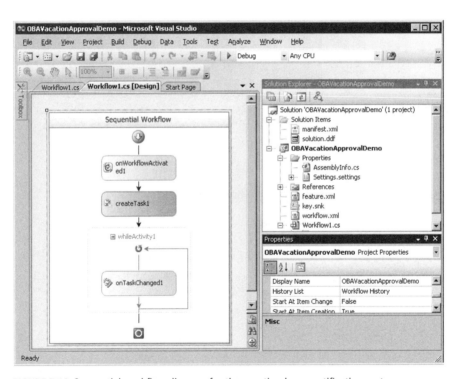

FIGURE 7-18 Sequential workflow diagram for the vacation leave notification system

You can double-click each activity to customize code behind just as you can double-click buttons on Windows forms solutions to add custom code. You can also define properties for each activity using the Properties window in Visual Studio 2008. Listing 7-3 shows the contents of the OBAVacationApprovalDemo sequential workflow class.

LISTING 7-3   OBAVacationApplicationDemo sequential workflow class

```csharp
[C#]
using System;
using System.ComponentModel;
using System.ComponentModel.Design;
using System.Workflow.ComponentModel.Compiler;
using System.Workflow.ComponentModel.Serialization;
using System.Workflow.ComponentModel;
using System.Workflow.ComponentModel.Design;
using System.Workflow.Runtime;
using System.Workflow.Activities;
using System.Workflow.Activities.Rules;
using Microsoft.SharePoint;
using Microsoft.SharePoint.Workflow;
using Microsoft.SharePoint.WorkflowActions;
using Microsoft.Office.Workflow.Utility;

namespace OBAVacationApprovalDemo {
    public sealed partial class Workflow1 : SequentialWorkflowActivity {

        private bool _taskCompleted = false;

        public Workflow1() {
            InitializeComponent();
        }

        public Guid workflowId = default(System.Guid);
        public SPWorkflowActivationProperties workflowProperties = new
        SPWorkflowActivationProperties();
        public static DependencyProperty approveTaskIdProperty =
        DependencyProperty.Register("approveTaskId", typeof(System.Guid),
        typeof(OBAVacationApprovalDemo.Workflow1));
[DesignerSerializationVisibilityAttribute(DesignerSerializationVisibility.Visible)]
        [BrowsableAttribute(true)]
        [CategoryAttribute("Misc")]
        public Guid approveTaskId {
            get {
                return
((System.Guid)(base.GetValue(OBAVacationApprovalDemo.Workflow1.approveTaskIdProperty)));
            }
            set {
                base.SetValue(OBAVacationApprovalDemo.Workflow1.approveTaskIdProperty, value);
            }
        }

        public static DependencyProperty approveTaskPropertiesProperty =
        DependencyProperty.Register("approveTaskProperties",
        typeof(Microsoft.SharePoint.Workflow.SPWorkflowTaskProperties),
        typeof(OBAVacationApprovalDemo.Workflow1));
    [DesignerSerializationVisibilityAttribute(DesignerSerializationVisibility.Visible)]
        [BrowsableAttribute(true)]
        [CategoryAttribute("Misc")]
        public SPWorkflowTaskProperties approveTaskProperties {
            get {
                return
```

```csharp
((Microsoft.SharePoint.Workflow.SPWorkflowTaskProperties)(base.GetValue(OBAVacationApprovalD
emo.Workflow1.approveTaskPropertiesProperty)));
        }
        set {
base.SetValue(OBAVacationApprovalDemo.Workflow1.approveTaskPropertiesProperty, value);
        }
    }

    private void approveTaskCreation(object sender, EventArgs e) {
        try {
            approveTaskId = Guid.NewGuid();
            approveTaskProperties = new
                Microsoft.SharePoint.Workflow.SPWorkflowTaskProperties();
            approveTaskProperties.AssignedTo =
                System.Threading.Thread.CurrentPrincipal.Identity.Name;
            approveTaskProperties.Title = "Vacation and Time off Workflow Task";
            approveTaskProperties.Description = String.Format(
                "This is a vacation and time off request " +
                "submitted by {0} [Employee Name] to {1} [Manager's Name]. " +
                "The employee is planning to take {2} days off.",
CustomFieldValue("Employee Name"),
                CustomFieldValue("Manager's Name"),
                CustomFieldValue("Planned days off"));
            approveTaskProperties.PercentComplete = (float)0.0;
            approveTaskProperties.StartDate = DateTime.Now;
            approveTaskProperties.DueDate = DateTime.Now.AddDays(10);
            approveTaskProperties.EmailBody = "Your vacation and time off request
                                                was approved by your manager.";
            approveTaskProperties.SendEmailNotification = true;
        }
        catch (Exception ex) {
            throw (new Exception("Unable to initialize workflow task.", ex));
        }
    }
    private string CustomFieldValue(string fieldName) {
        object item = this.workflowProperties.Item[fieldName];
        string s = this.workflowProperties.Item.Fields[fieldName]
                    .GetFieldValueAsText(item);
        if (s != null) {
            return s;
        }
        else {
            return String.Empty;
        }
    }
    private void approveTaskNotCompleted(object sender, ConditionalEventArgs e){
    e.Result = !_taskCompleted;
    }

    public static DependencyProperty afterApproveTaskPropertyChangeProperty =
    DependencyProperty.Register("afterApproveTaskPropertyChange",
    typeof(Microsoft.SharePoint.Workflow.SPWorkflowTaskProperties),
    typeof(OBAVacationApprovalDemo.Workflow1));
[DesignerSerializationVisibilityAttribute(DesignerSerializationVisibility.Visible)]
    [BrowsableAttribute(true)]
```

```
[CategoryAttribute("Misc")]
public SPWorkflowTaskProperties afterApproveTaskPropertyChange {
    get {
        return
((Microsoft.SharePoint.Workflow.SPWorkflowTaskProperties)(base.GetValue(OBAVacationApprovalD
emo.Workflow1.afterApproveTaskPropertyChangeProperty)));
    }
    set
{base.SetValue(OBAVacationApprovalDemo.Workflow1.afterApproveTaskPropertyChangeProperty,
value);
    }
}

private void onTaskChanged1_Invoked(object sender, ExternalDataEventArgs e) {
    if (afterApproveTaskPropertyChange.PercentComplete == 1.0) {
        _taskCompleted = true;
    }
}
}
}
```

Once you are done writing code for the vacation leave notification system, you can test the solution by using the Visual Studio debugger. When you debug the solution, Visual Studio deploys the solution to a SharePoint site and it adds the workflow template to a library or list. You can start an instance of the workflow template to test the solution while using standard debugging tools that help you debug your code as you would do with any other Visual Studio solution.

State Machine Workflows

As we explained earlier, state machine workflows respond to external events as they occur and represent a group of states, transitions, and events, which trigger transitions between these states. As shown in Figure 7-14 Visual Studio 2008 also provides a new SharePoint State Machine Workflow project template that provides a graphic workflow designer, a complete set of drag-and-drop activity controls, and the assembly references you need to build a state machine workflow solution.

To create state machine in Visual Studio 2008, start by creating a document library or list that you want to use for a custom solution. Next, in Visual Studio 2008, open the New Project dialog box and select the SharePoint 2007 State Machine Workflow project located under the Office node. In the name box, type the name of your solution. This last step opens the New Office SharePoint Workflow wizard, as shown in Figure 7-16.

The design, development, and debugging of state machine workflows is almost identical to that of sequential workflows. As mentioned before, the only difference is that state machine workflows are event-driven, and therefore, you can create event-driven workflow solutions. Figure 7-19 shows a state machine workflow diagram for the article publishing workflow application scenario we discussed earlier.

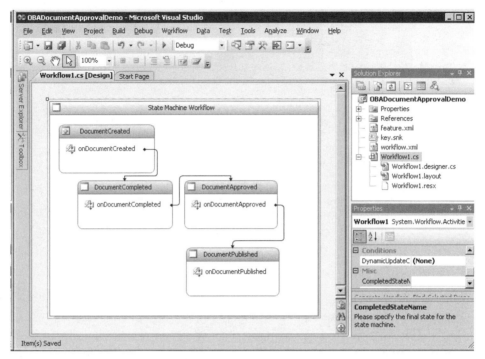

FIGURE 7-19 State machine workflow for document approval

Deployment

Visual Studio 2008 simplifies the deployment process by providing a deployment wizard that helps you create a workflow template package that you can use to deploy in different servers. Additionally, when you debug a workflow solution, Visual Studio 2008 deploys the workflow template and required configuration files to the SharePoint development site you used to create your solution. However, if you want to deploy the workflow template to a different server, you must perform additional deployment and configuration steps.

You can create a feature package to encapsulate a workflow solution and deploy it to different servers. A feature package is a CAB file with a .wsp file-name extension that contains the following files:

- **Feature.xml** XML-based file that contains a manifest listing the contents of a workflow solution. It provides high-level information, including the title, description, version, and scope of the workflow. Listing 7-4 shows a sample feature.xml file for the OBAVacationApprovalDemo solution.

LISTING 7-4 Sample feature.xml file for the OBAVacationApprovalDemo solution class

```
[XML]
<?xml version="1.0" encoding="utf-8" ?>
<Feature  Id="cf5c48e7-3428-4982-a039-898cbff616c2"
   Title="OBAVacationApprovalDemo feature"
```

```
   Description="Vacation and Time Off Approval Feature"
   Version="12.0.0.0"
   Scope="Site"
   ReceiverAssembly="Microsoft.Office.Workflow.Feature, Version=12.0.0.0,
Culture=neutral, PublicKeyToken=71e9bce111e9429c"
   ReceiverClass="Microsoft.Office.Workflow.Feature.WorkflowFeatureReceiver"
   xmlns="http://schemas.microsoft.com/sharepoint/">
<ElementManifests>
   <ElementManifest Location="workflow.xml" />
</ElementManifests>
   <Properties>
   <Property Key="GloballyAvailable" Value="true" />
   <!-- Value for RegisterForms key indicates the path to the forms relative to feature file
   location -->
   <!-- if you don't have forms, use *.xsn -->
   <Property Key="RegisterForms" Value="*.xsn" />
  </Properties>
</Feature>
```

- **Workflow.xml**   XML-based file that specifies details about the workflow assembly, metadata, and the custom forms (InfoPath forms or ASP.NET Web forms) needed for the workflow. Listing 7-5 shows a sample workflow.xml file for the OBAVacationApprovalDemo solution.

LISTING 7-5 Sample workflow.xml file for the OBAVacationApprovalDemo solution

```
[XML]
<?xml version="1.0" encoding="utf-8" ?>
<Elements xmlns="http://schemas.microsoft.com/sharepoint/">
<Workflow
   Name="OBAVacationApprovalDemo"
   Description="Vacation and Time Off Approval Workflow"
   Id="36cc9d57-d857-42ea-ad90-e461d58203ac"
   CodeBesideClass="OBAVacationApprovalDemo.Workflow1"
   CodeBesideAssembly="OBAVacationApprovalDemo, Version=1.0.0.0, Culture=neutral,
   PublicKeyToken=6f9ec6d2f579b3c8">
   <Categories/>
   <MetaData>
      <StatusPageUrl>_layouts/WrkStat.aspx</StatusPageUrl>
   </MetaData>
  </Workflow>
</Elements>
```

- **Compiled assembly**   The feature package installs a compiled workflow assembly into the Global Assembly Cache (GAC). We recommend that you sign the assembly using a strong key before you deploy the workflow solution to the server.

- **Custom forms**   You must include custom forms needed for the workflow. If the workflow solution uses ASP.NET Web forms, the feature package must provide instructions to deploy the forms to the Layouts folder of the server that will run the workflow solution. On the other hand, if the workflow solution uses InfoPath forms, the feature package must provide instructions to deploy the forms to the Features folder of the server that will run the workflow solution shown in Listing 7-7.

> **Note**   You can install InfoPath forms automatically to the server if you define the forms using the element of the feature.xml file.

Building a Feature Package   To build a feature package you start by defining the solution files and the destination directory of all workflow solutions that must be deployed to the front-end Web server. The previous configuration and installation instructions must be defined using a manifest.xml file and a CAB file.

- **Manifest.xml**   XML-based file used as a header file that defines the files that must be deployed to a front-end Web server. Listing 7-6 shows a sample manifest.xml file used for the OBAVacationApprovalDemo solution.

LISTING 7-6   Sample manifest.xml file used for the OBAVacationApprovalDemo solution

```
[XML]
<?xml version="1.0" encoding="utf-8"?>
<Solution SolutionId="36cc9d57-d857-42ea-ad90-e461d58203ac"
                    xmlns="http://schemas.microsoft.com/sharepoint/">
   <FeatureManifests>
      <FeatureManifest Location="OBAVacationApprovalDemo\feature.xml"/>
   </FeatureManifests>
   <Assemblies>
      <Assembly DeploymentTarget="GlobalAssemblyCache"
                          Location="OBAVacationApprovalDemo.dll"/>
   </Assemblies>
</Solution>
```

- **Solution.ddf file**   CAB file that specifies which files to include in the output CAB file. Listing 7-7 shows a sample solution.ddf file used for the OBAVacationApprovalDemo solution.

LISTING 7-7   Sample solution.ddf file used for the OBAVacationApprovalDemo solution

```
.OPTION EXPLICIT
.Set CabinetNameTemplate=OBAVacationApprovalDemo.wsp
.Set DiskDirectoryTemplate=CDROM
.Set CompressionType=MSZIP
.Set UniqueFiles="ON"
.Set Cabinet=on
.Set DiskDirectory1=OBAVacationApprovalDemo

Solution\manifest.xml manifest.xml

.Set DestinationDir=OBAVacationApprovalDemo
OBAVacationApprovalDemo\Feature.xml
OBAVacationApprovalDemo\workflow.xml
OBAVacationApprovalDemo\bin\debug\OBAVacationApprovalDemo.dll
```

Once you create the previous feature package files, you can create a .wsp package file using the makecab.exe command-line utility, as shown in Listing 7-8.

LISTING 7-8   Create a .wsp package file using the makecab.exe command-line utility.

```
makecab /f Solution\solution.ddf
```

Once you create the feature package, you use the stsadm.exe command-line tool to install and activate the workflow solution. Listing 7-9 shows how to install a feature using the stsadm command-line tool.

LISTING 7-9   Use the stsadm.exe command-line tool to install the workflow solution.

```
stsadm -o installfeature -filename <path of the Feature.xml file relative to the
12\TEMPLATE\FEATURES folder >
```

Listing 7-10 shows how to activate a feature using the stsadm command-line tool.

LISTING 7-10   Use the stsadm.exe command-line tool to activate the workflow solution.

```
stsadm -o activatefeature -name < folder in FEATURES directory containing the Feature
.xml file > -url http://Server/Site/Subsite
```

It is recommended that a server administrator deploys the workflow solution to a front-end Web server. Once the workflow solution is installed and activated, a site administrator must associate workflows with lists, document libraries, or content types.

Customizing Business Rules

So far, we've explored sample scenarios that have well-known business rules. For example, in the expense report scenario, the business rules are always the same. This workflow solution defines the direct manager as a single approver, and the content of the notifications is predefined as well. Depending on the expense total value, the workflow solution will either send a notification to the manager or to the accounting department. However, there are many real-world applications that have complex business rules. Routing for approval can depend on many business variables, and notifications can change depending on some other variables. Imagine that in the same expense reporting solution, you have to route an expense report to up to ten different managers, depending on the expense purpose, the expense total, and the date of submission. Additionally, depending on the expense purpose, the content of the notifications sent by the workflow will have some slight differences. This means that there may be multiple workflow solutions with different routing levels and notifications. In all previous solutions discussed in this chapter the approvers and notifications of the solutions are predefined, meaning that each workflow instance will always follow the same business logic and execute the same predefined activities. However, for OBA workflow solutions in which you need more flexibility, you must build a separate component that encapsulates complex business rules. Depending on the complexity of the business rules of your solution, you may either create a database that stores and validates all these business rules, create custom business layer classes or Web services, or use Excel 2007 as a business rule storage for decision sets.

Excel 2007 simplifies the rules capture and decision process for notifications and approvals. Implementing decision tables using Excel 2007 represents low costs for companies that already invested in 2007 Microsoft Office systems licenses. To add to the benefits, Excel 2007 provides a comfortable environment for rules administrators and requires minimal investment in training. Figure 7-20 shows routing rules in Excel 2007 and Figure 7-21 shows notification rules in Excel 2007.

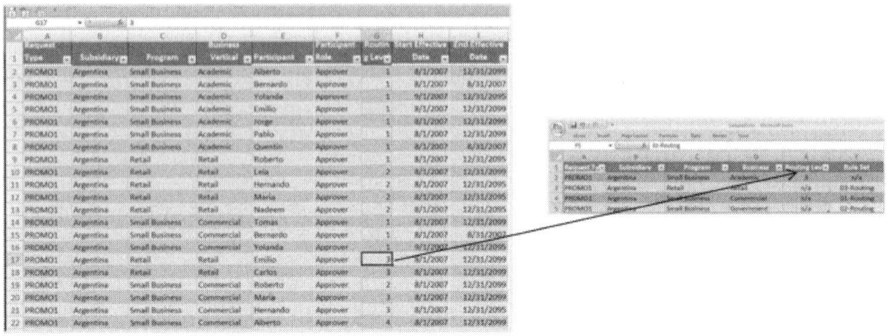

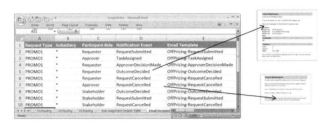

FIGURE 7-20 Routing rules in Excel 2007

FIGURE 7-21 Notification rules in Excel 2007

You can use Excel 2007 to store decision tables that capture approval, routing, and notification values. Thanks to the Open XML Formats, you can easily extract routing and approval domain information from Excel 2007 spreadsheets. Depending on your business needs, you can create a sequential or state machine workflow template using Visual Studio 2008. As part of your workflow template solution, you can use the Open XML Object Model API to retrieve business rules information from the decision tables stored in Excel 2007 spreadsheets.

Summary

Now that you have learned about the workflow capabilities offered by the 2007 Microsoft Office system, you can start thinking about different custom OBA workflow solutions that you can create for your company. You can use different Microsoft products and technologies to leverage your current technology investments and greatly simplify your business processes. Creating workflow solutions can be as simple as running configuration wizards using Office SharePoint Designer 2007, and as flexible as you can imagine if you use Visual Studio 2008 as an authoring wizard. What's most interesting is that you can enable workflow participants to use Office client applications, since they are already comfortable working with these programs. The possibilities are endless and rely completely on your business needs. Enjoy the process of building custom OBA workflow solutions. The results can be gratifying.

Further Reading and Resources

The 2007 Microsoft Office system is a true developer platform that helps connect LOB information and Office client applications. Workflow solutions integrate many different Microsoft products and technologies, and we want to provide as many as possible. The space is limited, but here is a list of key developer resources that can help you with a deep dive into workflow capabilities offered by different Microsoft products and technologies.

Windows Workflow Foundation (WF)

- Introducing Microsoft Windows Workflow Foundation: An Early Look: *http://msdn2 .microsoft.com/en-us/library/aa480215.aspx*

- Windows Workflow Foundation Samples: *http://msdn2.microsoft.com/en-us/library/ ms741723.aspx*

- Simple Human Workflow with Windows Workflow Foundation: *http://msdn2.microsoft .com/en-us/library/aa480178.aspx*

- *Essential Windows Workflow Foundation* (Microsoft .NET Development Series) by Dharma Shukla and Bob Schmidt (Addison-Wesley Professional)

Windows SharePoint Services

- Developer Introduction to Workflows for Windows SharePoint Services 3.0 and SharePoint Server 2007: *http://msdn2.microsoft.com/en-us/library/aa830816.aspx*

- Understanding Workflow in Microsoft Windows SharePoint Services and the 2007 Microsoft Office System: *http://www.microsoft.com/downloads/details .aspx?familyid=DBBD82C7-9BDE-4974-8443-67B8F30126A8&displaylang=en*

- How-To Video: Building a Basic Approval Workflow with SharePoint (MOSS 2007) and Visual Studio: *http://www.sheltonblog.com/archive/2007/11/21/how-to-video-building -a-basic-approval-workflow-with-sharepoint.aspx*

- Windows SharePoint Services 3.0: Software Development Kit (SDK): *http://www .microsoft.com/downloads/details.aspx?familyid=05E0DD12-8394-402B-8936- A07FE8AFAFFD&displaylang=en*

Office SharePoint Server 2007

- SharePoint Server 2007 Developer Portal: *http://msdn2.microsoft.com/en-us/office/ aa905503.aspx*

- SharePoint Server 2007 SDK: Software Development Kit: *http://www.microsoft .com/downloads/details.aspx?FamilyId=6D94E307-67D9-41AC-B2D6- 0074D6286FA9&displaylang=en*

- Workflow Information Center: *http://msdn2.microsoft.com/en-us/office/bb421687.aspx*

- Andrew May's WebLog: SharePoint Workflow Object Model Map for download: *http://blogs.msdn.com/andrew_may/archive/2006/05/31/ SharePointBeta2ObjectModelMapsDownloads.aspx*

- Microsoft SharePoint Products and Technologies Team Blog: Workflow: *http://blogs .msdn.com/sharepoint/archive/tags/Workflow/default.aspx*

- Business Document Workflow: *http://office.microsoft.com/en-us/sharepointserver/ CH101782961033.aspx*

- Workflow projects in CodePlex: *http://www.codeplex.com/Project/ProjectDirectory .aspx?ProjectSearchText=workflow*

- *Workflow in the 2007 Microsoft Office System* by David Mann (Apress)

InfoPath 2007 and Outlook 2007

- InfoPath Forms for Workflows: *http://msdn2.microsoft.com/en-us/library/ms573938.aspx*

- Building Simple Custom Approval Workflows with InfoPath 2007 Forms: *http://msdn2 .microsoft.com/en-us/library/bb629921.aspx*

- Scenarios for Using InfoPath and InfoPath Forms Services: *http://office.microsoft.com/ en-us/infopath/HA102119421033.aspx*

- Use InfoPath E-mail Forms in Outlook: *http://office.microsoft.com/en-us/help/ HA101645491033.aspx*

- Using InfoPath E-mail Forms: *http://blogs.msdn.com/tudort/archive/2006/02/22/ 536800.aspx*

Office SharePoint Designer 2007

- BlogOffice SharePoint Designer 2007: *http://blogs.msdn.com/sharepointdesigner*

- Microsoft Office SharePoint Designer 2007: Create a Workflow: *http://office.microsoft .com/en-us/sharepointdesigner/HA101005911033.aspx*

- Workflow Development in Office SharePoint Designer: *http://msdn2.microsoft.com/ en-us/library/ms414204.aspx*

Visual Studio 2008

- SharePoint Workflow Solutions: *http://msdn2.microsoft.com/en-us/library/ bb386211(VS.90).aspx*

- VSTO Team Blog: OBA: *http://blogs.msdn.com/vsto2/archive/tags/OBA/default.aspx*

Workflow Deployment

- Workflow Deployment Using Features: *http://msdn2.microsoft.com/en-us/library/ ms414556.aspx*

- How to: Deploy a Workflow Template: *http://msdn2.microsoft.com/en-us/library/ ms460303.aspx*

- Creating a Solution Package in Windows SharePoint Services 3.0: *http://msdn2.microsoft .com/en-us/library/bb466225.aspx*

- Signing an Assembly with a Strong Name: *http://msdn2.microsoft.com/en-us/library/ xc31ft41(VS.71).aspx*

- Stsadm command-line tool (Office SharePoint Server): *http://technet2.microsoft.com/ Office/en-us/library/188f006d-aa66-4784-a65b-a31822aa13f71033.mspx?mfr=true*

Open XML File Formats

- Introducing the Office (2007) Open XML File Formats: *http://msdn2.microsoft.com/ en-us/library/aa338205.aspx*

- Open XML SDK Documentation: *http://msdn2.microsoft.com/en-us/library/ bb448854.aspx*

- Manipulating Excel 2007 and PowerPoint 2007 Files with the Open XML Object Model (Part 1 of 2): *http://msdn2.microsoft.com/en-us/library/bb739834.aspx*

- Manipulating Excel 2007 and PowerPoint 2007 Files with the Open XML Object Model (Part 2 of 2): *http://msdn2.microsoft.com/en-us/library/bb727373.aspx*

- Preparing Open XML documents using MOSS and WF: *http://blogs.infosupport.com/ wouterv/archive/2007/04/12/Preparing-Open-XML-documents-using-MOSS-and-WF.aspx*

Office Development

- Office Developer Center: *http://msdn2.microsoft.com/en-us/office/default.aspx*

- Microsoft Office Interactive Developer Map: *http://msdn2.microsoft.com/en-us/office/ bb497969.aspx*

- Office Business Applications: Price Exception Management: *http://msdn2.microsoft.com/ en-us/library/bb977552.aspx*

- Erika Ehrli Cabral's blog: *http://blogs.msdn.com/erikaehrli/*

Chapter 8
Deploying Your Office Business Application in the Enterprise

You have seen many great examples of Office Business Applications throughout this book. You have seen how simple it is to leverage the power of the Office platform to create rich applications for your customers and users. Now you will see how straightforward it is to deploy these applications in your enterprise. Getting it to work on your machine is only half the battle. Now you must deploy your OBA into the wild. In the first half of this chapter, you will see how VSTO and ClickOnce make it easy to publish and update your client VSTO solutions. In the second half, we will focus on the server side of the application and look at some ways to package and deploy your Web parts, Web services, and workflows into your SharePoint environment.

VSTO Deployment

VSTO deployment has made the biggest advancements since version 2.0. ClickOnce is now the technology used to deploy your OBAs on the client. This means that your applications can be published, installed, updated, rolled back, and uninstalled using the ClickOnce technology. The ClickOnce cache also provides offline support for your applications, freeing your users to continue working even when not connected to the network. The ClickOnce security model based on inclusion lists is now used over the computer access security (CAS POL) model of .NET, which was used in previous VSTO releases. This greatly simplifies the security model and gives your OBAs a version-resilient security model.

After you develop your application, publish the version to a publish location. Users then install the application from the publish location. The developer can publish an updated version to the same publish location. Users who have the old version installed will get the new version automatically, or based on the interval specified by the publisher. New users will install the new version. If a problem is discovered the publisher can roll back easily to a previous version. Uninstallation is as simple as running the uninstall from the Add or Remove Programs dialog box as with any other Windows application.

Publish Wizard

In Chapter 2, you created an Outlook add-in project called OutlookAddinProject. You will deploy this project to an end user using the Publish Wizard. Open the OutlookAddinProject that you created in Chapter 2 or use a new Outlook project. The first page of the Publish Wizard dialog box, seen in Figure 8-1, asks you to provide a publish location. This is the location that all of the files needed to install and run the solution will be copied to. By default, it is a relative path to a folder called "publish." This will be created under your project folder. You can also specify a server location either to a UNC folder, an FTP server, or a Web server. The wizard provides some examples of valid locations. Click Next to proceed.

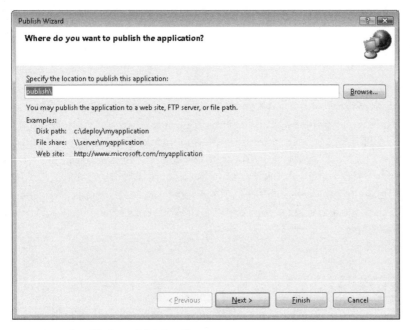

FIGURE 8-1 Specify the publish location.

The next page in the wizard, seen in Figure 8-2, asks you to specify the location that the user will be installing the application from. The publish location in the previous step was about where you want to copy the files to, and this page is asking where the user will install the files from. These may be the same location, but many times they are different. For example, you may publish the files to an FTP location, but the user will install the files using an HTTP location. The installation location is optional. You should only enter the value if you know the final installation location. You should also leave it blank or choose the From a CD-ROM or DVD-ROM option if users will be installing from a CD, DVD, or USB drive. You or the administrator can easily change this later. You will see how to do this later in the chapter. Click Next to proceed.

The last step of the wizard, shown in Figure 8-3, is to verify that you have entered the correct information before you click Finish to publish. Clicking on Finish will copy the solution files

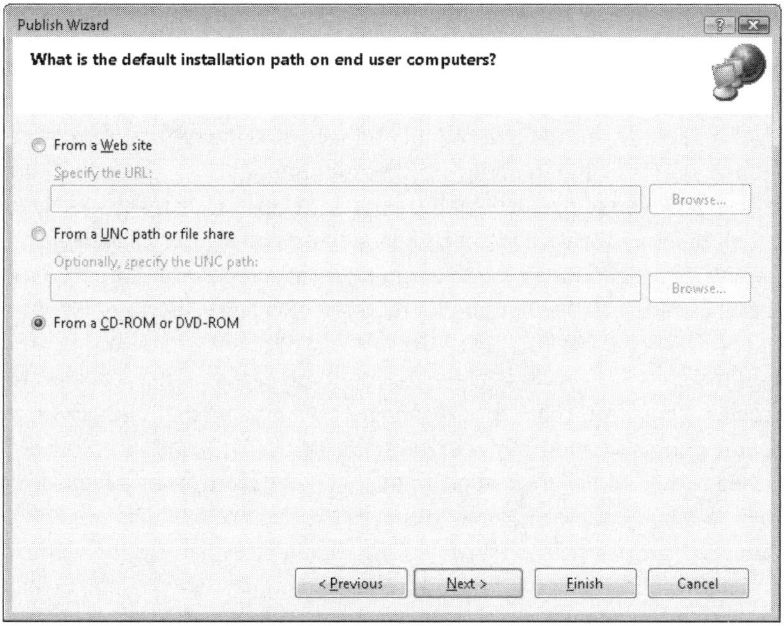

FIGURE 8-2 Specify the installation location.

to the publish location and create the required ClickOnce manifests and setup files required. You will see these in more detail later in the chapter. Click Finish to publish the solution.

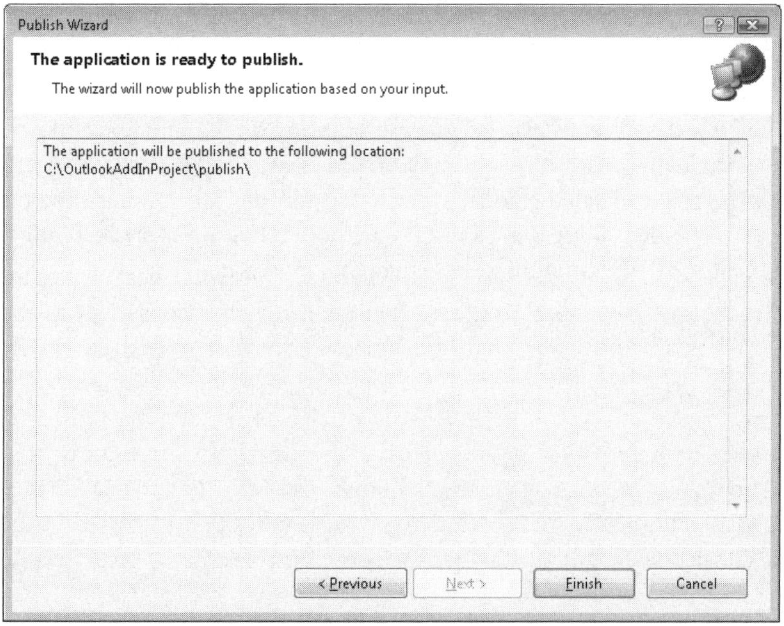

FIGURE 8-3 Verify and publish.

Installation

Once you have published the solution it is ready to be installed. Open the publish folder, or wherever the location is that you published to. You will see that there are two files in the root of the publish folder: setup.exe and OutlookAddInProject.vsto. The setup.exe project is the setup program that will install the solution and check for prerequisites. OutlookAddInProject .vsto is a ClickOnce deployment manifest for the solution. If you have already installed the VSTO Runtime, which also installs a handler for the .vsto extension, you will be able to double-click on the .vsto file to install the solution. In general, it is better for users to use the setup.exe, as this will check the machine for requirements and is the common way users install applications. The setup.exe installs the OutlookAddInProject.vsto deployment manifest. This deployment manifest file is an XML file that, among other things, has a pointer to the ClickOnce application manifest. The Application manifest is created in the Application Files subdirectory of the publish location. In the Application Files folder is one version-specific folder for each published version of the application. In this example, there is one subdirectory called OutlookAddInProject_1_0_0_0. The naming format of the OutlookAddInProject_1_0_0_0 subdirectory contains two parts. The first part of the subdirectory name is the name of the application, and the second part is the four-part version number: major, minor, build, and revision. Open this folder to see the version 1.0.0.0 files. This folder also includes a copy of the OutlookAddInProject.vsto deployment manifest. This is useful for rollback, which we will explore in the next section. Another interesting thing that the publish process does is that it adds the .deploy extension to all of your files, such as .dll and .mdb. This is a ClickOnce feature that enables the solution to be installed from an IIS Server. Without adding the extension, many file extensions are blocked on a hardened IIS server. By adding the .deploy extension, IIS allows the files to download to the client. The ClickOnce installer strips off the .deploy extension before caching the files so that the solution will work correctly.

Double-click on the setup.exe in the publish folder to begin the installation. Be sure to clean the VSTO project before installing if you are installing on the same box on which you are developing. To clean the project, right-click on the project and choose Clean from the context menu. This will uninstall the add-in, which is installed when you build the project. The first setup screen you will see is in Figure 8-4, although this may only flash briefly. This screen tells you information about the solution you are installing.

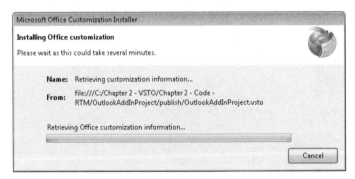

FIGURE 8-4 Installing the VSTO solution

The next screen you will likely see is the trust prompt. You will be prompted to trust the add-in if the add-in is not signed with a valid or trusted certificate or the add-in is not in the inclusion list. At this point, you should verify the install location, add-in name, and publisher and make a trust decision to install the add-in.

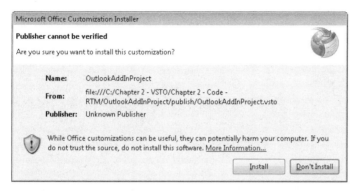

FIGURE 8-5 Verify and publish.

After you choose to trust the installation, you will see the installation progress screen, as seen in Figure 8-6.

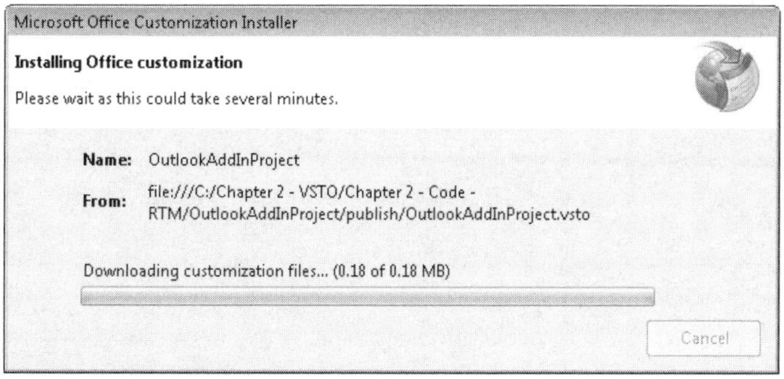

FIGURE 8-6 The installation progress

The VSTO add-in is now installed and ready to use. Open Outlook to verify that the add-in was correctly installed. Also at this point you can unplug and go offline. The add-in has also been installed into the ClickOnce cache. The confirmation dialog in Figure 8-7 tells you that the customization was successsfully installed.

You can verify that the add-in was installed correctly from the Outlook Trust Center. In Figure 8-8, you can see the add-in in the list of Active Application Add-ins. Selecting the add-in will show you detailed information. For example, you can see the path to the publish manifest as the location property.

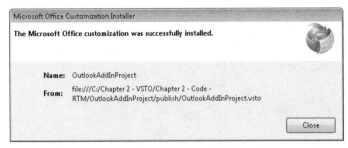

FIGURE 8-7 The VSTO solution was successfully installed.

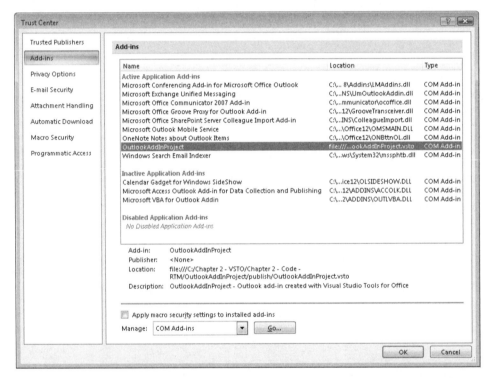

FIGURE 8-8 The Office Trust Center shows that the VSTO solution was successfully installed.

Update and Rollback

One of the biggest benefits of using VSTO and ClickOnce in your enterprise is the ability to automatically update all of the clients using the solution. This is impossible to do with VBA, which embeds the VBA inside of the document. VSTO solutions separate the document or application from the code. This simple difference allows for greater security and updating. In this scenario, you have deployed your VSTO application to your enterprise users and would like to add a new feature to your solution. Open the OutlookAddinProject that you published in the previous section. In order to demonstrate a simple change, open the Ribbon1.vb file and change the name of the OBA tab to OBA v2. Publish the solution again using the Publish Wizard, accepting all of the default values. When you open Outlook again, you will see that the new version has been installed automatically. So if you are following along with this, you actually will not see the latest changes. This is because by default the check for updates interval is set to seven days. If you wait for seven days and then open Outlook, you will see the changes. This was a choice to balance the network traffic and add a slight delay to check for updates with a reasonable default value. If you are developing and testing the deployment feature of your application, you want to change the value to check every time the application is opened. We will explore how to do this later in this chapter in the Publish Page section. For now, you can simulate this behavior by double-clicking on the OutlookAddinProject.vsto deployment manifest file in the root of the publish location.

FIGURE 8-9 The OBA v2 solution has been installed.

Rollback

Rollback provides the ability to back out of changes and revert to a previous version. You discover that the OBA v2 change that you deployed has a security bug. You need to take immediate action to fix the issue. You do not have time to find, fix, and test a solution. The only option you have is to revert to the previous version until you can fix the problem. Within each version-specific folder of the published solution, there is a copy of the deployment manifest for that version. Copy the deployment manifest from the version-specific folder you would like to rollback into the publish location folder, pasting it over the existing OutlookAddinProject.vsto file. Now when the application checks if it has the latest version, it will see that it does not and will install the 1.0.0.0 version again. Open Outlook to see that the OBA tab is now called just OBA again. Using this technique you can roll back or roll forward to any version that you have published. You can also change the deployment manifest to roll to another server.

Uninstallation

In the past, it was difficult to manage your Office add-ins. There was limited visibility into what was installed and where it was installed. The work done by the Office, VSTO, and ClickOnce teams comes together now to make it easy to manage your add-ins. You saw in

Figure 8-8 how Office shows you a unified list of all of the add-ins that are running and that Office knows about. This list is really a read-only view of the add-ins. To remove or unload the add-in, you can select COM Add-ins in the manage drop-down near the bottom of the Trust Center dialog box. Click Go to open the COM Add-ins dialog box (Figure 8-10). The COM Add-ins dialog box shows you a checked list of the installed add-ins. The checked items are items that are loaded and running currently. You can temporarily disable and prevent an item from loading by de-selecting the check box for that item. Or you can remove the add-in by selecting the item to remove and clicking the Remove button. This removes the add-in from Office, but this is not the recommended way to uninstall VSTO add-ins.

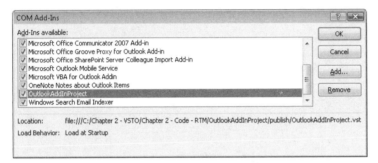

FIGURE 8-10 The COM Add-ins dialog box is used to remove add-ins.

The recommended way to uninstall the add-in is to use the Windows add and remove programs dialog box, seen in Figure 8-11. This is the standard way to uninstall programs in Windows, and now VSTO add-ins surface in this dialog as well. To uninstall, select the item and click Uninstall. This will start the uninstall process, which will completely remove the add-in.

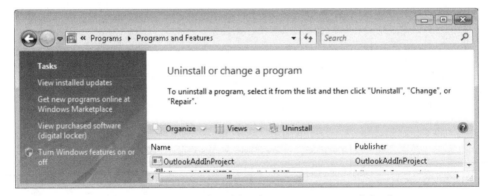

FIGURE 8-11 Uninstall the add-in using the add and remove programs dialog box.

Document Solutions

Document projects in VSTO such as Word, Excel, and InfoPath also use ClickOnce to deploy the solution. Document solutions have an additional way to install the application. Opening the document will install the ClickOnce solution just as it did if you double-clicked on the .vsto deployment manifest. With document solutions, just like with double-clicking the .vsto file, you must have all of the VSTO prerequisites installed first, such as the .NET Framework 3.5 and the VSTO version 3.0 runtime. The VSTO publish process adds a copy of the document to the publish location and to each version-specific folder. Open the WordDocumentProject project that you created in Chapter 2. Publish the project just as you did for an add-in project by right-clicking on the project and choosing Publish. Locate the publish folder and open WordDocumentProject.docx. This will open the document and install the document solution associated with this document. Since the process is the same as installing add-ins, you will see the same prompts, such as the Trust Center dialog box and the progress dialog box. Figure 8-12 shows version 1 of the document solution with 10 buttons in the action pane.

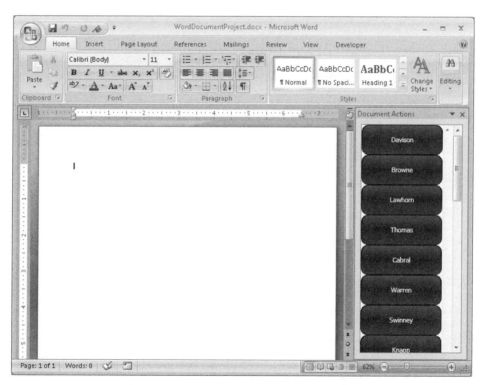

FIGURE 8-12 Version 1 of the document with 10 buttons in the action pane

You will now update the code shown in Listing 8-1 to show only five buttons in the action pane. Open the ThisDocument.vb code-behind file for the WordDocumentProject. Modify the LINQ query in the CreateCustomTaskPane subroutine with the code in Listing 8-1.

LISTING 8-1 Change CreateCustomTaskPane Linq query to take five items.

```
'get the customer emails from the SharePoint list
Dim CTPItems = (From contact In _
    SPListXElement.Elements("SPListItem") _
    Where contact.Element("Email").Value IsNot Nothing _
    Select New System.Windows.Controls.Button With { _
        .Style = u.GetStyle("BlackGlassButton"), _
        .Content = contact.Element("Title").Value _
    }).Take(5)
```

Republish the solution and open the document again to verify that the solution has been automatically updated with the new version. Again, as we mentioned in the previous section, you may not see the changes because the default setting is to check only every seven days. In the next section, we will explore how to have more control over these publish parameters.

Publishing Document Solutions to SharePoint

SharePoint is where you keep all of your documents in the enterprise, and this includes VSTO documents. You saw in the previous section how to publish a VSTO document solution to a file system. Now you will see how to use a VSTO document as a document template for a SharePoint library. There are a few basic steps required.

1. Publish your VSTO document to a file share.

2. Create a SharePoint document library with your VSTO document as the template.

3. Trust the SharePoint document library.

Although there are many details to each step, if you understand the VSTO deployment model discussed in Chapter 2 and the basic SharePoint library features, then this is very straightforward. The only new piece to this is that you need to explicitly trust the document using the Trusted Locations features of Office. The only factor that makes this difficult is that HTTP paths are disabled by default. But you will see all of the steps to configure this correctly.

The first step is to publish a VSTO document. You can use the WordDocumentProject that you created in Chapter 2. This must be published to a UNC or standard HTTP location. You cannot publish this to a SharePoint document library, but you can create a normal HTTP path on the same machine.

Next, you will add a new SharePoint document library called VSTOLibrary and specify a custom template using the WordDocumentProject file. Specifying a custom template will make your WordDocumentProject.docx the default template when a user creates a new library document. In the Actions menu, select Open with Windows Explorer. Copy the

WordDocumentProject.docx into the Forms subfolder. Close the Windows Explorer window and open the document library settings from the Settings menu. Click on Advanced Settings and set the path of the template URL to **VSTOLibrary/Forms/WordDocument.docx** and click OK. At this point, you will be able to click the new document action from the VSTOLibrary to open the document. It should fail to load the customization because you need to trust the library location.

The last step is to trust the SharePoint library folder location. In order to set the Trusted Location to an HTTP location, such as to your SharePoint server, you may need to modify the group policy objects. You can download the 2007 Office system administrative template files from the Microsoft Download Center and search for "2007 Office system Administrative Template files (ADM, ADMX, ADML) and Office Customization Tool version 2.0." For Windows Vista, copy all .admx files to the c:\windows\PolicyDefinitions\ folder. You should also copy all of the corresponding language pack .adml files to the en-us subfolder. Now start the group policy editor from the Run menu by typing **gpedit.msc.** You must first allow Word to trust a location not on this computer. To do this, expand the User Configuration, Administrative Templates, Microsoft Office Word 2007, Word Options, Security, Trust Center, and Trusted Locations, and then set Allow Trusted Locations not on the computer to Enabled. With this group policy setting enabled, open Word, then select the Office menu, then Word Options, Trust Center, and then click the Trust Center Settings button. Select the Trusted Locations tab on the left, and then click Add New Location. In the dialog box that opens, enter the **http://servername/library/** path and click OK. Also select the option to trust subfolders as well. This is important, as the document template will open from the form subfolder located under the library path.

You can now use the document library just as you would use any SharePoint library. The only difference is that you now have full VSTO solutions backing these documents. All of the other VSTO deployment features discussed in Chapter 2, such as automatic updates and rollback, still apply.

Publish Page

The publish page is a property page of the project, which contains all of the available properties for publishing the project. Right-click on the project and choose Properties from the context menu. Figure 8-13 shows the Publish tab of the Project Properties window. The Publish Now button will publish the application without starting the Publish Wizard. The Publish Wizard will use these property settings as well.

Publish Location   The publish location contains two properties. The first is the publish folder. The publish folder is the location to which VSTO will copy the published files. This corresponds to the first page of the Publish Wizard, seen earlier in Figure 8-1. The second property is the installation folder. This is the location from which the application will install the add-in. This can be a UNC folder, an HTTP or HTTPS Web site, or a relative path. This is

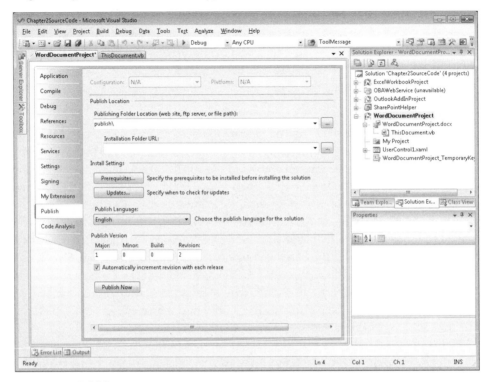

FIGURE 8-13 Publish page

the same property of the second page of the Publish Wizard seen in Figure 8-2. If you are installing from a CD/DVD or are not sure of the final installation location, you should leave this property blank.

Install Settings   The install settings section contains two properties. The first is a dialog box to set the prerequisites required by your application. Clicking on the Prerequisites button opens the Prerequisites dialog box seen in Figure 8-14. By default, the VSTO project sets three prerequisites: Windows Installer 3.1, .NET Framework 3.5, and Visual Studio Tools for the Office system 3.0 Runtime. You can set additional items if your application requires them. These will be built in the setup.exe when it is created. You can read more about how to add your own custom prerequisites to this list in the Visual Studio SDK.

The second property in the settings section is the Updates behavior button. Clicking on this will open the Customization Updates dialog box seen in Figure 8-15. There are three basic options: always check, never check, and check at a specific interval. The default value is set to check every seven days. This value tries to strike a balance between performance and timely updates. During development, you should set this value to check every time the customization runs so that you can see your changes as they are updated automatically.

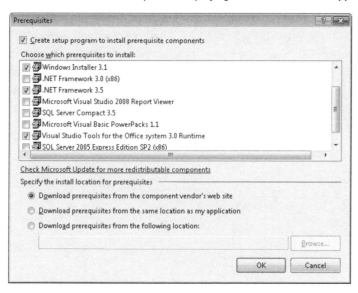

FIGURE 8-14 Setup prerequisites

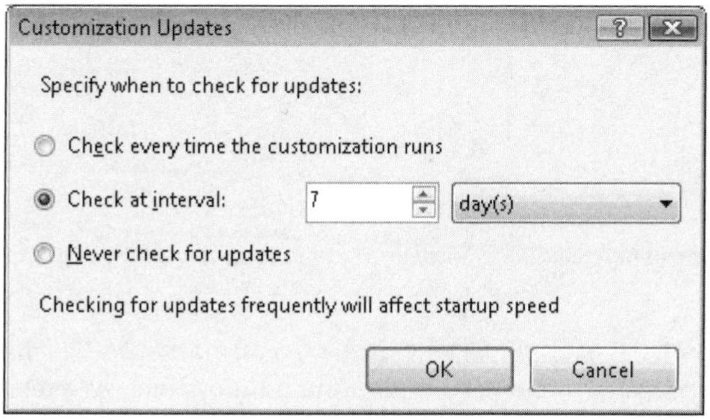

FIGURE 8-15 Set for interval checks

Publish Language   The publish language drop-down list box allows you to select the language for the install UI. This setting only affects the setup program and not the add-in itself.

Publish Version   The publish version is the version of your published application. The revision number automatically increases each time you publish if the automatically increment checkbox is checked. In a real application you should control the publish version number manually. The publish version number is different from the application version. When you publish an application, you specify a publish version number. This is the version that represents all of the components that are published together. Each individual component has its own version number, which you can see by clicking on the application tab and then the Assembly Information button. The Assembly Information dialog box, in Figure 8-16, allows you to specify the assembly version number and the file version number. Imagine you have an add-in that contains three assemblies, A, B, and C. All of these assemblies are at version 1.0.0.0. You publish version 1.0.0.0 of your application. In this case, the version numbers are the same as the publish version number. You make some changes to assembly A and give it a version of 2.0.0.0. B and C remain at version 1.0.0.0. You publish the application and give it a version of 1.5.0.0. (Since only assembly A was updated, you feel this should only be a point release.) Now your component versions are all different from the publish version. The publish version is the version label for a group of components at a specific version.

FIGURE 8-16 The Assembly Information dialog box is used to set the assembly and file version.

Changing the Install Location   It is common for a developer to not know the application installation location in the production environment during development. As a developer, you create the code, then install it on a test server, and then hand the code off to an administrator to deploy to a production server. The administrator needs a way to set the final installation location without republishing the application. The installation path can be changed using the setup.exe itself. Open a command window and run the following command.

```
Setup.exe /url="\\NewServer\NewInstallationPath"
```

The URL switch of the setup.exe takes the same path that you would enter in the Publish Wizard, a relative, UNC, or HTTP path. This is the path to the deployment manifest from the user perspective during installation.

Document projects also require that you change the _AssemblyLocation custom property dialog box (see Figure 8-17). To open the Custom property dialog box, click the Office button, Prepare, and then Properties, and then choose Custom properties from the drop-down list. The _AssemblyLocation property is a multi-value field delimited with a | (pipe) character. The first part is the location path and the second part is the GUID of the solution identifier for the document solution. You should change the location path only and not the solution identifier GUID.

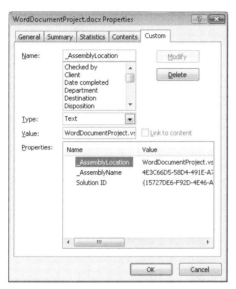

FIGURE 8-17 The _AssemblyLocation property stores the location path to the deployment manifest.

Update on Demand   The ClickOnce update options give you a wide range that should meet most of your needs. But what if you want to separate the check from the update? For example, you just want to notify the user that there is an update and let the user choose when it is appropriate to install the update. Maybe the update is large and the user will want to install it later. You could also have more complex rules for updates like making some updates mandatory and some optional. Or you could allow the user a period of time to install the updates. You might also have a scenario where you want to log on a server that indicates which version each user has and when it was last updated. All of these are excellent scenarios that are not supported out of the box. But you can enable these scenarios programmatically using the System.Deployment namespace. The following is a simple example of how to create a manual update feature for your OBA. This will create a Ribbon button that allows the user to update the application. If there are updates pending, it will install the new update. If the application is currently up to date, it will display the current version. Open the WordDocumentProject project that you created in Chapter 2. The first thing you need to do is add a Ribbon designer item to the project. Now add a button to a Ribbon tab, like the add-ins tab. Set the text of the button to be "Check for Updates." Double-click on the button to add an event handler. Add a reference to the System.Deployment assembly. Add the following imports statement to the top of the class file.

```
Imports System.Deployment.Application
```

Create a subroutine called UpdateNow, like in Listing 8-2. This will be called from the button1 click event.

LISTING 8-2 Manually check for application updates.

```
Private Sub UpdateNow()

    'Check if this application is deployed using ClickOnce
    If (ApplicationDeployment.IsNetworkDeployed) Then

        'Create an Deployment object
        Dim AppDeployment As ApplicationDeployment
        AppDeployment = ApplicationDeployment.CurrentDeployment

        If (AppDeployment.CheckForUpdate) Then
            'an update is available do you want to update now
            Dim updateItNow As DialogResult
            updateItNow = MessageBox.Show("A new version is available. " _
                                    & "Would you like to update the application now?", _
                                    "New Version Available", _
                                    MessageBoxButtons.OKCancel)

            If (updateItNow = DialogResult.OK) Then
                AppDeployment.Update()
                MsgBox("The application has been updated. Please restart the document.")
            End If

        Else
            MsgBox("The Application is running the latest version. " & _
                    AppDeployment.CurrentVersion.ToString)
        End If
    Else
        MsgBox("The application is not deployed")
    End If

End Sub
```

The UpdateNow subroutine starts by checking if this is a ClickOnce deployed application by calling the static method IsNetworkDeployed on the ApplicationDeployment class in the System.Deployment.Application namespace. This method will return true if the application is a ClickOnce application. Next you get a reference to the ApplicationDeployment object by calling the static method CurrentDeployment. Once you have a reference to the current ApplicationDeployment object you can call the CheckForUpdate method. This method returns a Boolean value of true if there is an update available. An update is defined as the current version does not match the deployment manifest version, which means that rollbacks are also considered updates. There is also another method called CheckForDetailedUpdate UpdateCheckInfo object. The UpdateCheckInfo object contains more details about the update, such as the version number and size of the update. You use the details from the UpdateCheckInfo object to make more complex scenarios, such as the ones mentioned earlier. If there is an update available, you prompt the user to install the update. If the user agrees, call the Update method on the current ApplicationDeployment object. Once the update is complete, the user will need to restart the application in order to see the new version. Listing 8-3 shows that the last step is to call the UpdateNow subroutine from the button1 click event.

LISTING 8-3 Call the UpdateNow method when the button is clicked.

```
Private Sub Button1_Click( _
        ByVal sender As System.Object, _
        ByVal e As Microsoft.Office.Tools.Ribbon.RibbonControlEventArgs) _
        Handles Button1.Click
    'Check for updates to the application
    UpdateNow()
End Sub
```

SharePoint Deployment

The second part of the OBA deployment story is about deploying the SharePoint parts of your application. There are many parts of SharePoint that you can customize and deploy as part of your solution. For example, you might consider building and publishing custom Web parts within your SharePoint site, which needs to be a part of the deployment process. We've covered the creation and publishing of Web parts in a couple of chapters (specifically, see Chapter 3 and Chapter 7), so in this chapter we're going to focus on three main areas:

1. How you deploy a solution and a feature that contain a single list. This is a simple example, but once you understand how to deploy one part of the model, it is the same for the rest.

2. A high-level discussion on how to deploy SharePoint workflow using VSTO.

3. How to deploy a VSTO client-side customization to your SharePoint site and then subsequently map this to a content type. A good example would be a custom budget template that loads data from a LOB system that you then bind to a custom content type on SharePoint.

Features

SharePoint is the center of many Office Business Applications. Most OBA applications contain many components, such as a custom list or library that uses a workflow to show InfoPath forms or uses Excel services. All of these components together make up your application. They all need to be installed and uninstalled together for your application to work properly. SharePoint allows you to bundle all of your various SharePoint components together as an atom unit in a feature. A feature is a collection of a number of elements that work together to provide an application. For example, you could have a feature that contains a number of lists, libraries, and workflows to make up an application. You will see how to create a simple feature in this chapter.

Features are defined as a folder in the features directory located at C:\Program Files\ Common Files\Microsoft Shared\Web server extensions\12\TEMPLATE\FEATURES on the Sharepoint server. In this example, you will create a feature called OBADiscussionList. This feature will contain a custom list for discussion OBAs and a workflow. Create a file under the OBADiscussionList folder called manifest.xml. Listing 8-4 shows a simple manifest XML file.

LISTING 8-4 Simple feature.xml file

```xml
<?xml version="1.0" encoding="utf-8" ?>

<Feature
   Id="11111111-2222-3333-4444-555555555555"
   Title="OBA List"
   Description="A Sample OBA List"
   Version="1.0.0.0"
   Scope="Web "
   xmlns="http://schemas.microsoft.com/sharepoint/">

   <ElementManifests>
      <ElementManifest Location="OBADiscussionElement.xml" />
      <ElementManifest Location=" ExpenseReportWorkflowElement.xml " />
   </ElementManifests>

</Feature>
```

The feature.xml file contains a root node called Feature. This has attributes such as Id, title, version, and description. The scope value is set to "Web," which gives this feature a site scope. The feature node also contains a collection of element manifest. Each element manifest defines a new component for the feature. For example, if your feature had a document library, a list, and a workflow, then you would have three ElementManifest nodes in the ElementManfests node collection. In the example seen in Listing 8-5, you have one for the OBAListElement. In this case, use an ID of 11111111-2222-3333-4444-555555555555; this will make it easier to debug and recognize your feature later on.

LISTING 8-5 Simple OBAListElement.xml element file.

```xml
<?xml version="1.0" encoding="utf-8"?>
<Elements xmlns="http://schemas.microsoft.com/sharepoint/">
  <ListTemplate
  Name="discuss"
  Type="108"
  BaseType="0"
  OnQuickLaunch="TRUE"
  FolderCreation="FALSE"
  SecurityBits="12"
  Sequence="350"
  DisplayName="OBA Discussion List"
  Description="An OBA Discussion List"
  />
</Elements>
```

In this feature, we are also going to include the workflow that you created in Chapter 7. Add the workflow.xml element shown in Listing 8-6 to the feature folder. See Chapter 7 for the complete listing and other components required for the workflow.

LISTING 8-6 Simple ExpenseReportWorkflowElement.xml element file

```
<?xml version="1.0" encoding="utf-8" ?>
<Elements xmlns="http://schemas.microsoft.com/sharepoint/">
    <Workflow
        Name="ExpenseReportWorkflow"
        Description="Use this workflow to track expense report status."
        Id="C6964BFF-BG8D-41ac-AC5E-B61EC111731C"
        CodeBesideClass="OBAExpenseReport.Workflow1"
        CodeBesideAssembly="OBAExpenseReport, Version=12.0.0.0,
        Culture=neutral, PublicKeyToken=71e3bce121e9429c"
        TaskListContentTypeId="0x01080100C9C9515DE4E24001905074F980F93160"
        AssociationUrl="_layouts/expenseReportAssociationPage.aspx"
        InstantiationUrl="_layouts/expenseReportInitiationPage.aspx"
        ModificationUrl="_layouts/expenseReportModificationPage.aspx">
    <Categories/>
    <AssociationData>
    …
    </AssociationData>
    <MetaData>
    …
    </MetaData>
    </Workflow>
</Elements>
```

Once you have defined the feature.xml and all of the required elements, you must copy the feature to the feature directory on the SharePoint server at C:\Program Files\Common Files\ Microsoft Shared\Web server extensions\12\TEMPLATE\FEATURES. The feature still must be installed using the stsadm.exe command line tool. The first step is to install the feature using the following command run on the server with administrator permissions.

```
stsadm -o installfeature -filename OBADiscussionList \Feature.xml
```

The next step is to activate the feature using the following command specifying the site to make the feature available.

```
stsadm -o activatefeature -filename OBADiscussionList \Feature.xml -url http://Server/Site/
Subsite
```

Once the feature is installed and activated on the server, the feature is available for end users to use. Open the SharePoint site and open Lists**.** Click on Create to create a new list. You can see in Figure 8-18 that the OBA Discussion list is now available.

After you click on the OBA Discussion List link, you will be taken to a screen to name the instance of the custom list. In Figure 8-19, you can see in the URL the feature id GUID that you created; in this example, it was a very recognizable pattern of 11111111-2222-3333-4444-555555555555.

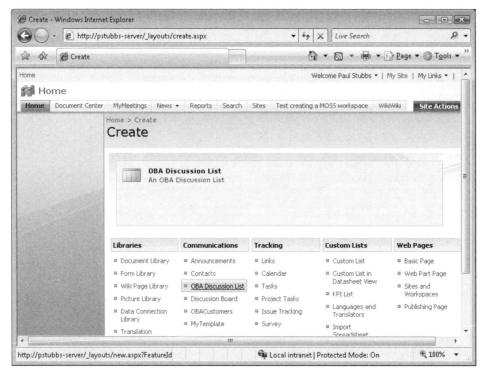

FIGURE 8-18 Create a new instance of our custom OBA Discussion list.

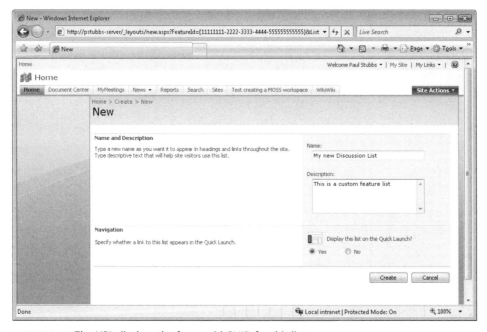

FIGURE 8-19 The URL displays the feature id GUID for this list.

SharePoint Workflow Deployment

In some sense, you can characterize VSTO as a "wrapper" technology around the Office system. What this means is that it represents the access layer to the object model for the different Office system products, such as Microsoft Word and Excel. Beyond the client, though, as you saw in Chapter 7, VSTO also has the ability to create and deploy workflow for SharePoint; thus VSTO is a wrapper technology for SharePoint as well. One of the key differentiators, though, is that even though you're similarly using VSTO to create a project for Word or for SharePoint workflow, the deployment is slightly different.

When building and deploying SharePoint workflow using VSTO, one of the key differences is that VSTO provides a wizard to guide you through the publishing of a specific workflow template, thus significantly reducing the number of steps that are required to build and debug the workflow project. As you go through the process of deploying the workflow, you associate that workflow with a particular SharePoint object—a list, for example. If you have not read Chapter 7, I would suggest taking a look at the Deployment section under SharePoint Workflow, as it provides some detail on SharePoint workflow deployment. Beyond reading Chapter 7, more general SharePoint Workflow documentation exists online at *http://msdn2.microsoft.com/en-us/library/ms460303.aspx.*

Summary

You have seen how easy it is to deploy your OBAs on both the client and server. VSTO and ClickOnce make deploying the application to enterprise users quick and secure. It gives administrators the control to install, update, and roll back the solutions from a central location. You have seen how you can bring together the client and the server by deploying your VSTO document customizations in SharePoint and as custom library templates. On the server side, you have seen how WSS features make deploying the components of your custom SharePoint applications more straightforward. Although there are many types of components that you can customize in SharePoint, the pattern is the same for all of them. You have seen a few examples, like lists, libraries, and workflows. An OBA application spans both client and server, and understanding how to deploy to both will make your application a success.

Index

Symbols and Numbers

.deploy extension, 200
.NET Framework
  ASP.NET, 12–13
  LINQ. *See* Language Integrated
    Query Link (LINQ)
  System.IO.Packaging, 43–44
  Workflow Foundation (WF), 162
.odc file extensions, 56
.wsp file extension, 188
6 Microsoft Office Business
    Applications for Office
    SharePoint Server 2007
    (Microsoft Press), 1, 21, 138

A

Access 2007
  Ribbon UI, 10
  workflows, 172
Actions Pane, 42–44
  customization, 60–61
Active Directory (AD)
  My Profile, 118
  Web Site and Security Framework,
    12–13
add-in solutions. *See* add-ins
add-ins, 23, 34
  installation, deployment, 200–201
  Office 2003, 24–26
  Office 2007, 26
  Office, smart client creation,
    30–34
  uninstallation, 203–204
  VSTO, 16
  VSTO 2005 SE, 19
Address rule, 33–34
ADF (application definition file). *See*
  application definition file (ADF)
ADO.NET, 14, 99–100
AJAX, 90
Alexander, John, 138
algorithm customization, 66–69
application definition, 157–159
application definition file (ADF),
  78–79
  creation, 100–104
  LOB system database addition,
    79–83
application server, back-end, 12
Approval workflow, 148, 173
architecture, 5
array creation, 33
ASP.NET

Web Site and Security Framework,
  12–13
  workflow forms, 168–169
Association form, 167
Attis, J. Dan, 138

B

back-end application server, 12
  Excel Services, 94–96
back-end information access, 14
BAL (Base Active Library), 163–164
Ballmer, Steve, 108
BAPI (Business Application
    Programming Interface), 67–68
Barker, Rob, 21, 138
Base Active Library (BAL), 163–164
BDC (Business Data Catalog). *See*
  Business Data Catalog (BDC)
BI (business intelligence). *See*
  business intelligence (BI)
Bichsel, Joanna, 21, 109, 138
BindingSource control, 48
Bitencourt-Emilio, Luis, 109
BlackGlassButton style, 40–43
Blank site definition template, 19
blog resources, 84
  Business Data Catalog, 109
  Excel Services, 109
  OBA, 109
  SharePoint, 109
  VSTO, 109
blogs, 121–126
bookmarks, 46
budget database, 56
Buenz, Adam, 21, 138
Bushan, Nene, 138
Business Actions Web part, 77
Business Application Programming
    Interface (BAPI), 67–68
Business Data Catalog (BDC), 4, 6–7,
  99–101
  blog resources, 109
  business intelligence, 77–83
  Definition Editor, 78–79, 83–84,
    100, 155–159
  Information Center, 108
  LOB data retrieval, custom task
    pane, 98–107
  Meta Man, 79
  My Profile, 118
  resources, 108
  SharePoint, 140–142
  Software Development Kit, 108
  TechNet forum, 108
Business Data Item Builder Web
  part, 78

Business Data Item Web part, 77
Business Data List Web part, 77
Business Data Related List Web
  part, 77
business intelligence (BI), 4–5,
  53–54
  client-side customizations, 56–60
  dashboard, 70–72
  Excel UI customization, 60–69
  further resources, 83–84
  MOSS 2007, 69–83
  OBA framework, 54–55
business productivity infrastructure,
  3
business rules, 191–192
Business Scorecard Manager, 54

C

Cabral, Erika Ehrli, 195
callback models, 35–36
CALs (custom activity libraries),
  163–164
CAML query, 93
Carter, Eric, 84
case study
  expense report, 176–178
  job recruitment, 90–107
ClickOnce, 16, 197, 200, 205, 217
Client applications, workflows,
  171–174
client-side business intelligence
  customization, 56–60
coding
  code reuse, 86
  custom, 6
  lack of, Business Data Catalog,
    99–100
  lack of, custom workflows, 175
  mash-ups, 137–138
  support, Office Fluent UI, 8
  workflows, 5
collaboration, 5, 15
  blogs, 121
  MyProfile, 117–121
  wikis, 126
Colleague Tracker Web part,
  114–116
Collect Feedback workflow, 148–
  149, 173
Collect Signatures workflow, 149,
  173
COM add-ins, 203–204
COM API
  SharePoint list access, 27–30
combo box, 66
Commandbars, Outlook, 38–39

About the Authors

Steve Fox is a program manager for Microsoft, where he's worked for eight years. His background is in the areas of social computing, search technology, natural language, and, more recently, Visual Studio Tools for Office (VSTO) and Office Business Applications (OBAs). He has presented information at many different conferences on VSTO and OBAs, and he is co-author of the book *6 Microsoft Office Business Applications for Office SharePoint Server 2007*. He lives in Seattle, Washington, where he spends his time reading spy novels, watching movies, playing hockey, and, of course, working.

Rob Barker has worked for Microsoft Corporation for the past seven years. He is a senior technical evangelist in Microsoft's Developer and Platform Evangelism group and focuses on Microsoft Office, SharePoint Products and Technologies, and Office Live development and architecture guidance. Check out his blog at *http://blogs.msdn.com/rbarker* for information about his upcoming projects.

Joanna Bichsel lives in Redmond, Washington, and works at Microsoft as a program manager on the Office Platform Strategy team. She focuses on Microsoft Office development, evangelizing the platform and helping provide architectural guidance and resources for developers and architects building enterprise solutions on Office. She blogs at *http://blogs .msdn.com/joanna_bichsel*.

Erika Ehrli Cabral works at Microsoft, where she is currently the site manager and content strategist for the MSDN Office Developer Center. She focuses on acquiring, authoring, and releasing technical content for Office and SharePoint developers. Previously, she was a development consultant working for Microsoft Consulting Services Mexico, where she is originally from and where she joined Microsoft five years ago. Check out her blog at *http://blogs.msdn.com/erikaehrli* for information about Office development and her upcoming projects.

Paul Stubbs worked as a program manager with the VSTO team in Redmond, Washington. In addition to VSTO, he worked with the Visual Studio Tools for Applications (VSTA) team, developing a new managed code application programmability development tool for InfoPath 2007 and independent software vendors. He is currently working on the Office team, developing programmability features for future versions of Microsoft Office. He has written for *MSDN Magazine* and has spoken at such events as TechEd and TechReady. He is also co-author of *VSTO for Mere Mortals: A VBA Developer's Guide to Microsoft Office Development Using Visual Studio 2005 Tools for Office*. He participates in the developer community on the Microsoft forums and on his blog, *http://blogs.msdn.com/pstubbs*.

2007 Microsoft® Office System Resources for Developers and Administrators

Microsoft Office SharePoint® Server 2007 Administrator's Companion

Bill English with the Microsoft SharePoint Community Experts
ISBN 9780735622821

Get your mission-critical collaboration and information management systems up and running. This comprehensive, single-volume reference details features and capabilities of SharePoint Server 2007. It delivers easy-to-follow procedures, practical workarounds, and key troubleshooting tactics—for on-the-job results.

Microsoft Windows SharePoint Services Version 3.0 Inside Out

Jim Buyens
ISBN 9780735623231

Conquer Microsoft Windows SharePoint Services—from the inside out! This ultimate, in-depth reference packs hundreds of time-saving solutions, troubleshooting tips, and workarounds. You're beyond the basics, so now learn how the experts tackle information sharing and team collaboration—and challenge yourself to new levels of mastery!

Microsoft SharePoint Products and Technologies Administrator's Pocket Consultant

Ben Curry
ISBN 9780735623828

Portable and precise, this pocket-sized guide delivers immediate answers for the day-to-day administration of Sharepoint Products and Technologies. Featuring easy-to-scan tables, step-by-step instructions, and handy lists, this book offers the straightforward information you need to get the job done—whether you're at your desk or in the field!

Inside Microsoft Windows® SharePoint Services Version 3

Ted Pattison and Daniel Larson
ISBN 9780735623200

Get in-depth insights on Microsoft Windows SharePoint Services with this hands-on guide. You get a bottom-up view of the platform architecture, code samples, and task-oriented guidance for developing custom applications with Microsoft Visual Studio® 2005 and Collaborative Application Markup Language (CAML).

Inside Microsoft Office SharePoint Server 2007

Patrick Tisseghem
ISBN 9780735623682

Dig deep—and master the intricacies of Office SharePoint Server 2007. A bottom-up view of the platform architecture shows you how to manage and customize key components and how to integrate with Office programs—helping you create custom enterprise content management solutions.

Microsoft Office Communications Server 2007 Resource Kit

Microsoft Office Communications Server Team
ISBN 9780735624061

Your definitive reference to Office Communications Server 2007—direct from the experts who know the technology best. This comprehensive guide offers in-depth technical information and best practices for planning, designing, deploying, managing, and optimizing your systems. Includes a toolkit of valuable resources on CD.

Programming Applications for Microsoft Office Outlook® 2007

Randy Byrne and Ryan Gregg
ISBN 9780735622494

Microsoft Office Visio® 2007 Programming Step by Step

David A. Edson
ISBN 9780735623798

Additional Resources for Developers: Advanced Topics and Best Practices

Published and Forthcoming Titles from Microsoft Press

Code Complete, Second Edition
Steve McConnell • ISBN 0-7356-1967-0

For more than a decade, Steve McConnell, one of the premier authors and voices in the software community, has helped change the way developers write code—and produce better software. Now his classic book, *Code Complete*, has been fully updated and revised with best practices in the art and science of constructing software. Topics include design, applying good techniques to construction, eliminating errors, planning, managing construction activities, and relating personal character to superior software. This new edition features fully updated information on programming techniques, including the emergence of Web-style programming, and integrated coverage of object-oriented design. You'll also find new code examples—both good and bad—in C++, Microsoft® Visual Basic®, C#, and Java, although the focus is squarely on techniques and practices.

More About Software Requirements: Thorny Issues and Practical Advice
Karl E. Wiegers • ISBN 0-7356-2267-1

Have you ever delivered software that satisfied all of the project specifications, but failed to meet any of the customers expectations? Without formal, verifiable requirements—and a system for managing them—the result is often a gap between what developers think they're supposed to build and what customers think they're going to get. Too often, lessons about software requirements engineering processes are formal or academic, and not of value to real-world, professional development teams. In this follow-up guide to *Software Requirements*, Second Edition, you will discover even more practical techniques for gathering and managing software requirements that help you deliver software that meets project and customer specifications. Succinct and immediately useful, this book is a must-have for developers and architects.

Software Estimation: Demystifying the Black Art
Steve McConnell • ISBN 0-7356-0535-1

Often referred to as the "black art" because of its complexity and uncertainty, software estimation is not as hard or mysterious as people think. However, the art of how to create effective cost and schedule estimates has not been very well publicized. *Software Estimation* provides a proven set of procedures and heuristics that software developers, technical leads, and project managers can apply to their projects. Instead of arcane treatises and rigid modeling techniques, award-winning author Steve McConnell gives practical guidance to help organizations achieve basic estimation proficiency and lay the groundwork to continue improving project cost estimates. This book does not avoid the more complex mathematical estimation approaches, but the non-mathematical reader will find plenty of useful guidelines without getting bogged down in complex formulas.

Debugging, Tuning, and Testing Microsoft .NET 2.0 Applications
John Robbins • ISBN 0-7356-2202-7

Making an application the best it can be has long been a time-consuming task best accomplished with specialized and costly tools. With Microsoft Visual Studio® 2005, developers have available a new range of built-in functionality that enables them to debug their code quickly and efficiently, tune it to optimum performance, and test applications to ensure compatibility and trouble-free operation. In this accessible and hands-on book, debugging expert John Robbins shows developers how to use the tools and functions in Visual Studio to their full advantage to ensure high-quality applications.

The Security Development Lifecycle
Michael Howard and Steve Lipner • ISBN 0-7356-2214-0

Adapted from Microsoft's standard development process, the Security Development Lifecycle (SDL) is a methodology that helps reduce the number of security defects in code at every stage of the development process, from design to release. This book details each stage of the SDL methodology and discusses its implementation across a range of Microsoft software, including Microsoft Windows Server™ 2003, Microsoft SQL Server™ 2000 Service Pack 3, and Microsoft Exchange Server 2003 Service Pack 1, to help measurably improve security features. You get direct access to insights from Microsoft's security team and lessons that are applicable to software development processes worldwide, whether on a small-scale or a large-scale. This book includes a CD featuring videos of developer training classes.

Software Requirements, Second Edition
Karl E. Wiegers • ISBN 0-7356-1879-8

Writing Secure Code, Second Edition
Michael Howard and David LeBlanc • ISBN 0-7356-1722-8

CLR via C#, Second Edition
Jeffrey Richter • ISBN 0-7356-2163-2

For more information about Microsoft Press® books and other learning products,
visit: **www.microsoft.com/mspress** *and* **www.microsoft.com/learning**

Microsoft®
Press

Additional SQL Server Resources for Developers
Published and Forthcoming Titles from Microsoft Press

Microsoft® SQL Server™ 2005 Express Edition
Step by Step
Jackie Goldstein ● ISBN 0-7356-2184-5

Teach yourself how to get database projects up and running
quickly with SQL Server Express
Edition—a free, easy-to-use
database product that is based
on SQL Server 2005 technology.
It's designed for building simple,
dynamic applications, with all
the rich functionality of the SQL
Server database engine and
using the same data access APIs,
such as Microsoft ADO.NET, SQL
Native Client, and T-SQL.
Whether you're new to database
programming or new to SQL Server, you'll learn how, when, and
why to use specific features of this simple but powerful database development environment. Each chapter puts you to work,
building your knowledge of core capabilities and guiding you
as you create actual components and working applications.

Microsoft SQL Server 2005 Programming
Step by Step
Fernando Guerrero ● ISBN 0-7356-2207-8

SQL Server 2005 is Microsoft's
next-generation data management and analysis solution that
delivers enhanced scalability,
availability, and security features
to enterprise data and analytical
applications while making them
easier to create, deploy, and
manage. Now you can teach
yourself how to design, build, test,
deploy, and maintain SQL Server
databases—one step at a time.
Instead of merely focusing on
describing new features, this book shows new database
programmers and administrators how to use specific features
within typical business scenarios. Each chapter provides a highly
practical learning experience that demonstrates how to build
database solutions to solve common business problems.

Microsoft SQL Server 2005 Analysis Services
Step by Step
Hitachi Consulting Services ● ISBN 0-7356-2199-3

One of the key features of SQL Server 2005 is SQL Server Analysis
Services—Microsoft's customizable analysis solution for business
data modeling and interpretation. Just compare SQL Server
Analysis Services to its competition to understand the great
value of its enhanced features. One of the keys to harnessing
the full functionality of SQL Server will be leveraging Analysis
Services for the powerful tool that it is—including creating a cube,
and deploying, customizing, and extending the basic calculations. This step-by-step tutorial discusses how to get started, how
to build scalable analytical applications, and how to use and ad-
minister advanced features. Interactivity (enhanced in SQL Server
2005), data translation, and security are also covered in detail.

Microsoft SQL Server 2005 Reporting Services
Step by Step
Hitachi Consulting Services ● ISBN 0-7356-2250-7

SQL Server Reporting Services (SRS) is Microsoft's customizable
reporting solution for business data analysis. It is one of the key
value features of SQL Server 2005: functionality more advanced
and much less expensive than its competition. SRS is powerful,
so an understanding of how to architect a report, as well as how
to install and program SRS, is key to harnessing the full functionality of SQL Server. This procedural tutorial shows how to use the
Report Project Wizard, how to think about and access data, and
how to build queries. It also walks through the creation of charts
and visual layouts for maximum visual understanding of data
analysis. Interactivity (enhanced in SQL Server 2005) and security
are also covered in detail.

Programming Microsoft SQL Server 2005
Andrew J. Brust, Stephen Forte, and William H. Zack
ISBN 0-7356-1923-9

This thorough, hands-on reference for developers and database
administrators teaches the basics of programming custom applications with SQL Server 2005. You will learn the fundamentals
of creating database applications—including coverage of
T-SQL, Microsoft .NET Framework, and Microsoft ADO.NET. In
addition to practical guidance on database architecture and
design, application development, and reporting and data
analysis, this essential reference guide covers performance,
tuning, and availability of SQL Server 2005.

Inside Microsoft SQL Server 2005:
The Storage Engine
Kalen Delaney ● ISBN 0-7356-2105-5

Inside Microsoft SQL Server 2005:
T-SQL Programming
Itzik Ben-Gan ● ISBN 0-7356-2197-7

Inside Microsoft SQL Server 2005:
Query Processing and Optimization
Kalen Delaney ● ISBN 0-7356-2196-9

Programming Microsoft ADO.NET 2.0 Core Reference
David Sceppa ● ISBN 0-7356-2206-X

---

*For more information about Microsoft Press® books and other learning products,
visit:* **www.microsoft.com/mspress** *and* **www.microsoft.com/learning**